OUTSIDERS

Outsiders

A History of European Minorities

Panikos Panayi

THE HAMBLEDON PRESS

London and Rio Grande

Published by The Hambledon Press, 1999

1 02 Gloucester Avenue, London NW1 8HX (USA)
Po Box 1 62, Rio Grande, Ohio 45674 (USA)

ISBN 1 85285 179 1

A description of this book is available from the
British Library and from the Library of Congress

Typeset by Carnegie Publishing, Lancaster
Printed and bound in the UK on acid-free paper
by Cambridge University Press

Contents

Maps

Preface

This book does not claim to be a complete history of minorities in Europe. To write such a history in a couple of hundred pages is unrealistic. Instead, it aims at explaining why minorities exist throughout the continent at the end of the twentieth century.

Outsiders identifes three different types of minorities. The first consists of dispersed groupings: people, united by religion or way of life, moving into and across Europe throughout the continent's history who have always felt themselves as minorities. They include both Jews and Gypsies. Secondly, there are localised groupings, whose origins again lie outside Europe, but who could remain largely anonymous until the growth of national states in the nineteenth and twentieth centuries. Thirdly, since the end of the Second World War, Europe has witnessed a mass migration of people across its borders, into already existing nation states, where the newcomers immediately find themselves outsiders.

Minorities may ultimately represent imagined groups, controlled both by the nation states which wish them to conform and by leaders within the minorities. Nevertheless, *real* differences certainly exist between ethnic minorities and majorities within individual states. The distinctions between ethnic majorities and minorities have, throughout European history, revolved around three characteristics in the form of appearance, language and religion.

The state, especially the nation state during the modern period, has had a central role in perpetuating the differences between majorities and minorities. Throughout European history, those in control of power have pointed to differences between in-groups and out-groups and have discriminated in favour of certain sections of the population. Ideology has always played a central role in this process. If in the middle ages it was based on religion, in the modern age nationalism has taken its place. These ideologies have served as justification for the implementation of policies which favour the majority at the expense of the minorities. The result of such policies has usually included legislative exclusion and often outright persecution resulting in killings. While Jews and Gypsies are obvious victims, very many others have suffered throughout the centuries.

At the time of going to press the themes covered by this book grip the international media's attention as NATO bombs Serbia in an apparently humanitarian attempt to help the ethnic Albanian Muslims of Kosovo. This group, with its own language and religion, shared by its Albanian neighbours, but not by Serbs, could remain anonymous in the Ottoman Empire, the system under which it developed. However, various forms of nationalism, especially Yugoslav during the 1990s, has made the Kosovo Albanians minorities and victims, like countless other groupings during the twentieth century.

Panikos Panayi
London, 1 April 1999

Acknowledgements

I would like to acknowledge my gratitude to the following for allowing me to reproduce maps and photographs: Cambridge University Press for the maps of 'The Ottoman Empire in the Sixteenth and Seventeenth Centuries', and 'Expansion of Rumania, 1861–1920', both of which are from Barbara Jelavich, *History of the Balkans*, vol. 1, 1983, and for use of 'Expansion from Moscow', from Robert Auty, Dimitri Obolensky and Anthony Kingsford (eds), *An Introduction to Russian History*, 1976; the Minority Rights Group, who hold copyright for the maps of 'The Vlachs' and 'Greeks in Albania', both of which are from Hugh Poulton, *The Balkans*, 1992; Gomer Press, for the map of 'West Friesland', from Meic Stephens, *Linguistic Minorities in Western Europe*, 1976; the University of California Press, for 'The Growth of the Habsburg Empire', from Robert Kann, *History of the Habsburg Empire, 1526–1918*, 1974; Professor David Childs for 'Loss of German Territory After World War 2', from his *Germany in the Twentieth Century*, 1991; Professor Richard Crampton for the map of the 'Ethnic Composition of Interwar Czechoslovakia'; Professor Sven Tägil, for the map of 'Swedes in Finland', which comes from his *Ethnicity and Nation Building in the Nordic World*, 1995; The United Nations High Commissioner for Refugees for the map of 'Cross-Border Population Displacements in the Caucasus Region'; *History Today* for the map of 'The Mongols in Europe in the Thirteenth Century'; Sir Martin Gilbert, for 'The Soviet Deportation of Nationalities, 1941–1945'; Oxford University Press for 'Population Movements, 1944–51' and 'Bilateral Labour Recruitments Existing in 1974'; Mark Thompson for 'National and Ethnic Distribution in Czechoslovakia'; Mcgraw-Hill for 'Population Movements, 1944–51', originally from O. M. Broek and John W. Webb, *A Geography of Mankind*, 1978. Attempts were made to trace the copyright holders of all other maps, but no response was obtained.

I would like also like to express my gratitude to the following organisations for providing financial assistance: the British Academy, the Nuffield Foundation, the Alexander von Humboldt Foundation and De Montfort University, which, collectively, allowed the employment of three research assistants and visits to libraries in London and Germany. I am very grateful to the three researchers who gathered information for the volume: Joanne Reilly, Paula Kitching and Matthew Britnell.

My own research for the book took place in five cities, involving a large number of libraries, and I am grateful to the staffs of all of these: in Leicester, De Montfort University, Leicester University and Leicester County Council; in London, the British Library of Political and Economic Science, the British Library, and the libraries of the School of Slavonic and East European Studies, the School of Oriental and African Studies, the German Historical Institute and the British Refugee Council, as well as Hornsey and Wood Green public libraries; in Osnabrück, the University library; in Berlin, the Staatsbibliothek; and in Stuttgart the libraries of the Institut für Auslandsbeziehungen and the Institut für Zeitgeschichte, as well as the Württembergische Landes-bibliothek.

I would also like to acknowledge the assistance of numerous individuals who helped me in numerous ways. The administrative staff at De Montfort were especially supportive, including Maxine Armstrong, Viv Andrews, Val Bell, Steve Gamble, John Mackintosh and Barrat Patel. My academic col-leagues, who helped in various ways, either by reading parts of the manuscript or offering advice with sources, include Lorna Chessum, Pierre Lanfranchi, Natasha Lemos, Mark Sandle and Gurharpal Singh. Outside De Montfort, I am grateful to Klaus J. Bade, Tony Kushner, Johannes Dieter Steinert and John Stevenson.

As ever, I am grateful to my parents, at whose home in Hornsey I stayed when I carried out the London research and where I also wrote some of the manuscript. Many students also helped to keep the work in perspective, including Stuart Blackmore, John Davis, Mundeep Deogan, Adam Gillogley-Mari and Lyndon MaCerlaine. The book is dedicated to Bethan Charles, Tammie O'Neil, Helen Ward and Lesley White.

1

Minorities, States and Nationalism

Types of European Minority

The long history of settlement within Europe has meant that there exists today within the continent as a whole an enormous variety of minorities. These minorities consist of those who were indigenous before 1945, many of whom moved into or across Europe hundreds of years before the twentieth century; and immigrants, migrants and refugees who settled in a new area after the Second World War. These minorities have become distinguished from dominant groupings by a wide variety of characteristics, whether religion, as in the case of the Jews and Balkan Muslims; language; allegiance to another state; or way of life, as in the case of Gypsies. There are three main categories of European minorities: dispersed peoples, localised minorities and post-war immigrants. All have the basic characteristics of constituting small numbers within a particular state, distinguishing themselves through appearance, language or religion, and having limited political power. They have, collectively, evolved as minorities over the course of periods varying from decades to centuries.

The dispersed European minorities themselves can be divided into four groups. The first of these, the Jews, already lived in Europe during the classical period and gradually moved west and north over subsequent centuries. Gypsies appeared in eastern Europe, originating in India, from about the twelfth century and, again, moved west and north. These two minorities have always been outsiders throughout European history, both before and after the age of the nation state. Slightly different are the two dispersed groupings, the Germans and the Muslims, concentrated in the eastern half of the continent. The former moved eastward from a variety of areas of core German settlement from as early as the tenth century, continuing throughout the middle ages and beyond. By 1919 they found themselves living throughout the newly created states which followed the collapse of the Austro-Hungarian and Ottoman Empires, but especially in Czechoslovakia, Hungary, Poland and Rumania. Muslims moved westward into eastern Europe, from further east in their case, as a result of encouragement by the Ottoman Empire. Like

the Germans, they found themselves as minorities in the new states which
followed the collapse of the great European empires at the start of the
twentieth century. A significant difference between Muslims and Germans
is that the former include the descendants of indigenous peoples who converted to Islam following the Ottoman invasions of Bosnia, Bulgaria, Cyprus
and Greece.

The other major category of indigenous minorities are those localised to
small areas of Europe or to individual states. These people, with their own
economic, social and cultural values, have become ethnic groupings because
of state creation and extension in areas where they live. Good examples of
such minorities include the Celtic fringe in Britain, essentially subjects of an
expanding English kingdom; the Sami people, who retained their differences
despite the continual northward movement of the Scandinavian states from
the middle ages; and the peripheral peoples of Russia and the Soviet Union,
who remained distinct from an expanding empire.

Another type of localised minority has been created by the process of
state creation through unification. In such a situation a dominant culture
emerges, usually that of the group which played the leading role in the birth
of the new state. State creation has occurred throughout the course of
European history. Examples have included the unification of Spain in the
fifteenth century, the creation of Italy and Germany during the nineteenth,
and the formation of Yugoslavia and Czechoslovakia at the end of the First
World War, each of which created minority groups. Numerous localised
groupings simply represent victims of boundary changes, resulting especially
from the peace treaties which concluded twentieth-century conflicts, especially the First and Second World Wars. In such situations the fate of
peoples in particular areas was far less important than the other concerns
of the victors. Such minorities have existed particularly in central Europe
and the Balkans: for instance, Hungarians in Rumania and Greeks in Albania.
A few minority groups remain within the heart of particular nation states.
Good examples of such peoples include the Vlachs, who live in various
Balkan states, and the Kurds of Turkey. The main characteristic of such
peoples consists of the fact that they came second in the development of
ethnic consciousness, which has meant that they find themselves trying to
form their own political structures, as in the case of the Kurds, in the
historical heart of particular nation states. In the case of the Vlachs political
consciousness has not taken off.

Migrants, immigrants and refugees make up the majority of post-war
arrivals. No other fifty-year period in the history of Europe has seen as much
immigration as has taken place since 1945. The entire continent has been
affected at some stage either by taking up population from or by surrendering

people to another part of Europe. Population movements in post-war Europe fall comfortably, though not perfectly, into three phases. The first covers the years immediately following the end of the Second World War and includes the population movements during the initial years of peace, which particularly affected the areas which the Nazis had controlled. The tens of millions of people on the move included victims of Nazism, in the form of foreign workers used by the German economy and former inmates of the camp system; German expellees from the victorious and vindictive regimes which followed the defeat of the Nazis; and victims of Stalinism, attempting to escape from that particular system of totalitarianism, but in many cases forced back by the agreements of the Allies at the end of the war.

The second phase of European migration, which ended in the early 1970s, essentially represented the search for labour supplies to act as fodder for the expansion of the European economies. Those states with colonies, notably Britain, France and the Netherlands, had obvious supplies of labour, but they also used workers from the European periphery, as did Germany and Switzerland and virtually all the rest of north-west Europe. Push factors played a subordinate role in this second phase of migration because the determining factor in causing population movement was the initiative of business and industry in the receiving state. However, in a number of states, including Turkey and Italy, the government of the sending society pursued a policy of exporting population as part of a solution to domestic overpopulation and underdevelopment. Tens of millions of people migrated to western Europe in this period. In the eastern half of the continent a few foreign workers moved to the German Democratic Republic, while millions of people migrated within the Soviet Union, especially Russians who moved to the Baltic Republics and Central Asia, partly in an attempt to develop the economies of those regions.

The third phase of post-war European migration, from the middle of the 1970s, involved several contradictory developments. First, the slamming shut of doors by the western European industrial democracies on migrants from all over the world. Secondly, an increase in the number of people who actually wished to move towards the wealthy parts of western Europe, especially following the political changes caused by the Cold War and its end. Many of the countries on the Mediterranean periphery, which had previously experienced emigration, now found themselves acting as importers of migrants from eastern Europe and North Africa. At the same time, the fact that the European Union allowed free movement of labour meant that many nationals of Italy, Greece, Spain and Portugal could now move into north and western Europe without the necessity for labour transfer agreements previously required.

The Definition of Ethnic Minorities

Four factors contribute to the existence of ethnic minorities, revolving around the issues of size, geographical concentration, difference and power. All of the minorities which exist in contemporary Europe possess each of the above characteristics, to some degree, and have done so throughout their history as minorities. A perfect minority, for the sake of argument, is smaller than the majority grouping, is concentrated in a particular location or number of locations, looks outwardly different and lacks power vis-à-vis the dominant population.

Paradoxically, in numerical terms it is sometimes possible for a 'minority' to constitute a 'majority'. The existence of the Apartheid regime in South Africa, with blacks outnumbering whites, represents the best example of such a situation. While this is not true in any contemporary European state, minorities often outnumber majorities in particular locations within individual states. Clearly, Scots and Basques outnumber English and Castilians within Scotland and the Basque land, but not within Spain or Britain. At the other end of the spectrum, Gypsies in eastern Europe and post-war immigrants, even though they tend to congregate in particular locations in towns and cities, always represent minorities wherever they live.

Congregation in particular locations plays a major role in the existence of minorities. This allows intermarriage and the consequent perpetuation of ethnically 'pure' members of a particular population, as well as the development of ethnic organisations in areas where a market exists for them. Once individual members of a group move outside an area of such concentration it becomes easy for them to lose their ethnicity, either by marrying a member of another group or by participating in the activities of the dominant population and consequently finding themselves sliding towards assimilation.

The existence of minority groupings rests fundamentally upon ethnicity and the differences consequent upon it. The origin of the word ethnicity lie in the Greek word, *ethnos*, which simply means nation. No difference exists between an ethnic group and a nation, in the strict sense of the meaning of the latter word of applying to a group of people with shared characteristics. This relates equally to immigrants, dispersed groups and localised minorities.

An ethnic minority shares one or more of a number of characteristics in the areas of appearance, language and religion. Appearance represents the most controversial signifier of difference, usually referring, at a fundamental level, to physiognomy or skin colour. Clearly, in the cases of Arab, Asian and Black immigrants in contemporary Europe, there is no doubt that they look different from the fairer settlers who have lived on the continent for thousands of years. Similarly, it would be dishonest to claim that, for instance, no difference exists in physical appearance between most Germans born in the north German plain and most Turks born in Anatolia. Historically, appearance has also played a central role in distinguishing one group from another in Europe. One of the fundamental contrasts between the Gypsies who arrived in Europe during the middle ages and the already established populations lay in the much darker skin colour of the newcomers, who had originated in northern India.

It would be wrong, however, to suggest that any group in Europe has a claim to absolute ethnic purity. The constant population movements during the whole course of the continent's history, and the intermixing of peoples which has taken place, makes this impossible. Just to take the example of the Germans, this group did not exist until the end of the first millennium. Similarly, to claim that all black or Asian people constitute the same ethnic group simply because of the colour of their skin would be an absurdity. Only racists would make this claim; or, contradicting them, anti-racists, who have developed black ethnicity as a reaction against the slurs of racists.

The appearance of groups also manifests itself in other ways, notably dress, which once again makes recent newcomers far more conspicuous than the old-established populations of Europe. A middle-aged Muslim woman in a Parisian street in the middle of summer, wearing her traditional dense clothing, is clearly different from a scantily clad, twenty-year-old, fair French girl. Yet dress may not signify very much in distinguishing two groups long-established in Europe, say Basques and Castilians, especially in an urban environment.

Food, which can be regarded as another aspect of appearance, also differentiates one ethnic group from another. The variation is greater between Europeans and post-war arrivals from overseas. It would again be difficult to distinguish between the diets of two long-established populations: living next to each other they have usually developed similar cuisines often involving a mixing of both traditions. Religion plays a role in the diet of many European ethnic groups, most notably Hindus, Jews and Muslims.

Appearance, encompassing dress and food, represents a basis for difference, but neither dress nor food are built upon to any great extent by ethnic ideologues. This cannot be said to hold true of language, perhaps the most important basis for the development of political ethnicity. Indeed, we need to recognise the fact that all modern literary languages are artificial constructs of the age of industry and nationalism. Preliterate societies communicate in dialects which thousands rather than millions of people speak. The act of creating a literary language in a particular area destroys the sum of its parts. Such an action represents a move towards a politically based ethnicity: no group can regard itself as a nation unless it possesses its own language. Once this has happened, led by the literate middle classes of a particular area, they can force the government of a state to grant them language rights, which can encompass everything from prescribing road signs in their literary language to enforcing its use in education.

While language is central to the claim of most ethnic groups wishing to describe themselves as distinct entities, religion is only slightly less important. It may have represented an act of standardisation in centuries past when the major religions first developed, but attending a religious service in many parts of Europe today is the most important way for members of some groups to display their difference from the dominant population in the state in which they live. For some minorities, notably Jews and Muslims, religion is and always has been more important than language, as many members of minority religions have spoken the tongue of the populations which surround them, most notably in the Balkans. However, other ethnic groups also differentiate themselves by their religion in some way or other from the dominant population. This is especially true of immigrants into Europe who have brought to the western half of the continent religions which hardly existed there before 1945, notably Islam, Hinduism and Buddhism. In other instances, notably Northern Ireland, historically evolved religious adherence forms the basis of difference, although in these cases religion has often been superseded completely by politics, to the extent that religion has little to do with ethnic identification other than in a symbolic sense.

Several basic differences clearly exist between European peoples and form the basis of ethnicity. However, we need to ask how consciously individuals, as opposed to groups, feel these differences. There can be no doubt that an immigrant who moves to any part of the world in any historical situation will notice the differences between his former place of residence and the surroundings in which he finds himself. In post-war Europe this is true of middle-class immigrants, moving from one industrialised state to another; but it is especially true of individuals who migrate from a Third World village to a large western industrialised city. Quite simply, they have moved from one world to another, surrounded by different buildings and different coloured people wearing strange clothes, living in a cold climate, speaking a language which they usually cannot understand, eating different food, practising a different religion and being involved in economic activities with which they have no familiarity. They may be traumatised or terrified, an experience shared by millions of immigrants into all parts of post-war Europe. Such people are profoundly conscious of their difference and greatly value the opportunity to use their own tongue with people of their own sort, one reason for ethnic clustering. The practice of their own religion in such a time of obvious spiritual need plays a large role in the continuance of religion in the new environment, so that the newcomers put great value on the construction of temples or churches. For such individuals the continuance of their traditional way of life, no matter how mutated it may become in their western surroundings, is a question of psychological survival.

It may theoretically be possible for a member of a long-established minority group to have no consciousness of his difference from the dominant population. Such a person, surrounded by people who speak his own dialect, might not come into contact with members of the dominant population. In view of the spread of education, transport and nationalism, this innocence is unlikely virtually anywhere in contemporary Europe. Indigenous minorities almost always represent a direct contrast to immigrants in the sense that they only become conscious of their difference when the dominant grouping, with its exclusive nationalist ideology, moves into their area. This is brought about in a variety of ways. The spread of literacy, for instance, is often in the language of the nation state in which a particular people lives. This gives rise to demands for minority language provision in schools. The spread of a national culture also makes a local population realise its difference, because of the difficulties it has in relating to images on a television screen or to information in a newspaper. The arrival of transportation can also have an effect, as it allows outsiders to move into an area, whether as administrators or as workers. In such situations, the local population becomes conscious of its difference.

In other instances, especially in the case of dispersed minorities, awareness of difference has existed for centuries. In the case of Jews for over two millennia, due, above all, to the perennial persecution which they have faced. This has reinforced their distinctiveness rather than done anything to lessen it. Similarly, Gypsies in post-war Europe are deeply conscious of their difference: both because of their distinct food, clothes, religion, language, occupation and residence patterns, and because of the hostility which they have faced from standardising nation states.

Ethnicity becomes an issue when people are faced with new situations, either because they themselves have moved into an area; because a dominant national ideology has encroached on their space; or because they face outright hostility from the populace and government in a particular state. In essence, ethnicity is a reaction to these new situations. Food, dress, language and religion do not represent differences except in a situation in which other people do differently. Only then do people become conscious of their difference and only then can political ethnicity develop.

Ethnicity becomes conscious and politicised following a series of developments. In the first place, a culture develops, springing from a literary language, which leads to books, theatre and music. In the case of the long-established groupings this process dates back over centuries, in the case of Jews even longer. Political ethnicity becomes possible with the backing of an ethnic media and the stereotypes which it perpetuates, developments which have taken place during the past two centuries. In many parts of Europe this encompassed the development of newspapers in the language of groupings in specific areas, such as the Basque land and Catalonia. Such groups may also develop a national myth through their media, even though they do not have their own nation states. In other instances, such as that of Gypsies, the lack of literacy or of any fixed settlement has hindered the development of political ethnicity.

In the modern period participation in the political process represents the most developed level of ethnic consciousness. Activism can take a variety of forms. Amongst immigrants it can simply consist of bodies campaigning for the rights of a particular group within the country of settlement. For indigenous minorities, the development of full-blown nationalist organisations represents at least a desire for autonomy and, usually, independence. Numerous examples of such bodies exist throughout Europe, including the Scottish National Party, the Vlaams Block, ETA and Sinn Fein.

The State and its Ideology

To numerical inferiority, geographical concentration and ethnic difference, we need to add lack of power. Where minorities control the state, they become the dominant grouping. The relationship with the state represents the axis around which all other aspects of minority and majority relationships revolve. The group which controls power imposes its own culture and ideology upon those perceived as different.

Minorities usually lack power not only politically but also economically. If they had economic power, they would probably control the state. In the overwhelming majority of European states, economic and political power have gone hand in hand throughout history. Newly arrived immigrants, Gypsies and peripheral groupings such as the Lapps represent examples of peoples who have neither political nor economic power. Nevertheless, the equation is not always so straightforward, as there are contemporary and historical examples of minorities with economic power. In the case of the Basques and Catalans, vis-à-vis the Castilian centre of Spain, their advanced economies have played a fundamental role in the birth of ethnic consciousness in their respective regions. Similarly, in post-Holocaust Europe, those Jews who survived Nazi brutality have proved themselves better educated and wealthier than members of the dominant groupings. In much of western

Europe this was also the case before the Holocaust; it represented one of the main reasons for hostility towards Jews.

Nevertheless, as a dispersed minority, Jews have never controlled political power in individual European states, even though those prepared to assimilate through the ages have secured positions of authority. Ultimately the group which controls political power represents the one which decides which sections of the population make up the insiders and which make up the outsiders.

While ethnic minorities have existed throughout European history, even though they may not always have been recognised as such, the minority populations which exist today do not all have an equally long history. On the one hand, Jews and Gypsies have represented minorities throughout their centuries long presence on the continent, in the former case because of their religion and in the latter due essentially to their appearance. Similarly, when immigrants moved into or across the European continent after 1945, they instantly became minorities because of the presence of already existing states, which had often played a large role in their importation. On the other hand, localised groupings, together with dispersed Muslims and Germans, have not always existed as minorities, even though they may have resided in a particular location for centuries. To take the example of the Kosovo Albanians. As a Muslim population they actually represented a privileged group under the Ottoman Empire; but, with the formation of Yugoslavia at the end of the First World War, they became a minority in a state essentially controlled by Serbs and, to a lesser extent, Croats. In this case, the rise of South Slav nationalism played a central role in the birth of a Kosovo Albanian minority.

This general point needs expansion. While some minorities have existed as such throughout European history and others have not, at the end of the twentieth century all peoples in Europe form part of either a majority or a minority. A difference exists between the modern nation state, with its all embracing ideology and control, and all the forms of government which preceded it: tribal, monarchical and imperial. In all of these there remained some possibility of anonymity for minorities. In the modern nation state no such opportunities exist.

To begin with tribal society, which existed in Europe a thousand and more years ago. In such societies the concept of minorities simply did not present itself as an issue. In the first place, tribal societies seldom had people with different ethnic characteristics within them, as separate tribes tended to keep themselves apart. Furthermore, the lack of any advanced culture or state organisation meant the absence of a sophisticated xenophobia which victimised minorities, even though primitive hostility towards other groups certainly existed in particular situations. The Angles and Saxons forced the already resident Celtic population towards the fringes of the British Isles, although to claim that this affected all 'native' Britons is questionable, because intermarriage certainly took place. One of the major characteristics of the tribal period was indeed the relative freedom of movement in an age before state control. The ethnic groups which were to emerge in Europe, either as nation states or the minorities within them during the modern period, had found their areas of long-term residence by the sixteenth century and in many cases hundreds of years before that.

It is the emergence of centralised states that makes the presence of minorities conspicuous and a problem; in some forms of government more than in others. Empires, as well as monarchical states, represented a fairly loose form of control within the European continent. They played a central role during the course of Europe's history, controlling vast tracts of land from the time of the Roman Empire, in its various forms, to the demise of the Habsburg and Ottoman Empires. All of these ruled over extremely divergent ethnic populations. The Habsburgs and Ottomans certainly had their favoured population groups in the form of German-speakers and Muslims respectively. In addition, they also carried out acts of persecution, especially, in the case of the Ottomans, during the period of conquest and in the final century of their empire. Yet the Ottoman Empire accepted difference as natural, especially in religion, the main signifier of ethnicity before the twentieth century. Residents living within the domains of the Habsburgs and Ottomans did not have a centralising culture imposed upon them because, in this loose and primitive form of organisation, literacy and technology remained limited. There were no mass circulation newspapers, no universal education and (of course) no television, each with its ability to preach the message of those in control in the form of a standardising nationalism. Consequently, in the agrarian non-technological societies and economies of the Ottoman and Habsburg Empires, different religious and linguistic groups could keep themselves to themselves barely conscious of their ethnicity, believing simply in their own God and striving to make a subsistence living. They recognised the existence of other peoples, but accepted the differences. They had no desire to eliminate them until nation states arose in the nineteenth and twentieth centuries.

While the empires of the Habsburgs and the Ottomans controlled much of central and eastern Europe for several centuries, a different situation existed in some of western Europe, with monarchical states controlling smaller areas. It has been argued that England was a nation state by the eleventh century at the latest, both because of the existence of an organised and effective government by the time of the Norman invasion and because of a cultural Englishness.[1] The idea has much to recommend it. But how English did the bulk of the population feel? Their main form of consciousness consisted of their religion. This was a non-technological age before mass education. The idea of England could not circulate through textbooks in a period when the church represented the main organ of propaganda. Nevertheless, the concept of England certainly existed among the educated elites. For minorities, medieval and early modern England could, nevertheless, be an extremely unpleasant place, most notably for the Jews, who suffered expulsion in 1290.

Similar patterns of statehood existed in other parts of western Europe before the rise of mass nationalism during the nineteenth and twentieth centuries, most clearly indicated by the persecution of Jews and Gypsies. Spain, after its creation at the end of the fifteenth century, provides a good example of an intolerant pre-modern agrarian state persecuting Jews, Gypsies, Moriscos, Basques and Catalans. In Spain, as elsewhere in Europe, religion played a fundamental role in creating and persecuting ethnic minorities before the age of nation states. During the crusading era of the twelfth and thirteenth centuries Jews represented the main victims of the all-embracing Catholic ideology which resulted in massacres and expulsions throughout western Europe. Heretical groups in the later middle ages, such as the Lollards and Hussites, also faced persecution as minorities. Religion became fundamental in holding states together following the birth of Protestantism during the sixteenth century. Between about 1520 and 1685 the history of western Europe can be seen as a period of embryonic nationalism based upon either Protestantism or Catholicism. Thus the classic Protestant kingdom, England, distinguished itself from its Catholic neighbours, especially France and Spain, whose Catholicism and consequent anti-Protestantism formed the basis of nascent nationalism in those countries. The French Wars of Religion pitted the Catholic majority against the minority of Huguenots. In eastern Europe, controlled by the Ottoman Empire for most of the early modern period, religion also formed the core issue in differentiating one group from another, yet it remained dormant as a basis of nationalism until the nineteenth century.

At the end of the eighteenth century, the dawn of the modern industrial era, in central and eastern Europe the Habsburg and Ottoman Empires still remained in control, even though they had reached the stage of terminal decline. Within these two domains lay a wide range of peoples, marked out by religion and language. Nevertheless, minorities did not cause a problem within them because of the absence of a centralising and standardising state and culture.

In the following two hundred years nationalism spread both downwards, to affect the entire population, and eastward, to become the only accepted form of state control. This has meant that ethnic minorities have become visible everywhere as all human beings have become conscious of their national or, alternatively, their ethnic identity. There is no longer anywhere to hide.

It has been held that nationalism in the modern sense does not date back further than the revolutionary turmoil that troubled the second half of the eighteenth century, meaning the American and French Revolutions. [2] Nationalism has been a Pandora's box: once opened, whether in the eighteenth century or before, it has been followed within the European continent by ever more groupings describing themselves as nationalities. This process constantly perpetuates itself. As one nation state comes into existence, minorities within it, as well as its neighbours, feel threatened. The collapse of Yugoslavia in the 1990s best illustrates this process, although the whole history of the emerging Balkan states, as the Ottoman Empire disappeared after 1800, demonstrates the way in which self-defence has played a role in the evolution of nation states.

The wars between England, France and Spain in the sixteenth and seventeenth centuries, and between Austria, Prussia and Russia in the eighteenth, undoubtedly had a role in the birth of the ideology of all these nations, but consciousness of it did not spread far beyond the ruling elites. In contrast to the monarchical regimes which came before them, the new nation states were the embodiment of the people rather than the monarchy. [3] Nationalism has essentially represented a transformation of the state since the eighteenth century to focus, in theory, upon the people who live within it.

At the end of the twentieth century the nation state is taken for granted as a natural, even eternal, political arrangement. [4] Nationalism is now simply orthodoxy. Very few people ever give a thought to the fact that they live in a nation state. The banality of nationalism is not only represented by concepts such as fighting for one's country, it is reflected by the everyday events of reading newspapers, in which news is dominated by events in each particular country. What really matters is not what happened the previous day but what happened, say, in England or to England the previous day.

To give another example of the banality of nationalism, we can point to the symbolic, mystic value of a passport. This allows individuals to cross national boundaries. Without it a person is, literally, a non-entity. In post-war Europe the passport is sacred. The reason for this is clear. One of the fundamental changes since the eighteenth-century Enlightenment has been the declining influence of religion, particularly during the last fifty years. Its place has been taken by nationalism. Indeed, it is no exaggeration to describe this ideology as having the same influence over contemporary

Europe as Christianity once had, in both its eastern and western varieties, before the Reformation. Its control is more complete because it is both political and ideological, whereas the medieval church had no direct political power outside the papal states.

This situation did not occur overnight, but the transformation did take place fairly rapidly, mainly during the nineteenth century: by 1914 millions of people were prepared to *die* for their country. The reasons for these developments lay in a complex series of changes in Europe, affecting economy, society, politics and culture. The main social and economic change in European society during the past two centuries has clearly been the transformation of virtually the entire continent from one in which the agrarian means of production dominated to one in which industry has become central. The spread of nationalism is closely linked with the process of industrialisation. While nation states may have deep-rooted origins, which represent a basis for their subsequent elaboration, they are human creations. Like the modern age and the industry which accompanies it, their essence is standardisation, rationalisation and centralisation. The end product therefore represents an artificial culture in the form of the nation state, as artificial as the industrial goods produced by the industry which dominates the new form of political organisation. These new political creations often initially came into existence for the benefit of the classes, notably the bourgeoisie, who had the most to benefit by the creation of an internal market. However, during the course of the nineteenth and twentieth centuries, the working classes have also been made to believe in the nation state. For the national movements emerging throughout Europe during the last two centuries, proletarians have often been used as fodder both in the political insurrections needed to overthrow imperial domination and in war against other nations.

By the start of the twentieth century nation states had become accepted as the only legitimate form of political organisation within Europe. This meant that the imperial powers centred on Constantinople and Vienna were doomed. The division of Europe into nation states was by this time inexorable, although there were many uncertainties about which individual countries came into existence. The new states in Europe, especially its eastern half, also contained minorities within their new borders because of the complexity of historically evolved settlement patterns. The determinants of the boundaries of new nation states included the linguistic and religious characteristics of particular areas, the size of individual ethnic groups, their ability to mobilise themselves into national movements and the attitudes of the Great Powers. These factors all remained important until the end of the twentieth century and the collapse of Communism. They also played a role in the state-building processes at the end of the two world wars, when the attitudes of the victorious powers played the determining role.

The essence of the nation state is political control. 'Nationalism is primarily a political principle, which holds that the political and the national unit should be congruent.'[5] It aims at standardisation and efficiency, achieved through the establishment of a series of institutions which promote the passage of culture through the whole economy. The most important of these is a national education system, which spreads knowledge of the national language and educates children primarily in the geography, history and literature of their own state. In addition, a series of more political organs hold the nation state together, including representative institutions, whatever the system of government; an army, in which those who claim citizenship must be prepared to die; and a national taxation system, an essential lubricant in keeping the nation state working. There also exist other symbols of nationalism. These include the national flag, the national anthem and a national football team, without which a country remains incomplete. Finally, the sacred national boundaries define the extent of the nation state.

Not all states in modern European history fit comfortably into the above definition. The Soviet Union, together with other federal states, such as Switzerland and Yugoslavia, allowed varying degrees of autonomy, demonstrated in language use, education and local self-rule. But above these there still existed, ultimately, the concept of a Soviet people, a Swiss people and a Yugoslav people, with central representative institutions, national citizenship, national flags and national anthems. Even in the Soviet Union, with its confused nationalities policy during its early years, the idea of a Soviet people began to spread after the Second World War, becoming legalised in the 1977 constitution. Furthermore, there also always existed the common denominator of Russian culture, despite aspects of local autonomy.[6]

It is impossible for all members of a nation state to fit into the straitjacket created by nationalism. This has led to the creation of minorities. In liberal democracies these may be social minorities, particularly in the early stages of industrialisation, when culture is first imposed from above, meaning that the working classes develop their own alternative culture.[7] The peasantry, in the short run, also usually remains outside either of these new cultures, continuing to live their lives as they always have done until the instruments of the nation state eventually manage to reel them into the body politic.

My concern lies centrally with ethnic minorities. The process of state creation from the end of the eighteenth century resulted in new minorities where they had not previously existed as such in the empires which controlled early modern central and eastern Europe. This is not to deny that these peoples with their own distinctive language and folklore had not already lived in these areas. While Albanians may have existed as a group for centuries, the creation of new states in the areas where they lived, with more direct control and with the implementation of a state culture which claimed to represent all members of the population living within the artificial boundaries drawn up, resulted in a reaction against the new, more direct form of political control by groups of people who spoke a different language, practised a different religion and felt themselves to be different in other ways.

The history of the creation and treatment of minorities in Europe has been a dramatic and tragic one. European ethnic groups have been the victims of some of the most brutal and systematic cruelty ever perpetrated, particularly during the Second World War. At the end of the twentieth century, looking towards a new millennium, minorities within Europe and the pressure of future migration remain central problems for the future of the continent.

2

Dispersed Minorities

Jews, Gypsies, Muslims and Germans

Jews and Gypsies represent the two quintessential European minorities, both because of the antiquity of their status as such entities and because of their ubiquitous nature, spread throughout the European continent. These characteristics together make them unique. No group in Europe other than the Jews has retained its status as a minority from the Roman Empire until the present, while few other groupings can, like the Gypsies, trace their status as an outgroup through almost a thousand years. Unlike virtually every other minority in Europe, the two have found themselves as minorities under all systems of government: empires, city states, monarchical structures and nation states.

Two groups which resemble the Jews and Gypsies consist of the Balkan and Soviet Muslims and east European Germans. Certainly, in terms of their widespread nature, while they may cover only one particular part of the continent, they have obvious similarities with Jews and Gypsies. All four groups, with a few localised exceptions, have not had the option of developing a nation state in the areas in which they have lived because of their lack of numbers and power, although both Germans and Muslims have been able to appeal to external forces, as has happened at various time periods and in specific locations.

All four of these groups, like the rest of the peoples of Europe, originated from outside the continent and usually moved into areas in which some sort of states already existed. While Jews, Gypsies and Muslims came from further east, the Germans moved eastward from central Europe where they had evolved as a people. The nature of settlement also varied between the four groups. Gypsies migrated to the European continent uninvited, a point which also applies to Jews, but not to all groups of Germans and Muslims. In contrast, the latter two moved to their areas of settlement because they had connections with an empire which controlled a particular part of the European continent, the Habsburgs in the case of the Germans and the Ottomans in the case of the Muslims. Even this explanation simplifies the true picture, because some settlements of Germans and Muslims grew independently of these two dynasties. The Muslims are a unique grouping within the four considered here, as some of them simply represent members of already resident populations who converted to Islam.

In terms of their evolution, the four groups reveal similar patterns, although each has distinct characteristics, peculiar to each grouping as a whole or to particular geographical locations. In the case of Jews, settlement in Europe began during the latter stages of Roman imperial control. Gypsies, in contrast, began to arrive in the early medieval period from northern India. Muslims moved to Europe with the Seljuk and Ottoman Turks in the same period, while the Germans began to migrate eastward from the tenth century.

The history of the four minorities during the rest of the medieval and early modern period varies. Three of the groups, the Jews, Gypsies and Germans, continued to migrate; the first, and to a lesser extent the second, due to persecution. Germans continued to move into parts of eastern Europe, largely as a result of invitations from local rulers, as late as the eighteenth century. In contrast, virtually all of the migration of Muslims had occurred by the sixteenth century, although conversions did take place subsequently.

The growth of nationalism had serious consequences for each of the four groupings. The standardisation required by the emerging European states throughout Europe in the nineteenth century meant that dispersed minorities could no longer remain anonymous in the politically and ethnically conscious democracies and autocracies which developed, even where they had been able to in the monarchical states which had previously controlled Europe. Worse still, even if they did not become victims of nationalism, specific ideologies began to emerge which proved to have cataclysmic consequences for Gypsies and Jews in the twentieth century in the form of racism and anti-semitism. Collectively, such ideas led to a public focus upon the position of Gypsies and Jews after 1850. But only during the Second World War did the racial and antisemitic views which had been emerging during the nineteenth century reach their fulfilment in the extermination camps built by the Nazis in Poland. In this process the principles of standardisation and industriali-sation also reached their ultimate conclusion: factory killing eliminated the imperfect Jews and Gypsies who spoilt the Nazi vision of an ethnically homogeneous, superior, Aryan population controlling eastern Europe.

While Germans and Muslims may not have become the victims of racism, they did suffer during the twentieth century as a result of nationalism, epitomised in the ethnic cleansing which has affected both groups. In the case of the Germans, the peace treaties reached at the end of the Second World War meant that German civilisation in eastern Europe, which had evolved over a thousand years, virtually came to an end in the space of just a few years. Most of the ethnic cleansing of Muslims occurred decades after the Second World War, epitomised most clearly in the treatment of Bosnians during the post-Communist war in Yugoslavia.

At the end of the twentieth century two of the ubiquitous minorities, Jews and Germans, have, as a consequence of the above processes, disappeared from large parts of the European continent. On the other hand, Muslims and Gypsies have, within eastern Europe and the Balkans generally, become more numerous. This was due to a population explosion characteristic of the modern age, which reached many national groupings of these two minorities during the second half of the twentieth century, even if in most cases they remain politically impotent.

Power relationships between minorities and governing regimes vary between the four dispersed groupings. Gypsies represent the most outcast in this sense because they have rarely played a role in any regime and their position has hardly changed. In contrast, Jews have often reached positions of power within states throughout modern European history, especially in the age of nationalism, which may help to account for the intensity of hatred that developed against them as conspiracy theories emerged claiming that Jews controlled particular states, acting as a 'Hidden Hand' working against the national interest: a fact which justified their elimination in the eyes of nationalists and antisemites. The position of Germans and Muslims as minorities has, on the other hand, changed over time. In the early modern period they generally remained favourably placed in areas controlled by regimes with which they had some connection. Their situation suffered considerable deterioration after the collapse of the Ottoman, Habsburg and Nazi Empires, as the states which took over the areas of German and Muslim settlement viewed them unfavourably.

First Settlements

Jews represent one the oldest groupings in the history of the European continent, both in terms of their own self-consciousness and the attitudes of states and peoples towards them. They have lived in Europe throughout its history. In some instances they may have been present, in small numbers in particular areas, before the arrival of the dominant groupings which went on to create nation states in those areas during the nineteenth and twentieth centuries. Precisely dating the first arrival of the Jews in Europe is a fruitless exercise, although some may have lived on the southern shores of the Black Sea before the Roman Empire.[1] Jews almost certainly came into contact with the Greeks before the time of Alexander the Great. They settled within the periphery of the Hellenic world, moving into the areas of Greek control

due to the constant succession of wars, the international traffic in slaves
and the general process of commerce. This movement intensified following
Alexander's conquest of Palestine in 333 BC. [2]

By the second century BC, Jews had reached the Italian peninsula, establishing a community in Rome. Their numbers in the European empire further
increased, after the capture of slaves following revolts in Palestine, so that
Jews reached as far as Gaul and Spain. In addition, traders from Palestine
also moved to urban settlements, especially Rome. In the first and second
centuries AD Judaea, under Roman rule, came under the control of a series
of ruthless leaders, leading to insurrections in the area, during which Jews
suffered heavy casualties. Something of an improvement in the position of
the Jews within the Roman Empire came in 212 when the Emperor Caracalla
issued an edict which gave citizenship to all free inhabitants of the empire
without distinction. [3]

By the time of the fall of the western Roman Empire, in the fifth century,
Jewish communities were scattered throughout the Italian peninsula, in
locations which included Naples, Sicily, Milan, Verona and Genoa, [4] as well
as further west and north in France, Spain and Germany, reaching significant
numbers in the last two locations. By the end of the Roman Empire a Jewish
community was to be found in all probability in every *municipium* of the
Roman Empire sufficiently important to have a forum and a hippodrome. [5]

In contrast to the Jews, the Gypsies of Europe arrived over a thousand
years later, completely uninvited. Like the Jews of Europe, the Gypsies started
in the east and gradually moved westwards, until they finally resided in
virtually every region in Europe before the growth of nation states during
the nineteenth century, which viewed both of the quintessential European
minorities as boils which lessened the perfect, but artificial, beauty of the
new political entities in the eyes of their creators.

The origins of the Gypsies lie in northern India, whence they began
migrating, for reasons which can only be guessed at, around the fifth century
AD. They reached Byzantium via Persia at some stage between the ninth
and eleventh centuries and then gradually spread westward. Evidence exists
to prove their presence in the whole continent by the early sixteenth century.
The Gypsies made their first appearance in parts of the Balkans, perhaps
driven there by the Turkish invasions of the area. [6]

Some of the earliest references to Gypsies in the Balkans refer to them in
Bulgaria and Rumania. Gypsy villages in western Bulgaria are mentioned in
a grant of land in 1378. [7] In Rumania they are first documented in Moldavia
and Transylvania during the fourteenth century as slaves. [8] Also in the fourteenth century they were present in Crete, Corfu, Serbia, Croatia and
Bohemia. [9] In the following century a Gypsy presence can be located for the

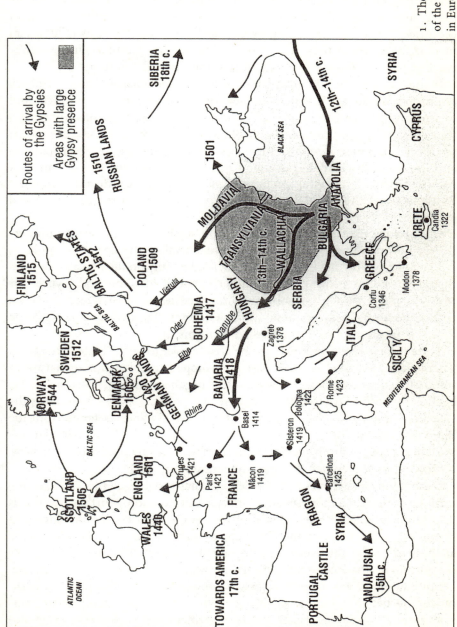

1. The Arrival
of the Gypsies
in Europe

first time further westwards. In 1423 they settled in Hungary in their thousands, following a charter which guaranteed them certain rights, issued by King Sigismund.[10] They reached Spain during the fifteenth century, where they were welcomed initially, but faced persecution, like other minority groups within the country, from the sixteenth to the eighteenth centuries.[11] The first recording of Gypsies in Germany was at Hildesheim in 1407, after which they appeared in several other German cities.[12] They reached parts of France and Italy during the fifteenth century.[13]

In the following hundred years they arrived in the north-western periphery of Europe. Within the British Isles, they first made an appearance in Scotland in 1505 and England in 1514.[14] In Ireland, meanwhile, there already lived a travelling group ethnically distinct from Romany Gypsies and usually known as tinkers, or tinklers, with Celtic roots and a Celtic language, Shelte, who also moved to England and Scotland.[15] In Scandinavia the Gypsies are first recorded in Sweden in 1512, moving to Finland during the sixteenth century.[16] By the start of the sixteenth century Gypsies had also reached Russia and Poland.

Chronologically, the first appearance of Muslims in significant numbers within Europe almost coincided with the arrival of the Gypsies. Similarly, both came from further east and both focused mainly on the Balkans. Beyond that comparisons prove difficult, either between Muslims and Gypsies or Muslims and Jews. The most obvious difference lies in the Muslim association with conquering peoples, notably the Ottoman Turks, but also with the Mongols in the case of Central Asian Muslims.

The Turkic peoples originate in the area known today as Outer Mongolia, where they existed as nomads who worshipped the elements of nature in the first millennium before Christ. They began migrating westward as far back as the second century BC and their first political manifestation was the Göktürk Empire, which lasted from 552 to 744 AD and stretched from the Black Sea across Mongolia and China almost as far as the Pacific. An important turning point in the history of the Turks was their adoption of Islam, completed by the end of the first millennium.

During the eleventh century the Seljuk dynasty stabilised the Turks, transforming them into a more sedentary people but expanding further westwards into Anatolia. The next major expansion, and the first one into the European mainland, occurred after the Ottoman dynasty became the Turkish rulers at the end of the thirteenth century. By the end of the following century the Ottomans had conquered Bulgaria, Macedonia and southern Serbia. Despite attempts by western rulers to prevent further advance, the Turks moved deeper into Europe during the fifteenth century, conquering Constantinople, Bosnia and Herzegovina. Suleimein the Magnificent (1520–66)

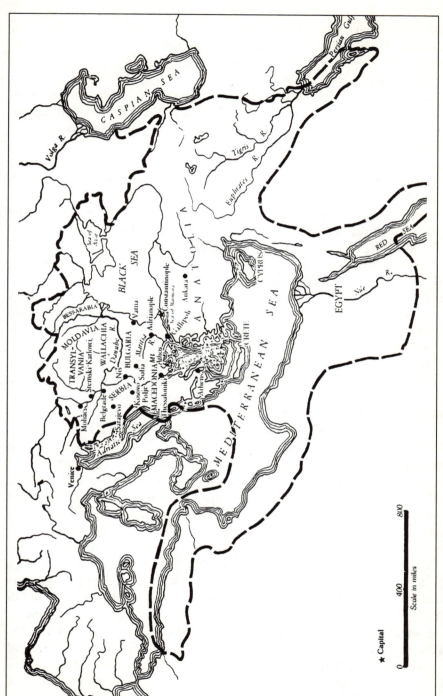

2. The Ottoman Empire in the Sixteenth and Seventeenth Centuries

led the Ottoman Empire to its zenith with the conquest of much of the Hungarian lands. Further east the Turkish Empire had reached the southern Ukraine and the Crimea and had stretched into parts of present-day Iraq as well as much of north Africa.

The history of the Turkish Empire in Europe from the end of the seventeenth century is one of decline due to conquest by the Habsburg and Russian Empires and the development of independent states in the Balkans during the nineteenth and twentieth centuries. [17] The centuries of Ottoman imperial rule in the areas they conquered left several legacies to the states which followed. One of the most important of these was the remnants of a Turkish population in some of the areas the Turks had ruled, as well as the survival of their religion in others. Significantly, this did not happen throughout the regions which they conquered, only in specific locations.

The Muslim populations of the Balkans are complex because they represent a mixture of settlers and converts, who do not always prove easy to distinguish and who the Ottoman Empire did not choose to differentiate. Both settlement and conversion sometimes took several hundred years. The former process began earlier and involved the Ottoman Empire importing ethnic Turks into particular areas of its vast domain: the best two examples consist of Bulgaria and Cyprus.

Bulgaria illustrates the complexity of the Balkan Muslims. Colonisation of Bulgaria by Turks took place from the fourteenth until the nineteenth centuries, with settlement reaching its height during the eighteenth century. The newcomers mostly moved into the plains of north-eastern Bulgaria around the Danube and the Black Sea. The second major Muslim group consisted of Pomaks, or Slavs who converted to Islam. They have lived predominantly in south-western Bulgaria and speak Bulgarian. Tartars form a third Muslim group, moving into the country from Turkestan and speaking Turkish by the twentieth century. The Gagaouz are an extremely complicated group, speaking Turkish and wearing Turkish dress but believing in the Greek Orthodox religion. Finally, some Bulgarian Gypsies converted to Islam. [18]

Similarly, in Cyprus the presence of Turks is explained by a similar complex of circumstances. Throughout its history the island has endured constant invasion and colonisation but, by the medieval period at the latest, the dominant grouping had become speakers of a Greek dialect and adhered to the Orthodox faith. This was the situation in 1571 when the Ottoman armies conquered the island and expelled the Venetians who ruled it. Almost immediately about 20,000 Turkish soldiers settled in Cyprus in return for land which had belonged to the Venetian nobility or Roman Catholic Church. In addition, some immigration of Turks may have subsequently taken place from Anatolia and the Balkans. Many conversions took place in the early centuries of Muslim rule to gain the benefit of full Ottoman citizenship; in the late nineteenth century a small number of Muslims still regarded Greek as their mother tongue. [19]

Further east, in what became the Soviet Union, historically evolved settlement patterns played a role in the presence of some of the Muslim groups which found themselves in the Russian Empire and then the Soviet Union, as illustrated by the history of the Tatars, who have lived in various locations. All are remnants of the Golden Horde of Turkic tribes led by the Mongols under Batu Khan that invaded Russia during the thirteenth century, when it became part of an empire stretching from Poland to China and from the Black Sea to Siberia. The Golden Horde dissolved during the fifteenth century, to be succeeded by the Khanates of Kazan, Astrakhan, Crimea and Siberia, which in their turn began to disappear as Russia moved eastward from the sixteenth century. [20]

3. The Mongols in Europe during the Thirteenth Century

The German people seem to have emerged as an identifiable group from the ninth century, developing through the integration and assimilation of several ethnically distinct groups, especially Germanic tribes, Celts and Slavs. [21] In the history of the German people since that time states have existed which have covered various parts of German-speaking Europe, but none of them has had political control of all settlements. The Habsburg and Nazi Empires, with their domination of much of eastern Europe, came closest to this. Other states controlled by German rulers have tended to have suzerainty over a greater or larger area east of the Rhine.

Like many of the Muslim populations of the Balkans and the Soviet Union, imperial control played a role in the development of German communities in eastern Europe, although in this case many of the historically evolved settlement patterns had little to do with the Habsburg dynasty. In most instances, the presence of Germans predated Habsburg control, while in others communities moved into specific areas after direct recruitment by rulers in parts of eastern Europe wanting to develop particular regions of their territories. When they gained control of particular regions, the Habsburgs often brought in new German populations. The first migration of Germans into eastern Europe began around the end of the first millennium. The process has similarities to that of twentieth-century labour migration into western Europe, in the sense that predominantly economic factors determined the movement and that ruling states, often very primitive at this stage of European history, invited the newcomers into their domains.

Modern Poland contains some of the largest communities of Germans. This is due both to the antiquity of their settlement in the area and to the fact that twentieth-century Poland has taken over a significant part of Prussia, the kingdom which played the leading role in the formation of modern Germany. The first Polish state, established in the tenth century, invited numerous German monks, peasants, artisans and knights into its territory during the twelfth, thirteenth and fourteenth centuries. The Teutonic Knights played a major role in converting the entire Baltic coast to Christianity, while Hanseatic merchants controlled its economic development.

In areas covered by contemporary Czechoslovakia, German settlement dates back to the twelfth and thirteenth centuries, when the rulers of Bohemia invited Germans into their lands in order to help economic development. German elements began to enter Hungary towards the end of the first millennium as missionaries and economic migrants. In the middle ages these were followed by further settlers and military personnel, as Hungarian control of central Europe spread further south and east into areas which the Mongols had ruled. Germans arrived in the west of Hungary from the middle of the twelfth century and worked as farmers, craftsmen and traders. They founded countless towns from the thirteenth to the fifteenth centuries.

Because of the centuries long control by Hungary of much of present-day Rumania, the history of German residence here is inextricably linked with German settlement in Hungary. In the twelfth century migrants from the Rhineland, central Germany and Flanders migrated to Transylvania, in response to an invitation from King Geza II. Their settlements were defended in the following century by the Teutonic Knights and the Transylvanian Germans obtained considerable local autonomy.

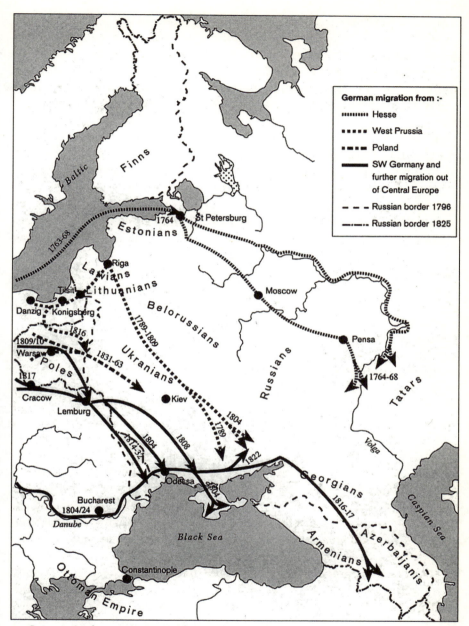

4. German Settlement in Russia during the Eighteenth and Nineteenth Centuries

German settlement in what was to become Yugoslavia occurred from the eighth century, with the migration of Bavarians southwards from the eastern Alps, although these became assimilated into the Slovene population of the area. In the fourteenth century there followed the movement of Thuringian and Franconian peasants into the previously uninhabited Koeve (Gotschee) region of contemporary Slovenia, where Germans lived until the twentieth century.

Although some Germans had been present in Moscow from the sixteenth century, the major movement of this minority into the Russian heartland occurred during the eighteenth century, following Catherine the Great's Imperial Manifestos of 1762 and 1763, inviting foreigners to settle within the country. She wanted to use the newcomers to furnish the capital capacity, technical and other skills which the native Russian population could not provide,[22] and to settle them in the border regions of the Volga and southern Ukraine. In response to the manifestos about 27,000 Germans moved to the Volga, while 10,000 migrated to the Black Sea region.[23] Many of these emigrants moved from Hessen, a major area of emigration in eighteenth-century Germany, due mainly to excess population growth.

In contrast to subsequent periods of European history, one of the distinguishing characteristics of the early years of settlement of dispersed minorities consists of the ease with which peoples could move into Europe and settle, relatively unmolested, in areas unaffected by nationalism. This first period of settlement simply represented the seeds of subsequent ethnic developments which did not, in some cases, reach fruition until the twentieth century.

Evolution

The evolutionary process was not linear. The settlement of Jews, Gypsies, Muslims or Germans in any particular location did not mean that, by the age of nationalism, an ethnic group would develop in that particular area, even if this in fact often happened. In the intervening years further important developments occurred which increased the size of minorities in particular locations. Apart from the obvious population explosion of the nineteenth and twentieth centuries, which affected some groups earlier than others, further migration (as well as, in the case of Muslims, conversions) fundamentally changed both the size of ethnic concentrations as well as their locations. The development of the medieval and early modern state also played a role in this process, practising persecution which resulted in the expulsion and redistribution of populations, processes which became commonplace and affected countless millions of people after 1900.

In the centuries which followed the fall of the Roman Empire, Jewish communities continued to exist in Spain, France and Italy, facing persecution and even expulsion, as they did in the areas to which they migrated further north on the Rhine, Elbe and Upper Danube, as well as England, where they began to appear in significant numbers following the Norman Conquest. Persecution increased, particularly during the phase of Christian fanaticism engendered by the Crusades. This resulted in pogroms in several towns, notably York and Cologne but also in other locations in England, France and Germany. A contemporary account described the disturbances in England in 1190:

> Many of those who were hastening to go to Jerusalem determined first to rise against the Jews before they invaded the Saracens. Accordingly, on 6 February, all the Jews who were found in their own houses at Norwich were butchered; some had taken refuge in the Castle. On 7 March, namely at the time of the fair, at Stamford, many were slain. On 16 March, at York, it is said that nearly 500 were put to death, attacking one another with mutual wounds, for they preferred to be struck down by their own people rather than perish at the hands of the uncircumcised. On 18 March, the feast of Palm-branches, as it is said, forty-seven were slaughtered at St Edmunds. Wherever the Jews were found they were massacred by the hands of the Crusaders.

Following the pogroms Jews faced expulsion from England, France and Germany, as well as from Spain and Portugal, from the thirteenth to the fifteenth century, due to a growth in general intolerance caused mainly by state creation and extension. [24]

These events played a role in the growth in the numbers of Jews in the eastern half of the European continent during the middle ages, although they had lived in numerous locations before this time. For instance, some Jews had settled in the area covered by Yugoslavia during the period of the Roman Empire and continued to live in Macedonia throughout the Byzantine period. [25] Jews also settled in Poland from the fifth century AD. [26] The persecutions which took place in western Europe helped these communities to grow as they accepted victims of the intolerance. According to the authority on the subject, the Ottoman Empire provided a principal refuge for Jews driven out of western Europe by massacres and persecution between the fourteenth and the twentieth centuries, which meant that the Jewish communities of Thessaloniki and Constantinople became some of the most vibrant in the continent. [27] The Jewish populations of Poland and its sister kingdom Lithuania also increased significantly from the end of the middle ages into the early modern period, which meant that by the middle of the eighteenth century they made up one fifth of the population of Poland and one third of the population of Lithuania. [28]

By 1800 other significant developments had taken place affecting European Jewry. Persecution in central and eastern Europe, covering Poland and the Ukraine but also resulting in expulsion from parts of the Habsburg Empire, meant a westward movement towards Holland and England, the latter having readmitted Jews from the 1650s, after expelling them in 1290.[29] Perhaps the most important development in the history of eighteenth-century European Jewry came as a consequence of the partitions of Poland which meant the incorporation into the Russian Empire of hundreds of thousands of Jews, a figure which added to the Jewish communities already living around the Black Sea from as early as the fourth century AD.[30] The final major eighteenth-century development was an increase in the religious toleration of Jews, which meant that they obtained or began to obtain civil rights in western Europe under the influence of the Enlightenment and the French Revolution.[31]

In medieval and early modern Europe persecution followed the Gypsies wherever they went. In Germany, as elsewhere, they were perceived as robbers, thieves and murderers, a perception not helped by the religious turmoil of the sixteenth and seventeenth centuries. As with Jews, the ultimate sanction used by monarchical states and cities consisted of expulsion, which took place in numerous European locations during the fifteenth, sixteenth and seventeenth centuries.[32] Referring specifically to the later sixteenth century, one source has gone as far as to speak of the sustained genocidal persecution and enslavement of European Gypsies, put down to a variety of factors including economic crisis and the upheaval caused by the Reformation, as well the threat of the Ottoman Empire in the east.[33]

The late seventeenth and eighteenth centuries were a period of severe repression of the Gypsies in central and eastern Europe. In Bohemia mass killings took place, while the Habsburg Enlightened Despots, Maria Theresa and her son Joseph II, tried a policy of forced assimilation, including the prohibition of nomadism and the use of Gypsy languages, as well as the forcible removal of children from parents, actions which today would be regarded as genocide. Such policies were abandoned with the death of Joseph II in 1790.[34] In the Balkans the normal condition of a Gypsy was that of a slave until the nineteenth century.[35] In Russia legislation was passed in 1759 to prevent the entry of Gypsies into St Petersburg and in 1767 a tax was imposed upon all Gypsies.[36]

In western Europe the situation was not much better. In Spain a law of 1745 declared that refractory Gypsies should 'be hunted down with fire and sword', while several attempts had been made between the fifteenth and seventeenth centuries to deport Gypsies.[37] Deportation was also standard practice in both France and England.[38] In the latter a series of Acts was passed between the sixteenth and eighteenth centuries which forbade Gypsies from travelling: indeed, until 1783, Gypsies could be imprisoned or expelled just for being Gypsies. [39]

Unlike the Jews, Gypsies did not experience a process of emancipation during the eighteenth century because of their completely different social and economic position. This meant that they remained illiterate and, consequently, unable to influence the consciences of either the Enlightened Despots or the emerging liberal democratic states. In fact, because of their completely outcast status, the emancipation of Gypsies did not really become an issue – in contrast to the ambiguous relationship of Jewry with European rulers.

In this sense the evolution of the other two dispersed groupings also differs significantly from that of Jews and Gypsies, as they had quite a different relationship with state authorities in the areas where they resided. This is particularly true of the Muslims, who had a privileged position in the areas controlled by the Ottoman Empire, but applies also to Germans, especially in areas which came under Habsburg rule.

The Ottoman system of government did not discriminate purely in favour of Turks but, instead, recognised the position of all religious groupings by formally organising members of different faiths into communities called millets, which by the eighteenth-century existed for Armenians, Catholics, Jews, Muslims and, largest and most powerful of all, Orthodox Christians. While this system worked effectively in an age of imperialism, the states which followed in the age of nationalism, which began with the movement for Greek independence in the early nineteenth century, undermined the system because of the tighter control and standardisation of people required by the nation state. Consequently, the nation states which followed in the areas of the Balkans with pockets of Muslims inevitably had visible minorities within their borders. This visibility became particularly obvious during the countless Balkan wars which took place after 1800.

The period of Ottoman rule saw few such conflicts. Instead, apart from the relative peace of ethnic relations within the Balkans, one of the other major developments consisted of the conversion of parts of the existing populations to Islam. In some areas the relatively privileged position of Muslims abetted this process, although it did not always represent the determining factor in exchanges of faith.

Former Yugoslavia illustrates this process, particularly Bosnia-Herzegovina. Many historians of Bosnia begin its history in the sixth and seventh centuries AD, when the region covered by Yugoslavia was settled by the Slavic peoples migrating from the area now covered by Iran. The Slavs included both Serbs and Croats who have had a similar and connected history from the earliest times. [40] The development of Christianity in the area began in the seventh century following the arrival of missionaries from Rome and Constantinople, leading to the development of Catholicism in the north and west and the growth of the Orthodox Church in the south and east. In addition, from the tenth century, a Christian belief particular to the area, Bogomilism, also developed, named after its founder, a Bulgarian Orthodox priest, and subsequently known as the Bosnian Church. From the twelfth until the fifteenth century a Bosnian state existed which fluctuated in size. The Ottomans began moving into the area during the fourteenth century, making significant inroads during the following century but not completely taking it over until the start of the sixteenth.

Unlike the situation in Bulgaria and Cyprus, there was virtually no movement of Turks into Bosnia, so that all present-day Muslims in the area have the same ethnic origins as the Orthodox Croats and Serbs. Much conversion took place during the sixteenth century, when not only Islam but also the Orthodox Church, which was favoured by the Ottomans, gained converts from the Catholic and the Bosnian churches. Nevertheless, by the start of the seventeenth century, if not before, Muslims had become the largest religious group in Bosnia. [41]

The most important reason for conversion appears to have been the disorganised nature of religion in the area, with few priests, which meant that the shift from folk Christianity to folk Islam was not very great. [42] The two religions remained similar and the conversion from Christianity to Islam could take several generations. One authority confidently stated that Muslims in contemporary Bosnia-Herzegovina were made up in the following way:

> 10–12 per cent are descendants of Bosnian-Hercegovinian Croatians of the Bogomil sect, 70–75 per cent come from Bosnian-Hercegovinian Croatian Catholics, 12–13 per cent come from Croatian Muslims of the neighbouring Croatian provinces and Montenegro, 2–3 per cent are of Turkish ethnic origin, and 1–2 per cent are of Vlach origin. [43]

As elsewhere in their empire, the Turks ruled Bosnia through the millet system, each religious group having its own schools, welfare system and courts. By 1870 Bosnia had Muslim majorities in all but one of the geographical divisions of the country, making up the largest grouping in the state as a whole with 870,128 of the 1,746,399 inhabitants, followed by 636,208 Orthodox Christians and 220,353 Catholics. [44]

The second most important concentration of Muslims in the Balkans was in Macedonia, which has an ethnic mix of a complexity which makes it stand out even in the Balkans. The various groups which make up the Muslims are one reason for this complexity. They can be broken down into three. First, ethnic Turks, who moved into the region from the sixteenth century and whose settlement followed the pattern of Turkish migration into Bulgaria. After 1945 they numbered between 100,000 and 200,000 people according to official figures. The second group of Muslims in Macedonia consists of native Slavic peoples who converted to Islam and whose official figure was 40,000 in 1981. Albanians represent the largest Muslim group in Macedonia, concentrated in the part of the republic bordering Albania. They constituted the largest minority: 377,726 out of a total population of 1,912,257 in 1981. [45]

Albanians also live in the province of Kosovo within Serbia, which has an ethnic situation as complex as that of Macedonia, again with more than one Muslim group. In the first place there are a small number of ethnic Turks. These are far outnumbered by Albanians who actually constitute the largest ethnic grouping in the province, easily surpassing Montenegrins and Serbs. The Albanians converted to Islam during the seventeenth century when the Turkish rulers of the area used economic incentives to win their allegiance. [46] Religion represented the core of their ethnic consciousness. Because of their religion, they experienced no obstacles to advancement within the Ottoman Empire.

In the Russian Empire, the Muslim population increased in size from the sixteenth century, as the realm of the Tsars expanded and brought adherents of Islam into its southern and eastern peripheries, indicating another method of Muslim minority creation, in which a controlling state encroached on a new area. The complexity of ethnic groups on the Russian fringe, most of them beyond our geographical scope, make the Muslim groups within the Balkans look straightforward. Essentially, the history of Central Asia involved colonisation of the area by Arab, Mongol and Turkic peoples during the middle ages, followed by the conquest of the region by the Russian Empire, beginning in the sixteenth century and lasting well into the nineteenth. The Soviet Union inherited the Tsarist land mass and developed a series of policies toward its Muslim minorities.

As a result of the Russian advance into Central Asia, the number of Muslims in the empire had reached 13,907,000 by 1897, making up 11 per cent of the total population. [47] Before the age of nationalism, only four groups, the Volga Tatars, the Crimean Tatars, the Azeri Turks and the Kazakhs, had some rather vague notions of belonging to a separate and distinct nationality. The rest simply saw themselves as Muslims or as attached to the place where they lived.

Of these groups, the Crimean Tatars came under Russian control during the eighteenth century, having previously constituted part of the Ottoman Empire. By the time of the 1897 census, the 188,000 Tatars made up just one-third of the population of the Crimea, surpassed by Russians and Ukrainians, who constituted 45 per cent. [48] The other major historical area of

Tatar settlement in Russia consisted of the Khanate of Kazan. The twentieth-century Tatars in the region consist both of remnants of the Golden Horde and of other local groups, including Bulgars who moved into the area from lands around the Danube from the middle of the seventh century. The Russians conquered the Khanate of Kazan by the middle of the sixteenth century. During the following two centuries the Muslim population of the area faced persecution, forcing many to move eastward. [49]

The Azeri, or Azerbaijani, minority of the Soviet Union, living in eastern Anatolia, has different origins to the Tatars. In ancient times the area had been invaded by both the Persians and the Greeks, although other migrations and invasions followed subsequently. A turning point in the demographic history of the region came in the eleventh century with the invasion of the Seljuk Turks, which resulted in conversion to Islam. An Azeri language, of Turkic origin, developed. With Tsarist expansion over the following centuries, the area gradually fell into the Russian orbit, leading to annexation in 1828. [50]

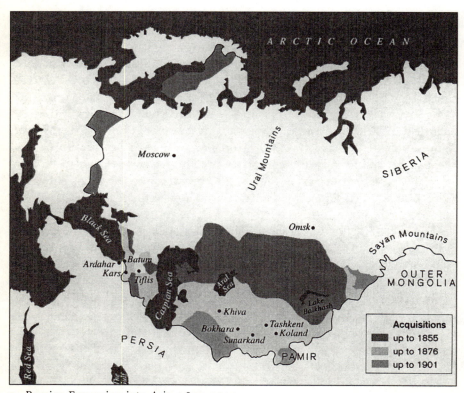

5. Russian Expansion into Asia, 1800–1914

The expansion of the Habsburg Empire into central and south-eastern Europe usually resulted in the arrival of fresh numbers of Germans into particular areas already inhabited by members of this group, rather than their importation for the first time. This meant a consolidation and expansion of already existing areas of settlement, a process most closely resembling the growth of the Ottoman Empire, although the absence of conversions clearly differentiates the expansion of Muslim and German settlements.

The Habsburg dynasty began to rise to prominence in the thirteenth century when Rudolph I became the first member of his house to become head of the Holy Roman Empire, which dominated much of central Europe. From 1438 this dynasty ruled the empire until its demise in 1806. It grew significantly from the sixteenth to the nineteenth centuries to incorporate major territories in central and eastern Europe, including Bohemia, Hungary, Transylvania, Croatia, Dalmatia and Bosnia. The pattern of administration of these areas changed with the passage of time, with much local autonomy at the end of medieval period followed by centralisation during the eighteenth century, then a growth in nationalist movements in the nineteenth century and some devolution. [51]

Germans moved into several new areas with the encouragement of the Habsburgs. These included the Tyrol, which came under the control of the dynasty as early as 1363, witnessing an influx of German settlers in the following centuries. In areas covered by contemporary Czechoslovakia, taken over by the Habsburgs in 1526, when the Habsburg Empire gained control of Bohemia, a Germanisation of the urban populations occurred during the eighteenth century, especially in the cities and border areas, although the German- and Czech-speakers remained tolerant towards each other. The annexation of Hungary by the Habsburgs also led to large-scale organised migration, instigated by a series of Habsburg rulers from the late seventeenth to the early nineteenth centuries. This movement began after the expulsion of the Turks from Hungary in 1683, although most of the newcomers settled in regions which would subsequently become part of Rumania, Russia and Yugoslavia.

In Rumania settlement occurred in the Banat from Württemberg, Breisgau, Alsace and Lorraine, with encouragement from the Habsburg Emperor Charles VI during the early eighteenth century. Further Germans from Bohemia, Württemberg and the Rhineland began to enter Bukovina at the end of the eighteenth century after it was retaken from the Turks. [52] Most of the Germans migrating towards what was to become Yugoslavia at this time went to Voyvodina, while others followed during the nineteenth century, so that by 1910 Germans made up 311,162 out of an incredibly diverse total population of 1,350,477. [53] The eighteenth-century Habsburg expansion

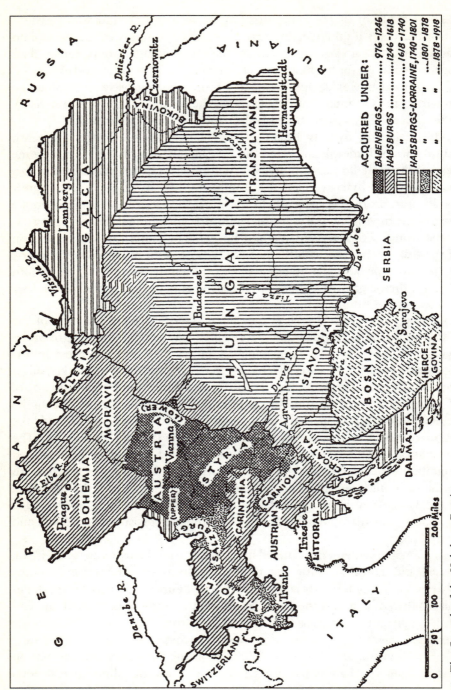

6. The Growth of the Habsburg Empire

also resulted in German migration into Croatia and Slavonia, its western neighbour. Finally, some movement of Germans took place into Bosnia-Herzegovina after its annexation by Austria-Hungary in 1878.

The Consequences of Nationalism and Racism

The migratory processes which had led to the evolution of the Jewish, Gypsy, Muslim and German populations, over thousands of years, came under serious threat as a result of the rise of nationalism and its twin racism. Unlike the informal empires, which generally accepted difference, the new ideologies demanded conformity. Those who did not have the right ethnic credentials faced a level of persecution never previously witnessed in European history, ultimately leading to the Nazi death camps. While in other cases the rise of nationalism and racism did not result in genocide, it often led to other forms of ethnic purification. The easiest way to achieve such aims lay in simply altering borders, a process which required the support of the great powers. Throughout the nineteenth century, as nationalism arose amongst eastern European peoples, the writing was on the wall for the dispersed minorities who happened to find themselves located in the wrong place. During the twentieth century, and more importantly in 1918 and 1945, the great powers gave their consent to boundary changes which had disastrous consequences for the minorities that happened to find themselves in newly created or adjusted states. There often followed processes of ethnic cleansing, either immediately or decades later. Those who remained inevitably faced some sort of hostility from the standardising nation states which had come into existence.

The most extreme forms of persecution against the Jews, and to a lesser extent against the Gypsies, occurred as a result of the growth of racism and antisemitism. Racism began to gain in power from the mid nineteenth century due to several developments. First, the transformation of Darwin's theories of evolution into Social Darwinism, which simply applied his ideas of natural selection of species of animals into natural selection of races of human beings, developing into a hierarchy of different races. The other development that helped this process was the first major encounter of Europeans with Africa and its inhabitants, as a consequence of imperial expansion, which appeared to reinforce ideas of a hierarchy of races. In continental Europe concepts of racial hierarchy also focused upon the differences between European groups. Extreme German nationalists, in particular, looked eastward towards lands which they wanted the newly-created German state to annex and where lived, what they viewed as, inferior Slavic races. Finally, throughout Europe, most potently manifesting itself in

France, Germany, Russia and (to a lesser extent) Britain, antisemites turned Jews into a race which threatened the racial purity and economic well-being of domestic populations. The Nazis ultimately perfected a system of government based upon the concept of superior and inferior races, in which Germans ruled over and dealt with Jews, Gypsies and Slavs in differing ways.

Hostility towards Jews clearly does not represent a new phenomenon, as it has existed throughout European history. The new antisemitism of the nineteenth century paradoxically began to emerge at a time when Jews had achieved full civil rights. In many ways the emerging Judeophobia represented a reaction against such developments. The new antisemitism became stronger than its medieval ancestors, inextricably linked with the growth of nationalism and the necessity for conformity that it demanded. Its ideology focused upon those who remained different, most notably the Jews, so that racism simply replaced medieval Christianity in its inability to tolerate the archetypal minority group. At the end of the nineteenth century strong antisemitism gripped France, Germany and Russia, in all of which it became a central political issue, although few European states remained completely free from its influence.

The most significant events in the history of nineteenth-century European Jewry occurred in the eastern half of the continent. The population explosion which affected the whole of Europe during this period meant that up to five million Jews lived in Russia, mostly within Poland, by the end of the nineteenth century.[54] This growth occurred at the time Russia experienced its first significant period of industrialisation and modernisation, the consequences of which included an influx of Orthodox Russians, following peasant emancipation under Alexander II, to urban areas. Many of these people came into contact with Jews, concentrated in towns and cities, for the first time. More significantly they found themselves in competition with Jews during this early and most exploitative period of industrialisation. This, combined with the inherent but growing antisemitism of the Russian Orthodox Church, now virtually becoming Tsarist policy, led to an explosion of murderous pogroms against Jews.[55] Even when such violence did not take place, Jews became victims of other forms of persecution, including restrictions on their residence in Moscow, which the authorities strictly enforced:

> In Moscow proper, inquisitional raids are made suddenly by night on the houses of well-known families – those of physicians, lawyers, apothecaries, etc. Between one and two a.m. they prosecute a most careful search in all the rooms, in the bedrooms of married and unmarried women. The latter are disturbed so that it may be seen whether they have concealed in their apartments those who, by the new laws, have been deprived of the right to remain in the city.[56]

The growth of the Jewish population and the rise in antisemitism resulted in a westward migration of Jews, usually bound for the USA. Not all emigrants travelled so far, preferring instead to settle at various points of the journey. About 100,000 remained in Paris,[57] a similar number in Great Britain,[58] while about 80,000 settled in Germany.[59] The effect of this immigration was to increase the antisemitism already existing in these states, as well as to add a new working-class and Orthodox element to the Jewish populations of western Europe.

Hostility towards Jews inevitably increased during the First World War, when conformity to the nation state became more of a necessity, leading to charges in both Germany and Britain that Jews were not serving in the army.[60] The post-war peace treaties, which reconstructed eastern Europe, completely changed the national distribution of the Jews on the continent. The most important development was the creation of a Polish state. This had the largest concentration of Jews in Europe, totalling 2,853,318 in 1919 (or 10.5 per cent of the population), living mostly in central and eastern Poland and focused within urban areas. By 1939 the total number had grown to approximately 3,300,000, still constituting about 10 per cent of the population.[61] A large number of Jews also remained in the Soviet Union, despite the loss of Polish territories, concentrated mostly within the areas of the old Pale of Settlement in the east and south east covering the republics of Ukraine, Belorussia and Russia, totalling, in the Soviet Union as a whole, 3,020,000 by the outbreak of the Second World War.[62] Remnants of the Jewish community formerly residing in the Pale of Settlement also found themselves living in the newly created Baltic Republics. In Latvia, for instance, Jews made up 5 per cent of the population of 1,500,000 in 1939.[63]

Virtually every eastern European state had a sizeable Jewish population during the inter-war years. Rumania acted as home to 800,000 Jews,[64] while in Hungary the Jewish population totalled 480,000 in 1938.[65] Elsewhere in eastern Europe over 180,000 Jews lived in the newly-created Czechoslovakia.[66] In the Balkans, Yugoslavia contained over 60,000 Jews residing mostly in urban areas, notably Sarajevo where a community had existed for hundreds of years and where they made up over 5 per cent of the population.[67] In Bulgaria, which had also contained a Jewish community since the days of Ottoman rule, the Jewish population did not exceed 50,000 in this period,[68] while Turkey still contained 81,872 Jews in 1927, more than half of whom lived in Istanbul.[69]

Compared with the Jewish populations of eastern Europe, those living in the western half of the continent remained far fewer during the inter-war years. In fact, the communities of many eastern European cities, especially within Poland, exceeded that of the Jewish population of some of the western

European states. The Nazi seizure of power, and their acceptance of emigration for much of the period before 1939, affected both the Jewish population
of pre-war Germany and that of the countries to which German Jews migrated.
In 1933 German Jewry totalled about 500,000 souls, but by the outbreak of
the Second World War this figure had declined to 200,000. To these, however,
should be added a further 240,000 brought in by the Nazi annexation of
Austria and Czechoslovakia, although emigration had also taken place from
these new additions to the Reich before the outbreak of war. [70] At first the
refugees moved mainly to neighbouring states, including Belgium, France,
Holland, Switzerland, Czechoslovakia and Austria, [71] although many clearly
left the last two of these after 1938 when Nazi annexation of these territories
created a new threat. Britain proved one of the most generous European
states from 1938, allowing 50,000 to enter, compared with the 40,000 who
went to France, 25,000 to Belgium and 10,000 to Switzerland. [72] Just as the
late nineteenth-century newcomers added a new element to the Jewish populations of western Europe, so in the same way did the refugees from Nazism.
All of those who escaped left someone behind, as the recollection of one
young refugee clearly illustrates:

> I left home in the evening with the whole family to see me off. At the station
> we were ushered into an enormous waiting room which was packed with children
> and parents weeping, crying and shouting. It occurred to me there for the first
> time that our grief was no longer a personal one. We all belonged to a group,
> but not a group that was determined through social, economic or intellectual
> dividing lines; we were all refugees. We were ordered to take leave of our relatives
> and go straight to the train, which had sealed windows and once we were all
> inside it the doors were sealed as well. Shortly before the train was due to leave
> our relatives appeared again on the platform. From behind the sealed windows
> I saw my parents again, rigid and unsmiling like two statues, for the last time
> ever. I was sixteen years old. [73]

No minority in European history has ever experienced the trauma faced
by European Jewry during the Second World War, when the Nazis tried to
wipe out thousands of years of civilisation of the quintessential European
minority in order to perfect the racial hierarchy and change the geography
of Europe, as outlined by Adolf Hitler in *Mein Kampf*. The new order, to
be ruled by Aryan Germans, facilitated in their task by Slavic peoples as
slaves, necessitated the eradication of Jews because of their perceived racial
impurity, a myth developed because of their distinctiveness throughout European history. The 'Final Solution' meant ending a 'problem' in European
history which the Nazis felt they could solve as a modern party.

The fulfilment of their aim varied from one area to another and the factors
which determined the extent of their success, and the survival rates of Jews,

included the nature and extent of German occupation in each particular state and the levels of antisemitism and sympathies of the local non-Jewish population. Areas annexed by the expanded Third Reich or contiguous with it, passing under direct Nazi rule, also tended to be those with the strongest antisemitic traditions and, consequently, those which lost the highest proportion of their Jews. Those under less direct control and with less developed traditions of antisemitism were those with the lowest death rates, notably Italy and Bulgaria. There remains no scientific equation which determined the rates of survival: Greece, with less developed traditions of modern antisemitism, nevertheless suffered significant Jewish losses.

The core areas of central Europe, Germany and Austria, experienced some of the highest Jewish death rates. Lucy Dawidowicz estimates that only about 28,000 Jews survived the Holocaust in Germany and Austria.[74] A city such as Munich, with a Jewish population of 9000 in 1933, had this number reduced through the policies of emigration and murder pursued during the following twelve years to just 430, a number which included those who had gone into hiding and those not considered 'full Jews'.[75]

Polish Jewry suffered a fate as bad, or worse than, that of their co-religionists in Germany. This was a state with potent traditions of modern antisemitism, manifesting themselves most violently in the pogroms which had affected the area in late Tsarist Russia and, more potently still, in the early days of the new Polish state. During the inter-war years antisemitism was official policy, despite guarantees about the status of minorities under the 1921 constitution. Restrictions particularly focused upon the entry of Jews into various professions and also affected their community and cultural life. Manifestations of the hostility included the development of seating ghettos in university classes.[76] The invasion of 1939 led to direct German control, although clearly some fusing of German and Polish antisemitism took place. Poland provided the ground upon which the Final Solution was implemented, allowing the Nazis first to experiment with the establishment of ghettos, then set up the six death camps in which the extermination of European Jewry became a reality: Auschwitz, Belzec, Chelmno, Majdanek, Sobibor and Treblinka. Jews from the whole of Europe were transported to these killing factories. One of the millions of victims, Abraham Lewin, living in the Warsaw ghetto, recorded, in one of his last diary entries before disappearing to one of the camps, his sense of foreboding:

Once again a few dark, melancholy and very, very gloomy days have gone by. The few who have survived continue to live their lives, which are filled with baseness and bitterness. On the surface everything is quiet and it seems that they do not want to disturb the peace of those who have been left alive. But deep in our hearts is gnawing away the perpetual dread that never lets up for one moment and eats away at us like a moth. [77]

In statistical, non-personal terms antisemitism in Second World War Poland meant the virtual elimination of Jewish life from Polish soil, which had one of the oldest and most developed Yiddish traditions in eastern Europe, reducing the Jewish population to around 250,000 souls, a fall of 90 per cent. [78]

A few Polish Jews attempted to move eastward into the Soviet Union on the outbreak of war; others were temporarily saved by the fact that they fell into the eastern half of the country annexed by the Soviet Union, as agreed by the Nazi-Soviet Non-Aggression Pact of August 1939. However, with the Nazi advance into the Soviet Union after the launch of Operation Barbarossa in June 1941, the Nazis soon began to implement the racial order they had already practised in Poland during the preceding two years. Once again, local antisemitism, which had manifested itself in violence in the Russian borderlands from the late nineteenth century until the end of First World War, assisted Nazi policies. The Nazis were further helped by local anti-Soviet nationalist inhabitants in the Baltic States and the Ukraine who willingly participated in hunting down and killing Jews in the occupied lands. Overall as many as two million Jews were murdered in the Soviet Union, meaning that Jewish losses were about proportionally four times as heavy as those of the Soviet population as a whole. [79]

Large-scale murder also happened elsewhere in eastern Europe. Hungary had a strong antisemitic tradition. This had resulted in the passage of discriminatory legislation throughout the inter-war years and acted as the background to the deportation of its Jews to Poland, [80] meaning that the Jewish population shrank from about 825,000 to 255,000. [81] In Czechoslovakia, annexed by Hitler just before the outbreak of war, about 240,000 Jews were killed; leaving just 22,000 in the Czech areas and 3500 in Slovakia. [82] Rumania lost about 300,000 out of its 757,000 Jews. [83] In Yugoslavia, with a limited antisemitic tradition, although one did exist among Bosnian, Croation and Serbian nationalists,

the Holocaust wiped out an estimated 55- to 60,000 Yugoslav Jews, approximately 80 per cent of the pre-war Jewish population of the country. Some were shot in the streets, others died in Yugoslav concentration camps; many were sent to the crematoria of Auschwitz and death camps elsewhere. [84]

Just 50,000 remained at the end of the war. [85] Even worse happened in Greece.

At the outbreak of War there were between 70,000 and 80,000 Jews in Greece, of whom over 50,000 lived in the city of Salonika. Fewer than 10,000 survived, and some of the oldest Jewish communities in Europe perished as a result. [86]

Bulgaria represented the classic exception to the rule in eastern Europe and the Balkans in the fact that it saved virtually all its Jews because the government did not hand them over for deportation to the death camps. [87]

In western Europe the picture varied from one country to another for similar reasons to those in the eastern half of the continent. Britain, with the exception of the Channel Islands, remained untouched, although a milder form of antisemitism certainly existed within the country's shores. The state did little to assist victims of the Holocaust, allowing only about 10,000 Jewish refugees to enter during the Second World War. [88] A similar number, 11,535, were saved by Franco's Spain, [89] while some also moved to Turkey, especially those on their way to Palestine. [90] In Scandinavia, meanwhile, much effort went into supporting and hiding Jews within Denmark – with assistance from Sweden. Norway's record was not so good. [91] Nor was that of Holland, which witnessed the deportation of 110,000 of its Jews to the Nazi extermination camps in Poland, meaning that only about 30,000 Dutch Jews survived the Second World War. [92] France had one of the deepest antisemitic traditions in western Europe, stretching back centuries and surfacing in the Dreyfus Affair of the 1890s; one which also set the political agenda during the 1930s. France passed its own racial laws under the Second World War Vichy regime – as well as setting up its own concentration camps. Nevertheless, about 70 per cent of the 350,000 Jews living in France in 1939 survived. [93] Italy, without much of an antisemitic tradition, had one of the most impressive survival rates, losing only 8000 of its 57,000 Jews, [94] due to a popular refusal to surrender to the Nazi will, despite the alliance of Mussolini and Hitler. [95]

In all, Lucy Dawidowicz estimates that 5,933,900 out of 8,861,800 Jews in the countries occupied by the Nazis were murdered, meaning a death rate of 67 per cent. [96] (The figure excludes the Jewish population of Britain, which totalled close to 400,000 by the end of the Second World War.) [97] Genocide has not affected the development of any other European minority so greatly. The situation of the surviving Jews was desperate, even on liberation. One American soldier who entered the Buchenwald camp in Germany wrote the following:

> On the sight of an American uniform a horde of gnomes and trolls seem to appear like magic, pouring out of doorways as if shot from a cannon. Some hop on crutches. Some hobble on stumps of feet. Some glide like Oriental genies. Almost all wear striped convict suits, covered with patches, or grey black remnants of Eastern clothing. [98]

After the Second World War, the remaining years of the twentieth century resulted in further developments which altered the composition of European

Jewry. In the first place, antisemitism did not die, especially in eastern Europe. This played a large part in the migration of Jews to Israel. The worst affected communities included those in Bulgaria, Poland and the Soviet Union. The mention of the first of these seems surprising in view of the fact that Bulgarian Jewry had survived the Holocaust largely intact. Nevertheless, an outburst of antisemitism immediately after the end of the Second World War meant that Bulgarian Jewry declined from its 1945 level of 46,500 to just 7676 by 1951.[99] In Poland, the strong historical traditions of antisemitism continued, manifesting themselves most potently in violence leading to as many as 1500 deaths among survivors of the Holocaust immediately after the end of the Second World War.[100] These events encouraged emigration to Israel, as did state-led antisemitic campaigns during the 1950s and 1960s. In all, the 120,000 Polish Jews who had survived the Holocaust had declined to about 5000 by the end of the 1960s.[101] The Soviet authorities also carried out overt anti-semitic campaigns on several occasions after the Second World War, while hostility towards Jews also showed itself openly following the collapse of the Soviet Union. These developments led to mass emigration to Israel. However, in 1989 the USSR still contained 1,487,000 Jews, still easily the largest com-munity in Europe.[102] Emigration to Israel also took place from most of the other east European Jewish communities, due both to intolerance towards them, as well as greater economic opportunities in the new state.[103]

Nevertheless, the decline of the Jewish communities in eastern Europe has not occured simply because of persecution and emigration. Falling birthrates and intermarriage have also played a role, factors which have also affected the Jewish populations of western Europe. In most of the states in which they have survived, the Jewish populations are more educated and economi-cally more successful than the dominant population, meaning that their demographic characteristics are those typical of the middle classes: freedom in choosing a partner, later age of marriage and fewer children. In the case of Britain, declining fertility rates and marriage with Gentiles have been responsible for the fall in the size of the Jewish population from 450,000 in 1955 to 330,000 in 1985.[104]

At the end of the twentieth century European Jewry has reached the most stable and successful point in its history of over 2000 years. While antisemitism still exists, the most overt racism which has surfaced on the continent since the Second World War has, with the exception of Poland in 1946, focused upon other minorities. This may largely be a reaction against the policies of the Nazis. The lessening of Jewish consciousness has also played a role in the increasing tolerance of Jews, although this lessening of consciousness may be due to antisemitism in the first place. Just as important, however, is the increasing secularisation of post-war society and the declining importance of religion. Nevertheless, Judaism is very much alive in Europe at the end of the twentieth century. In Russia, for instance, the collapse of the Soviet Union gave Jews a new lease of life,[105] while in Britain the institutions of the Jewish community, in the form of synagogues, schools and welfare institutions, are as strong as ever.[106]

While not underestimating the Gypsy Holocaust, the Nazis did not destroy an entire civilisation as they destroyed Yiddish culture in much of central and eastern Europe. The main reason for the survival of Gypsies lay in the fact that, while the Nazis saw them as racially inferior, their elimination was not at the top of German priorities. In contrast to Jews, they were secondary. Consequently, Gypsy civilisation survived in post-war eastern Europe only to suffer new forms of persecution in the newly-created states supported by the Soviet Union.

During the nineteenth century the Gypsies of Europe increased as a result of the population growth that affected all of the peoples of Europe. The major concentrations lay in eastern Europe. Hungary, for instance, housed 50,040 Gypsies in 1873, a figure which had increased to approximately 200,000 by the outbreak of the Second World War.[107] In Bulgaria, meanwhile, the Gypsy population had risen to 54,557 by the end of the nineteenth century.[108] One observer described a settlement there:

> Close to our camp was a small Gypsy *mahalo* of about eight houses and four tents. The tents, though made of inferior cloth, were rather more elaborate than ours, having three or more arch-pieces. The houses were longer than usual, and built against the slope of the hill, in which they were partly excavated, so that, at the back, they were considerably below the level of the surface of the earth ... The inhabitants, amiable people who received us with Gypsy hospitality, were all smiths; and we found them busy at their trade in a large hut with a wide veranda, which seemed to serve as a common workshop.[109]

One of the biggest Gypsy concentrations in Europe lay in Rumania, where the Romany population had suffered slavery from the medieval period until the mid nineteenth century. By 1930, 262,501 Gypsies lived in Rumania, making up 1.5 per cent of the overall population.[110] Czechoslovakia contained just 32,857 Gypsies in 1930, making up only 0.2 per cent of the population.[111] Poland saw an expansion of its Gypsy population during the nineteenth and early twentieth centuries, as a result of immigration from Rumania.[112] In Bosnia the Gypsy population reached about 10,000 during the late nineteenth century.[113]

Moving to western Europe, the nineteenth-century Gypsy population in England remained small in relation to that of the overall population, reaching 30,642 according to the 1911 census which counted 'persons found dwelling in barns, sheds, tents, caravans and the open air'. Concentrated in southern England and speaking, by the end of the nineteenth century, a combination of Romany and English, they made their living by a wide range of activities. One writer from 1815 described a settlement near Dagenham in the following way:

> The construction of their tents is well known to be wooden hoops fastened into the ground, and covered with a covering of blankets or canvas, which resembles the tilt of the waggon; the end is closed from the wind by a curtain. This gang was called by the name of Corrie. It consisted of an old man, his wife, a niece, and their son and daughter with ten children; said to be all from Staffordshire. The men were scissors grinders and tinkers.

While much of the hostile legislation of the early modern period may have disappeared, further measures followed in nineteenth-century Britain curtailing the settlement and movement of Gypsies.[114] In nineteenth-century France Gypsy robber gangs developed, although writers tended to exaggerate their numbers.[115] By 1895 over 400,000 itinerant people lived within the country.[116] In Spain Gypsies had become settled by this time, living in their own quarters within towns.[117]

As with the Jews, the early twentieth century resulted in a deterioration in the position of Gypsies throughout Europe as nation states increased their control over their populations, attempting to standardise those who did not fit into the acceptable pattern, a process that culminated in the Nazi extermination policies. Several European states passed legislation against Gypsies during the inter-war years. In Czechoslovakia a 1927 law required all nomads to carry passes, which could be withdrawn at any time. In the following year a pogrom in the village of Pobedim wounded eighteen Gypsies and killed six.[118] Gypsies also faced extreme hostility in Albania.[119] The centralising Soviet system had problems with its Gypsy population, which may have reached 200,000 by 1939, attempting unsuccessfully to turn Gypsies into a sedentary group, although the Soviet authorities also had a positive influence on the Gypsies, formalising their cultural activity and education.[120]

In Germany, the state was unremittingly hostile. Attempts at controlling the Gypsies intensified with the foundation of the German state in 1871. A turning point in their control came in 1926 with the passage of the Bavarian Law for the Combating of Gypsies, Travellers and the Workshy, which allowed the incarceration of Gypsies in workhouses for up to two years. The Nazis introduced further measures for rounding up Gypsies and set up a research unit within the Ministry of Health, under Dr Robert Ritter, to examine Gypsies for scientific reasons. Viewed as a racial threat to the purity of German blood, the Nazis forbade their marriage with Aryans and opened camps to house them before 1939. Such measures caused much distress amongst the German Gypsy population, as one of their number, who was a child at the time, later recalled:

> In the middle of the 1930s our life was haunted by the fear of persecution. My mother always reported that Gypsies would be taken to concentration camps. The streets of our own quarter were filled with stories of Gypsy families who had already been deported. Fear was spreading. My mother seemed to be indifferent about her own life but worried about me and my future. As I was often outside, she must have thought that I was in danger. When I came home in the evening her tired eyes brightened. She smiled at me when I opened the creaking door.

After the outbreak of war the Nazis decided upon a 'Final Solution to the Gypsy Question'.[121]

While estimates of the number of Gypsies murdered by the Nazis vary, Grattan Puxon and Donald Kenrick have documented 219,700 deaths,[122] although Puxon believes that the actual number was closer to 500,000.[123] The Nazis used similar methods of extermination on Gypsies to those used on Jews. Following the invasion of Poland the Gypsies initially found themselves concentrated in ghettos. In November 1941 they were gathered in the Lódz ghetto with a view to their extermination, subsequently being sent to the death camp at Chelmno. At Auschwitz a separate sub-camp was created for Gypsies, B II e, where they suffered the experiments of Josef Mengele. Of 23,000 people sent there, 20,078 died.[124]

The fact that the Nazis were not as determined to exterminate European Gypsies as they were to eradicate the Jews of Europe meant that the former had a higher survival rate. However, as with the Jews, the fate of the Gypsies varied from one part of the continent to another. In Germany, as we might expect, Gypsy life was virtually destroyed,[125] but this was not repeated in other parts of Europe. Even in Poland, the kingdom of death, over 20,000 survived. As their historian writes, they

> managed to evade the camps, gas chambers and executions. Some of them now came out of the depths of the forests where they had managed to survive; others returned from the concentration camps where they had not yet been exterminated; still others came back from the Soviet Union as repatriated persons. A very few highland Gypsies had managed to survive the war in the mountain fastnesses that their ancestors had inhabited.[126]

In Czechoslovakia persecution took place with the establishment of camps after the arrival of the Nazis, although deportation also took place to Auschwitz. Nevertheless, mass extermination did not take place because the war ended too soon for this to happen. In addition, the establishment of an independent Slovak state actually helped Gypsies to survive, so that the number of Gypsies in Czechoslovakia increased during the course of the Second World War. [127] In the Soviet Union the situation was different again, as up to 35,000 Gypsies were killed by the Nazis, including almost all of those in Latvia and Estonia; but, like the Jewish population of the Soviet Union, those who lived beyond the area of German occupation were protected by the Soviet authorities. [128] Elsewhere in Europe between 36,000 and 39,000 Gypsies were murdered in Rumania, while around 30,000 suffered a similar fate in Hungary. In Albania, in contrast, the Gypsy population remained virtually untouched. [129] The situation of Gypsies in Yugoslavia varied according to the fates of the areas in which they lived. The highest death rate was in the Nazi-supported Croatian state, where over 25,000 Gypsies were killed, while 12,000 of the 60,000 Serbian Gypsies suffered a similar fate. The safest were those living in Macedonia and Slovenia. [130]

The main reason for the higher survival rate of the Gypsies, compared with Jews, may find its main explanation in the fact that the latter minority held positions of power throughout European economic and political institutions, while the former remained a group which controlled little. Partly as a consequence of this, but also due to the antiquity of Jewish settlement in Europe, an ideology directed specifically against Jews, antisemitism, developed, making Jews a unique minority. Few other groups have had a global ideology directed against them. Add to this the history of Judeophobia, developed over thousands of years, and the explanation for the different treatment of Jews and Gypsies seems clear. Nevertheless, if the Nazis had won the Second World War, the Gypsies would have faced extermination. They had no place in the new world order envisaged in *Mein Kampf*, the blueprint for Nazi policies during the Second World War.

Gypsies have also had very little place in the visions of the states which have succeeded the Nazis in Europe, especially in its eastern half: they remain the most distinct minority on the continent and the most persecuted, particularly amongst the dispersed groupings and especially in eastern Europe. A series of developments characterise the history of the post-war gypsies. The first is their demography. In contrast to Jews, they have experienced a population explosion rather than a decline, especially in eastern Europe, where the dominant populations have increasingly viewed them as a threat because of this. In Czechoslovakia, for instance, the Gypsy share of the population increased from 0.83 per cent in 1947 to 2.03 per cent by 1980; by the middle of the 1990s, their total number approached 500,000. In Hungary, where Gypsies have a birth rate two or three times as high as the rest of the population, their numbers are approaching one million, a similar figure to Rumania. [131]

The demographics of the Gypsies fits in with their social and economic condition. In all of the states in which they live, they tend to reside in the worst accommodation and to pursue their occupations on the margins of society. Whereas in England they have continued with their itinerant ways, despite the attempts of the state to prevent them from doing so,[132] in most of continental Europe they have now become a sedentary group, in many cases due to force. In Czechoslovakia this involved the removal of wheels from their caravans and the shooting of their horses. The victims often carried on living in the worst accommodation, or moved into slum housing. The Czechoslovak state also attempted to proletarianise its Gypsies, as did other regimes in this part of the continent, meaning that their involvement in more traditional forms of employment has declined.[133] Nevertheless, at the end of the twentieth century, the Gypsies remain the quintessential European outgroup, in contrast to the assimilating Jews, who have undergone significant changes since the end of the Second World War.

The Muslim populations of the Balkans and the Soviet Union did not, like Jews and Gypsies, face a European wide hostility during the nineteenth and twentieth centuries. Instead, they have endured animosity in the various states created as a result of the nineteenth-century growth of nationalism throughout the Ottoman Empire. In the new states their position as representatives of the former imperial power, inevitably viewed negatively by the emerging nationalists, made their plight especially precarious. In the Soviet Union they became, like all other minorities, victims of Stalinism.

Within the Balkans, the creation of Bulgaria in 1878 offers an example of Muslim minority creation upon the birth of a new nation state. Whether measured by religion or by ethnic allegiance, that is as Muslims or as Turks, the minority fluctuated in size between half a million and a million from the late nineteenth to the mid twentieth century, making up between 10 and just over 20 per cent of the population. Persecution resulted in emigration, beginning before the First World War. It was formalised in the Turko-Bulgarian agreement of 18 October 1925, which allowed voluntary emigration of Turks from Bulgaria and Bulgarians from Turkey, although some Turks were forced to leave during the 1930s. In all approximately 100,000 left between 1925 and 1929, followed by others after the Second World War. Those who remained faced extreme persecution during the 1980s. With the collapse of Communism, they reemerged as a significant ethnic minority, establishing their own organisations, but continued to face hostility. By 1992 they numbered 1,112,531 out of a total Bulgarian population of 8,489,317, a proportion of 13.1 per cent.[134]

The Muslim minority of Bosnia did not actually become one in the modern sense of the word until perhaps the final decades of the existence of

Yugoslavia, in the sense of facing hostility from a standardising state. Before reaching that stage it went through several others, the first of which involved passing from Ottoman control to Austrian rule between 1879 and 1918. When the First World War ended, Bosnia became part of the newly-created Yugoslavia, made up of Serbs, Croats and Slovenes. The Bosnian Muslims made up just 6 per cent of the population at this time.[135] Since the end of the nineteenth century the size of the Muslim population has increased, even though the numbers of Serbs and Croats in Bosnia have grown faster. While the number of Muslims grew from 673,246 in 1895 to 1,905,829 in 1991, during the same period the population of Bosnia as a whole increased from 1,568,092 to 4,354,911, meaning that the proportion of Muslims has remained constant at between 35 and 36 per cent.[136] Adherents of Islam also lived in other areas of Yugoslavia including Serbia, where they formed a small grouping in pockets near the border with Bosnia and Montenegro.[137]

The Bosnian Muslims hit the world headlines in the 1990s, when the state became a major theatre in the Yugoslav war, after a referendum voted for independence in the spring of 1992. Because the Muslims made up under 40 per cent of the population, this caused resentment amongst Serbs and Croats both within Bosnia and outside it, leading to the bloodiest scenes in the Yugoslav war, as well as ethnic cleansing. In fact, the US sponsored peace deal in 1996 simply confirmed the reality of the ethnic cleansing that had occurred, as well as encouraging more of it, although the new constitutional structure required all three population groups to play a role in the running of the new Bosnia. The causes of the war lay in the fact that thousands of years of settlement patterns came under threat from the perfection in the ethnic composition of national populations demanded by nationalism.[138]

In the case of Albanians, both as a majority and a minority, one of the main reasons for their growing sense of nationhood during the late nineteenth century, representing a classic reason for many groups feeling a sense of nationhood, was simply that they reacted against the neighbouring states, Serbia and Greece, which were expanding and would swallow them up as minorities. They were supported by the great powers, notably Austria Hungary, which feared an enlarged Serbia, in the creation of their own state in 1912; but by this time many of the areas of residence of Albanians, such as Kosovo and Macedonia, already belonged to other successor states of the Ottoman Empire.[139]

Greece has an ethnic situation with regard to Muslims and Turks at least as complicated as those of Bulgaria and Yugoslavia. Unlike these two states, the Turks and Muslims of Greece are concentrated in one area, western Thrace, which borders Turkey. Turks appear to have settled here from the twelfth century and the area was conquered by the Ottoman Empire in 1354, remaining in Turkish hands until 1913 when it was taken over by Bulgaria, which had been victorious in the First Balkan War. France occupied the area at the end of the First World War, following the defeat of Bulgaria, and it passed into Greek hands under the Treaty of Sèvres in August 1920. There then followed a Greek advance, which made inroads into Anatolia; but the Turks fought back.

The Treaty of Lausanne of 1923, which ended the war, determined Greek-Turkish minority relations for decades to come. In the first place this is one of the best early twentieth-century examples of ethnic cleansing, significantly taking place in the Balkans, as the treaty facilitated population exchange between Greece and Turkey, meaning that 638,253 Greek refugees from Asia Minor moved to Macedonia, while the entire Muslim population of Macedonia, 348,000 people, left for Turkey, to add to a further 125,000 who had departed on the eve of the First World War.[140] Nevertheless, remnants of the respective populations were allowed to remain in the form of 110,000 Greeks in Constantinople and 191,669 Turks in western Thrace.[141] The Treaty of Lausanne guaranteed the rights of these two groups, but these rights have subsequently been constantly violated by both sides.

The numerical make-up of the Muslim population of western Thrace is difficult to ascertain, but the following seem to make up its constituent parts. In the first place, the majority consists of ethnic Turks, settlers who moved into the area during the Ottoman occupation. Secondly, there are converts who began changing their religion from the end of the fourteenth century. In addition, there are also a small number of Gypsies. To these we can also add a small number of Turkish-speaking Christians. In total it seems that between 100,000 and 120,000 'Turks' now live in western Thrace.[142]

Cyprus represents a classic example of the disastrous consequences of nationalism. In the age before nationalism the Greek and Turkish communities managed to coexist, especially in economic processes, although the best evidence of this mutual tolerance is the existence of numerous mixed Turkish and Greek villages. In 1891, thirteen years after the British took over the island, 346 out of the 702 population centres consisted of mixed communities, a figure which had fallen to just forty-eight by 1970. In addition, the Turkish population lived throughout the island during the late nineteenth century, even though it was more concentrated in some areas than others. Throughout the succeeding period Greeks have outnumbered Turks, the proportion changing from 24.4 per cent Turks in 1881 to 18.1 per cent by 1973.[143]

The dualism which has developed in Cyprus since the late nineteenth century has at least three fundamental causes. First, the origins of the division essentially lay in the Ottoman millet system. Although the Greek Orthodox

Church had a privileged position within this structure, it remained in a secondary position to the Muslims. Despite the mutual tolerance of the two communities, their religions remained completely separate, they had their own languages and rarely intermarried.[144]

This situation was simply a precondition and in itself cannot explain the schism which has taken place during the twentieth century. Two further core elements need to be added to this. The first was the divide and rule policy of British imperialism, operating on the principle of playing one community off against another. This maintained and reinforced the dualistic ethnic legacy of the Ottoman Empire.[145]

Even more important than British policy was the growth of nationalism, both Greek and subsequently Turkish. From the late nineteenth century Greek nationalism began to take root within the country, eventually growing into the Enosis movement of the post-war period. In view of the development of the modern Greek state, which had expanded precisely through the ideology of the 'Megali Idea', wishing to take over the Greek-speaking parts of the Mediterranean, it seems impossible to conceive of a situation in which Cyprus would not have been drawn into this vortex. To Greek nationalists, within both Greece and Cyprus, there seemed no reason why Cyprus should not follow other equally dubiously Greek areas of the Mediterranean in uniting with Greece. Unfortunately for Pan-Greeks, Cyprus came too late and was faced, simultaneously, by Pan-Turanism, which, just as strongly, desired to make Cyprus part of Turkey.

The crisis point arrived in the 1950s, with the growth of the movement for Enosis with Greece, which was anathema to the Turkish Cypriots and the mainland Turkish government which supported them; consequently the Cyprus problem became a Greek-Turkish conflict. The apparent solution lay in the creation of an independent Cyprus in 1960, in which both communities shared political power. Greece and Turkey, along with Britain, acted as guarantors of the settlement, which turned out to be a disaster, because, as a compromise, no side – either internally or externally – felt fully committed to it.[146]

The period between 1960 and 1974 therefore witnessed a situation in which the Turkish minority, backed by the Turkish government, increasingly withdrew from political and civic life, while episodes of ethnic violence occurred on several occasions. The almost inevitable conclusion arrived in 1974, when, following an attempt by the Greek junta to overthrow the democratically elected government of Archbishop Makarios, the Turkish army invaded Cyprus, in accordance with its 1960 treaty obligation to protect the Turkish minority on the island. The Turkish army has still not left and the island has undergone almost complete ethnic cleansing, being divided into the

Turkish backed northern half and the independent Greek Cypriot south. For those people who lost their ancestral homes and property, the 1974 invasion has left a deep scar.[147]

The legacy of the Ottoman Empire in the Balkans and the Mediterranean is extremely complex. Without the Ottoman invasions of the area the ethnic situation would clearly have been different, although still complex in view of its geographical location which makes it the first port of call for peoples moving from the east. Most of the purely political ethnic issues of the Balkans result from the legacy of Ottoman rule, whether or not Muslim populations are involved; yet we can hardly blame the Ottoman Empire for the developments which followed its demise. Its system worked well in an age when religion ruled. The advent of literacy and nationalism, and the development of concepts of nationhood based upon common origins, went beyond religion. The new nation states demanded adherence of all citizens to a new tighter system of political control. Local autonomy, which the Turks had respected by the millet system, suffered. The standardisation demanded by nationalism inevitably meant the escalation of serious ethnic problems which the Ottoman system had coped with effectively during its centuries of control in the area. The remnant Muslim populations stood out as representatives of the old system, becoming victims through a retrospective vindictiveness.

In the Soviet Union Islam survived, despite the extreme repression directed against it during the early days of Stalin in the late 1920s and 1930s. This

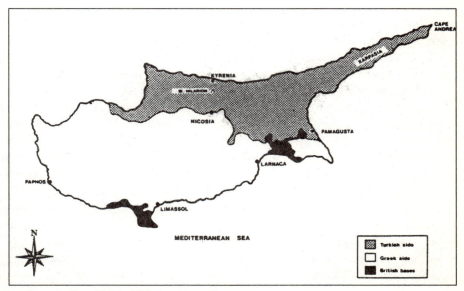

7. Cyprus after the Turkish Invasion of 1974

meant the arrest and deportation of nearly all religious functionaries, the closure of virtually all of the 25,000 mosques which had existed in 1917, as well as Muslim schools, and the threat of dismissal of Soviet officials practising the religion. Some revival took place during the Second World War, although further repression followed under Kruschev. Nevertheless, Islam has emerged to play a major role in the successor states of the Soviet Union in Central Asia and Transcaucasia.[148]

By the end of the nineteenth century a national consciousness developed in a series of Muslim groupings in the Russian Empire, burgeoning in the First World War and Revolution. All these groupings faced varying levels of repression from the 1920s until the 1980s. For instance, during the First World War the Crimean Tatars agitated for separation from the Russian Empire, enduring hostility from Russians because of their alleged Turkish connections. After a struggle in the area, an autonomous republic was established in the Crimea in 1921.[149] During the 1930s the process of Sovietisation meant an attempt at assimilation and the resultant alienation of the Crimean Tatars. Consequently, some Tatars fought on the side of the invading Nazis during the Second World War. Although others played a part in the Red Army, Stalin's vengeance was total. Immediately after the expulsion of the Germans in April and May 1944, all Tatars who had served in the German armed forces were executed. The rest of the population faced deportation to the Urals, Siberia, Kazakhstan and Central Asia, mostly Uzbekhistan. Of the 110,000 people deported, about 46 per cent died in an action tantamount to genocide.[150] After the Second World War the Crimean Tatars remained non-entities within lists of Soviet ethnic groups, but began campaigning for their rights in the 1960s, eventually returning home. In the post-Soviet Ukraine they have developed their own political parties.[151]

The Tatars of the Volga Basin also developed a national consciousness during the nineteenth century, especially after the 1860s when the Tsars attempted to impose Russification and Christianisation. Like the Crimean Tatars, those in the Volga Basin established their own state in 1917. Once again, the Bolsheviks dissolved it in the following year, although in 1919 they set up the Bashkir Autonomous Soviet Socialist Republic, followed in 1920 by the Tatar Autonomous Soviet Republic within the Russian Soviet Federated Socialist Republic (RSFSR), although most Tatars lived outside these areas. This consequently did not satisfy Volga Tatar leaders, who were eliminated during the Stalinist purges of the 1930s. In addition, the thriving Tatar press was also severely curtailed, while attempts to eliminate Islam only proved effective in the short run. A national revival occurred following the death of Stalin and Tatarstan emerged as an ethnic republic in the post-Soviet Russian Federation.[152]

In Azerbaijan, a series of political parties striving for independence had risen by the outbreak of the First World War. An independent Azerbaijan, with Ottoman help, was established in 1918, without the consent of the Armenian population, but collapsed when the Bolsheviks regained the area, which had temporarily fallen under British control, in 1920. In 1922 Azerbaijan joined the Soviet Union as part of the Transcaucasian Federation, together with Georgia and Armenia, but in 1936 both joined the USSR as separate republics. Like other parts of the Muslim Soviet Union, Islam and nationalism withered away during the inter-war years, although compensations included an increase in literacy. This literacy continued to rise until the end of the Soviet period, when nationalism took off amongst the Azeris. Nevertheless, nationalism had also developed amongst the Armenians, who made up significant minorities in Nagorno-Karabakh and Nakhichevan, within the republic of Azerbaijan. This state of affairs resulted in ethnic violence during the last days of the USSR, acting as a catalyst in its collapse. The violence continued into the 1990s when both Azerbaijan and Armenia became independent states. [153]

The modern history of the German minorities of eastern Europe follows, up to a point, that of the Balkan Muslim population. Like Muslims, Germans became minorities in the new states created as a result of the growing nationalisms in the late nineteenth and early twentieth centuries. In the case of the Germans, great power politics played a large role in their fate, specifically the fact that Germany lost both the First and Second World War, which meant that Britain, France, the USSR and the USA divided the continent purely according to their own wishes. In both world wars the Great Powers completely ignored the interests and wishes of the German minorities of eastern Europe.

In Poland the existence of a German minority came about with the creation of a Polish state in 1918, although, at this stage, the minority was smaller than it was to become at the end of the Second World War. East Prussia remained part of the newly-created German Weimar Republic, even though it was separated from the rest of Germany by the Polish corridor around Danzig. The number of German speakers within the newly acquired territories had stood at 2,100,000 before the outbreak of the First World War, but this had fallen to one million by 1939. [154] Most of these had lived in Prussian controlled areas but a few were remnants of the part of Poland gained by the Habsburg Empire during the late eighteenth-century partition of the country by Austria, Prussia and Russia. The decline in numbers during the inter-war years resulted from a migration to Germany at least partly caused by discriminatory minority policies pursued by Polish governments. [155]

The Second World War led to dramatic developments. In the first place, in the intense hatreds aroused by the German invasion, around 5000 ethnic Germans were murdered during the first days of the war.[156] The Germans later repaid Polish brutality with exorbitant interest, as the Poles contributed the third largest number of victims of Nazism, after Jews and Russians.[157] The local German population did not do particularly well during the war and ultimately lost out completely. Not only were they overlooked by the Nazis in preference to Germans who moved into the country from Germany itself, they also faced the economic and political hardships in the most brutal theatre of the Second World War, including early victimisation by Polish soldiers, as Martha Kutzer recorded:

> On Sunday, 3 September 1939, soldiers again forced their way into our home to conduct a search for weapons. The men had to wait out in the yard. The soldiers demanded the motorcycle owned by my son, the Rev. Richard Kutzer. My son had to keep his arms raised while a soldier got on the motorcycle asking how it worked. Eventually my son was taken away by the soldiers. They were just kids, sixteen or seventeen years old. Just as they got to the corner of the street I saw them hit my son in the stomach with a rifle butt. I saw this from a window. My son stumbled about a bit. Then one of the soldiers hit him again, this time across the shoulders. My son fell to the ground, writhing in pain. They stood him upright and ordered him to raise his hands again. Then they led him away. My husband, Otto Kutzer, and a man named Richard Hoffman, saw this. Both are now dead as well.[158]

The division of Europe at the end of the Second World War inevitably recognised geographical reality in the age of contiguous nation states and separated East Prussia from Germany. This area, shared between Poland and Russia, meant the creation of a potentially much larger German minority problem in Poland, aggravated further by the annexation of East Brandenburg and Silesia, areas east of the rivers Oder and Neisse which now formed the boundary of Germany. The areas taken over by Poland were inhabited by 9,500,000 Germans before 1939.[159]

This never became a reality because of the massive movement of Germans out of eastern Europe accepted by the victorious Allies. This migration had begun with the Russian advance westwards which reached German soil at the end of 1944, and which was accompanied by yet more brutality, in this instance resulting in the murder of about 100,000 Germans by Russian forces.[160] As a consequence, the number of Germans east of the Oder-Neisse line fell from its 1944 figure of 11,924,000 to just 4,400,000 by May 1945. These people fled into German territory, especially Saxony, Thuringia and Bavaria.[161] Most of the rest followed in the early post-war years as a consequence of the Allied decision to resettle ethnic Germans in rump Germany,

8. Loss of German territory after the Second World War

forming a major element, along with expelled Germans from countries further south, in the early post-war refugee crisis. As a consequence, between 200,000 and 300,000 Germans were left in Poland after the Second World War,[162] although further large numbers fled out of the country when opportunities for migration developed following the collapse of Communism in the country.

In Denmark and Belgium, Germans did not suffer quite the same fate as those in Poland, even though these areas had experienced German occupation during the Second World War. In accordance with Hitler's ideology, as western Europeans, Danes and Belgians were on a higher racial plane than peoples in the east. The German presence in these areas was mainly due to the fact that they bordered core Germany and, consequently, as boundaries changed over the centuries, population constituents changed.

Denmark has always been a borderland, with its southern edge traditionally the northern extent of Germany. During the middle ages German merchants and artisans settled in Schleswig, followed by religious refugees during the Reformation. As a border area, it inevitably contained a Danish minority. At the end of the First World War, in accordance with the Treaty of Versailles, but also as one of the many methods of punishing the Germans, a plebiscite was held in the whole of Schleswig. While the southern part voted to remain in Germany, 75 per cent of those in the north chose to join Denmark, a union which took place in 1920.

Inevitably, minorities were left on both sides of the new border, even though about 15,000 Germans moved out of north Schleswig between 1919 and 1921. This minority, in common with German settlements throughout the world, had developed a highly organised political, religious, educational and social life. The German minority's relationship with the majority population deteriorated as a result of the German occupation of the area during the Second World War, but no mass exodus occurred out of the country, leaving about 23,000 German speakers in Denmark. Since 1945 the number of German speakers has fallen to less than 20,000, due essentially to the subtle pressures of assimilation, such as intermarriage, which is not regarded as a problem amongst two ethnic groups with much in common. Nevertheless, German ethnic organisations and schools have continued to exist.[163]

The German-speakers of east Belgium have an almost identical history to that of their southern Danish counterparts. The area has traditionally been a border region which has fallen in and out of the various German states over the centuries, marking a traditional western German language boundary. As a result of the political changes which shaped eastern Belgium during the nineteenth and early twentieth centuries, involving the transfer of territory to and from the country, the German population varied in size. The Nazi invasion of the country during the Second World War resulted in mutual hatred between the German and Walloon populations of the area; but, as in Denmark, the wounds were healed shortly after the end of the war. The total number of German-speakers of the area stood at about 110,000 by 1970.[164]

By the outbreak of the First World War the population of the south Tyrol consisted of 232,700 German-speakers and just 7100 Italian speakers, as well as 11,700 people who spoke other languages.[165] German national feeling amongst the local population had begun to develop at the end of the eighteenth century and had become sophisticated, both politically and culturally, by the outbreak of the First World War.[166] However, Italian nationalists had regarded the region as coming within their orbit during the nineteenth century and, in 1915, the Allies promised the region to Italy as one of the rewards for joining the First World War on their side. Consequently, Italy annexed the south Tyrol in 1919, in opposition to the wishes of the local population. Mussolini imported Italians, totalling 81,000 in 1939, into the area.[167] This process continued during the Second World War, together with movement of German-speakers to Germany, under an agreement between Mussolini and Hitler. Significant Italian immigration into the south

Tyrol has also taken place since the Second World War, so that by 1971 Italians formed one third of the population.[168] Politically, a series of treaties between Austria and Italy has attempted to safeguard the position of the German minority. Most recently, the south and north Tyrol have moved together under the aegis of the European Union in an attempt to form the Autonomous European Region Tirol, suggesting a possible solution to other indigenous European minority problems.[169]

The creation of Czechoslovakia in 1918 inevitably resulted in the emergence of a German minority in that state. With the development of irredentism in the area, which intensified with encouragement from Hitler, a major conflict developed between Czechs and Germans, becoming so serious that it eventually led to the disappearance of Czechoslovakia in 1939, after the Nazis had initially annexed the western borderlands (the Sudentenland) in October 1938 under the pretext of protecting the German population of the area.

Inevitably the 4,000,000 Germans who lived in Czechoslovakia by the end of the Second World War became its victims at its conclusion. In fact, the Czechoslovak President, Eduard Beneš, decided as early as 1938 that all Germans would face expulsion at the end of the Second World War, which duly happened, together with an annulment of their citizenship. Most of these deportations occurred in 1946, although they began before and continued afterwards. In this way, 800 years of German settlement in Bohemia almost came to an end. The German proportion of the population declined from 22.3 per cent in 1930 to 1.3 per cent by 1950.[170]

In Hungary the vindictive 1920 Treaty of Trianon, which settled Hungary's fate at the hands of the victorious First World War Allies, severely reduced the size of the country, especially by the granting of Transylvania to Rumania. The treaty also meant that the number of Germans in Hungary declined from about 2,000,000 in 1910 to 550,000 in 1920. Although this figure increased to 700,000 between 1938 and 1941,[171] because of the return of some territories lost at Trianon, the Germans of Hungary suffered the same fate as similar populations in neighbouring countries, although a substantial residue of approximately 220,000 remained until the 1990s.[172]

It was only the expansion of Rumania at the end of the First World War, as a result of the Treaties of Trianon and St-Germain, which created a German minority in the modern Rumanian nation state, as hardly any Germans lived in the kingdom created during the late nineteenth century. By 1930 the German population of Rumania stood at about 750,000.[173] They were mostly involved in agriculture and included both Catholics and Protestants. After 1933 they came under the control of the Nazis, as did the whole country on the outbreak of the Second World War.

The German population shrank gradually during this conflict. In 1940 the Soviet Union annexed Bessarabia and Bukovina, which meant that over 200,000 Germans left these areas by 1943; mostly to be resettled in regions taken over by the Nazis. In addition, the temporary gain of territory by Hungary meant the reduction of the German population to two-thirds of its size before 1939.[174] When the Red Army entered Rumania in the late summer of 1944 more ethnic Germans fled, while those who remained faced reprisals. Nevertheless, over 350,000 Germans lived in Rumania in 1977, although this number declined drastically by the last days of the Ceaçescu regime, to approximately 80,000 in December 1991.[175]

Over half a million Germans lived in Yugoslavia in 1921, concentrated mostly in the Voyvodina but also residing in other parts of the new state, in which they had settled since the middle ages.[176] The various German communities had their own newspapers, schools and cultural organisations. Inevitably, the Nazis took an interest in them during the 1930s. After the invasion of the country by the Axis powers in 1941, the ethnic Germans found themselves in a privileged position. In addition, the SS recruited some of them into its service.

The association of the ethnic Germans with the Nazis meant, however, that the military defeat of the occupying forces made evacuation of the German populations inevitable, beginning at the end of 1943. When Soviet troops approached Voyvodina, in September 1944, the Germans who did not flee faced internment, a loss of citizenship and even deportation to Soviet labour camps, a process to which 100,000 people may have fallen victim,[177] in some cases remaining there until the early 1950s. As a consequence of the emigration of the Germans from Yugoslavia, just 61,000 remained in 1953, falling to a meagre 9000 in 1981,[178] a process helped by West German recruitment of Yugoslav foreign workers.

Further east, in Russia, the Germans had developed a thriving ethnic community during the course of the nineteenth century, expanding from the original areas of settlement in the eighteenth century and establishing schools, social clubs and churches. The 1897 Russian census recorded 1,790,489 persons who counted German as their native language, making up 1.4 per cent of the population, although the figure included more than half a million people living in Finland and the Baltic states.[179]

The early years of the USSR led to some positive developments in the position of its German population, such as the establishment of an Autonomous Soviet Socialist Republic of the Volga Germans. However, as happened in eastern Europe, the Second World War resulted in traumatic developments for the Germans in the Soviet Union. In the first place, along with the rest of the Soviet population during these years, the Germans suffered as a result of famine, disease, collectivisation and repression of religion.

The nadir in the history of the Germans in Russia came during the Second World War when, under accusations of acting as an internal front for the invading Nazi armies, the Soviets dissolved the Volga Republic and deported the German populations out of European Russia and into Siberia and Central Asia, a process which took several years. As with other Soviet deportations, the expulsion of the Germans resembled the actions of a genocide, resulting in thousands of deaths and the depopulation of 2900 of the 3000 German settlements in European Russia. As a consequence of the expulsion of the Germans from European Russia, the numbers of Germans in the Soviet Union decreased from 1,543,000 in 1941 to 1,250,000 in 1946. Most of the decline was caused by the movement of Germans out of the Soviet Union, either into Germany or, in a few thousand cases, beyond the European continent. Some of the Germans who were deported were allowed to return to their original places of residence, although the majority remained in the new areas, recreating their own communities, in the way that Germans have done throughout the world. By 1989 the number of Germans in the Soviet Union had increased to 2,035,807, although by this time only about half of them regarded German as their native language. Despite this, hundreds of thousands chose to make their way to Germany following the collapse of Communism, so that in 1990 alone more people made this journey than had done so throughout the period between 1955 to 1981. They followed several hundred thousand Germans who fled from the section of East Prussia annexed by the Soviet Union at the end of the Second World War.[180]

The story of the Germans in eastern Europe moved from one of expansion during the middle ages and, especially, the early modern period, to one of attempted and sometimes successful elimination as a consequence of the Second World War and of the resentments caused by the Nazi invasions in the states with German populations. As result of the events of the twentieth century, the Germans who continued to live outside the borders of Germany after 1945 inevitably consisted of remnant populations, which declined further when Communism collapsed in eastern Europe.

In this sense they have very close connections with the other three ubiquitous minorities. All have pre-modern origins and all have been shaped by migration and, to a greater or lesser extent, by the collapse of empires, as a result of the two world wars and the demise of Communism. All of the groupings existed as peoples before the age of nationalism and, in the case of Gypsies and Jews, had historically faced extreme persecution. The technology, demands and striving for perfection of the modern age and its ideology, nationalism, manifesting itself in its instrument of power, the nation state, meant that these groupings faced a level and extremity of persecution impossible before the twentieth century.

The technological and bureaucratic advances of the modern age meant factory killing, perfected in the Nazi death camps, became a possibility. Ethnic cleansing is also a twentieth-century advance as the modern age strives for purity, which nationalism dictates can only be achieved by homogenising the entire population of a particular state. This perfection is attempted by deportation and extermination of the impurities within the newly-created national and racial systems called nation states. However, few of the nation states created during the nineteenth and twentieth centuries could achieve the perfection they desired, so that remnant populations continued after the end of the Second World War. Nevertheless, even after the traumas of this event, the same striving for perfection continued, resurfacing in a violent way after the collapse of Communism and the certainties that rested upon it.

Due to the brutality of the Second World War, which brought to the surface the worst excesses of the age of nationalism, only the lucky survived into the post-war period, especially in the case of Jews and, to a lesser extent, Gypsies. While millions of ethnic Germans may have outlived the war, relatively few remained in their lands of birth. Muslims do not fit comfortably into this picture, but nationalism in eastern Europe did affect their numbers and distribution, although, like the Gypsies, their numbers increased in many areas due to an increase in fertility rates. In the case of some of the dispersed minorities, continuing intolerance since 1945, especially in the Communist regimes of eastern Europe, has resulted in further ethnic cleansing.

3

Localised Minorities

As well as dispersed minorities, there also exist groupings which find themselves in particular regions, sometimes living within an individual nation
state, in other instances crossing over the boundary of more than one. They
emerged as minorities during the age of nationalism as a consequence of the
standardisation and boundary changes which have accompanied the establishment of nation states throughout the European continent.

Like dispersed minorities, none of the localised groupings had their origins
in the regions where they now live. In fact, if we are prepared to go back
far enough, every people in Europe is made up of immigrants. This statement
applies equally to the dominant groupings that have eventually gained control
of particular regions. For a variety of reasons, one particular people took
over a specified area first, which means that those who do not have the
correct ethnic credentials find themselves, sooner or later, in the position of
minorities.

The process of change from a tribal group arriving on the European
continent into an emerging dominant or minority population sometimes
took thousands of years. Most of the peoples of Europe can trace their history
back hundreds or even thousands of years. In the various empires which
have existed throughout the course of European history, particularly the
Habsburg and Ottoman empires, the existence of minorities did not become
an issue until the rise of nationalism in the nineteenth century. Before that
time people could exist without having an ethnic consciousness. In the case
of the Ottoman Empire, for instance, only religion mattered for the rural
populations living in the Balkans. While the peoples of the empire may have
spoken their own unique languages, most peasants did not come into contact
with people who used another tongue, which meant that they had little
concept of ethnic consciousness, a situation which existed, in some cases,
into the twentieth century.

With the growth of nationalism during the modern era people have been
forced to choose an ethnic identity. The standardising processes which have
characterised the modern nation state, involving the spread of a language
and, more directly, persecution of particular populations, have enforced this.

These developments have meant that minority groupings have inevitably become conscious of their differences.

While the spread of nationalism may characterise the modern era, the processes which resulted in minority creation have far deeper origins, going back in the case of some migrations several thousand years. Initial arrival into a particular area represented just the first step in the process of minority, as well as majority, creation. In the meantime, a series of other transformations occurred before nation states and minorities within them emerged.

In some instances the changes which have taken place since the end of the eighteenth century have built upon the dynastic control of particular territories before the age of nationalism, in which a particular monarchy expanded its domain over a period of hundreds of years, resulting in the evolution of a core, dominant population with control over peoples on its periphery. The peripheral peoples may always have been outsiders and may always have suffered some degree of persecution, but the growth of both core and marginal nationalism formalised this process. The best examples of such developments consist of the United Kingdom and Russia.

In other cases minorities became victims of unification, a development which has affected parts of Europe since the fifteenth-century creation of Spain, followed, in the nineteenth and twentieth, by the emergence of Germany, Italy and Yugoslavia. The problem with such unification processes lay in the fact that they did not involve equal partners, which meant that the largest states imposed their own values and ignored those of the smaller populations, which may have had their own language or religion. The processes of standardisation characteristic of modernity have meant that minorities became conscious of their difference.

During the nineteenth and twentieth centuries, especially in central and eastern Europe, new states also emerged which found that they had minority populations on their boundaries. Great power politics facilitated such processes, as the creation of new states during the nineteenth and twentieth centuries often did not take into account the wishes of the local population.

Finally, a few European minorities have emerged within the heartland of particular nation states, often because their ethnic consciousness crystallised after new nation states had developed within the areas in which they lived. Once again, in the age before the emergence of national conformity, such groups could continue with little consciousness of their ethnic identity.

All minorities which exist within Europe have clear similarities in the fact that their status became more obvious during the nineteenth and twentieth centuries. The nationalisms and sub-nationalisms which developed almost invariably emerged through elite groupings, usually of merchants and industrialists, pursuing their own economic interest of creating a market for their goods. Their task of developing ethnic consciousness became easier during the modern age as literacy spread, which meant that they could indoctrinate the populations within their borders into believing that they were a particular nationality. By the second half of the twentieth century it had become impossible for individuals in Europe to live without a nationality. All the new states of the modern age have, trapped within artificially created borders and cultures, peoples who have no desire to take a particular nationality.

Peripheral Minorities

The development of some nation states and the minorities which evolved within them simply built upon previous historical processes. These involved the expansion of dynastic control into areas inhabited by populations with differing ethnic characteristics from those at the centre. While exclusion and persecution often took place during the dynastic era, the new nation states made this inevitable.

The Sami people offer a good example of such processes in action. They inhabit the northern and western periphery of Scandinavia and predate most of the groups which subsequently went on to develop nation states in the area, arriving from further east during the first millennium BC. Initially, they lived further south and west but, with the invasions of Scandinavia by Finns, Norwegians and Swedes, they were forced to retreat into their current peripheral areas, although the states which expanded northwards legally recognised their existence as minorities from as early as 1751. By the end of the nineteenth century the Lapps found that their freedom of movement had been curtailed as a consequence of the development of borders between the emerging Scandinavian states. In addition, they faced pressures to assimilate in all of the countries in which they lived, involving the adoption of dominant religions and education systems, although the major transition to Christianity had taken place during the seventeenth century. By the early 1980s the total Sami population stood between 58,000 and 100,000, with at least 17,000 in Sweden, a minimum of 35,000 in Norway, about 4000 in Finland and around 2000 in the Soviet Union.[1]

The history of the British Isles involved the expanding control of the English language in league with commerce and industry controlled by the English ruling classes. The process, begun in the Dark Ages, was not completed until the nineteenth century, by which time the Scots and Welsh had become part of the body politic. Despite the ruthlessness of the process, this did not apply to the Irish, except for those irredentists who remained in the north who, working in league with the British Parliament, partitioned Ireland in 1921 and created a seemingly insoluble ethnic problem.

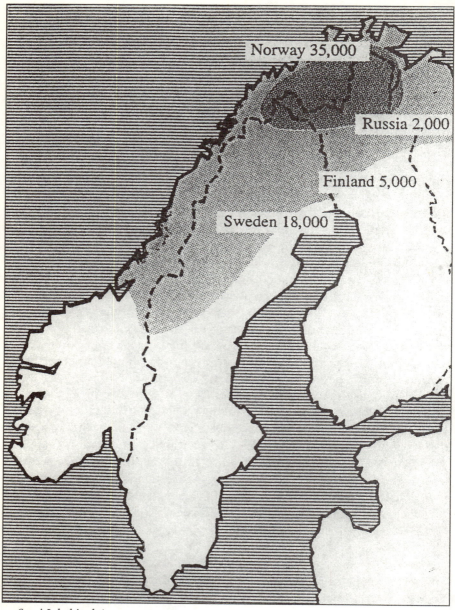

Norway 35,000

Russia 2,000

Finland 5,000

Sweden 18,000

9. Sami Inhabited Areas

Before the arrival of the Romans in Britain in 43 AD, tribal societies of Celts, speaking dialects of a common language with similar religious patterns, lived throughout the British Isles, having migrated from locations further east. The Roman invasion had a more profound impact upon England than they did upon the Celtic fringe, which continued with many of its traditional patterns of life.

After the fall of the Roman Empire the British Isles was affected by the Dark Age mass movement of peoples which occurred throughout Europe. In the case of England, the main group of newcomers consisted of 50,000 to 100,000 Angles, Jutes and Saxons who entered the south and east of the country from northern Germany and Denmark during the fifth and sixth centuries. By the end of the eighth century this group controlled the whole of England and parts of Scotland and Wales, having conquered and pushed the native Britons more and more to the periphery. The Irish and northern Scots remained distant from this process, continuing with their own Celtic way of life and primitive political organisation.

English monarchy and statehood essentially began with the Normans (building on the foundations of the Anglo-Saxon state), despite the fact that they imposed a French ruling culture which was gradually replaced by English by the fifteenth century. From the eleventh century England gradually gained control of the peripheral parts of the British Isles. Wales provided the easiest prey, having already fallen within the English orbit. The sixteenth century formalised the incorporation of Wales into the English orbit with the Acts of Union of 1536 and 1542, establishing English as the language of government, although the use of Welsh continued in religion and everyday communication for centuries.

The union of England and Scotland was a bloodier process, involving conflicts between English and Scottish rulers, but by the time King James VI ascended the English throne as James I in 1603 the two countries had moved closer together. The Act of Union of 1707 enshrined the connection between the two states, despite the rebellions which occurred both before and after the event.

English interference in Ireland has been bloodier still and has lasted for almost a millennium, during which time a series of English rulers, progressing through every system of government which the British Isles has experienced, has subjected the population of Ireland to acts of brutality which destroy any self-congratulatory myths about English gentleness. By the eighteenth century an Irish proto-nationalism had developed, although as a reaction against it the irredentist Orange Order was born. The Act of Union with Ireland in 1800 was unsuccessful almost from the start and the political history of Ireland since then has essentially consisted of an Irish attempt to end British control of the island, progressing through a series of stages and eventually leading to the unsatisfactory compromise of 1921, which failed to expel the English entirely from Ireland.

After the Act of Union of 1707 the peripheral sections of the British Isles became more and more subject to English control. Despite the fact that this process of internal colonialism guaranteed Scotland and Wales an equal footing with the English in the British Parliament at Westminster, the interests of Scotland, Wales and Ireland have inevitably remained secondary, if only because of their geographic position and population size within the Union compared with England.

The English idea of Britain spread through the high culture which conquered with the spread of the English language, a process assisted by the spread of literacy and English literary culture. In the early seventeenth century nearly half of the population of Scotland may still have been Gaelic-speaking,[2] a figure which had fallen to less than 2 per cent by the 1971 census.[3] Similarly, the use of Welsh fell from the middle ages, suffering especially due to industrialisation and the immigration of English people into south Wales during the late nineteenth century. By 1900 only 50 per cent of the population spoke Welsh, falling further to 18.9 per cent in 1981.[4]

From the nineteenth century Scottish and Welsh Nationalist movements have developed, growing from the economic base of industrialisation within these two areas, initially cultural but becoming political by the interwar years. As a reaction, the British Parliament made concessions to the rise of Celtic nationalism in the form of, for instance, allowing Welsh and Gaelic language instruction from the late nineteenth century and the establishment of Scottish and Welsh Offices, which might also be seen as instruments of imperial control. Such issues surfaced dramatically after 1945 as ethnic politics in Britain affected Wales, Scotland and, above all, Northern Ireland.[5]

Although it took control of a much more extensive territory, which meant that it ruled larger and more diverse populations, and practised more extreme acts of intolerance, the evolution of Russia and the Soviet Union and its minorities mirrors that of Britain in the sense that a core has expanded to take control of a periphery. As in the British case, during this centuries long process, the rulers from Moscow (both Tsars, especially during the nineteenth century, and secretaries of the Communist Party, during the twentieth), tried to standardise their population through the spread of a Russian and then Soviet consciousness. Inevitably, the elites in the peripheral territories reacted against the spread of such all-embracing nationalism and developed their own; often, during the early twentieth century, with the support of the Communist Party.

Russian history began in the first millennium, with the migration of Slavs from the Carpathian mountain region into the exposed plain stretching from eastern Europe into central Siberia. The first specifically Russian state came into existence in the tenth century, developing around Kiev, under Viking rulers, who also accepted eastern Christianity as their religion. By the end of the eleventh century the new state had begun to disintegrate, a process confirmed by the Mongol invasions of the thirteenth century. The invaders ruled a large expanse of territory for more than a century, although the control remained indirect, with little interference in the affairs of the Slav princes.

Out of the informal Mongol control emerged a state which has continuously existed around Moscow since the fourteenth century. The expansion of the state began to take place, especially to the north, during the second half of the fifteenth century under Ivan III. By the end of his reign, in 1505, the Mongols were on the defensive. The rule of Ivan the Terrible, from 1533 to 1584, meant further significant expansion, particularly into Siberia and beyond the Volga, as the Khanate of Kazan was defeated in 1552, resulting in the elimination of any threat that may have remained from the Mongols. The Romanovs, who became Tsars in 1613, expanded further, especially under Peter the Great (1672–1725), whose conquests reached the Baltic; and Catherine the Great (1762–96), who gained territory with the partitions of Poland and reached the northern shores of the Black Sea, following victories over the Ottoman Empire. The nineteenth century brought Georgia, Finland, central Poland, the Caucasus and Turkestan into the Russian Empire, together with a stabilisation of the border with Afghanistan.[6]

The 1897 Russian census revealed the ethnic consequences of the previous five centuries of imperial expansion, counting sixty-four different nationalities. Great Russians made up 55,667,500 out of a total population of 125,666,500. Ukrainians came second with 22,380,600. No other group counted more than ten million, while the smallest minority, the Voguls, totalled just 7600.[7] This mass of population practised over fifteen different religions.[8]

The Tsarist policy of Russification was a failure; the country remained to the end a vast mosaic of numerous peoples.[9] Previously, as in all successful empires, centralisation had been counter-balanced by the granting of concessions to local rulers and traditions. Under Nicholas I (1825–55) Russian culture was introduced into the education systems of Poland, Belorussia and Lithuania, while the Orthodox Church intensified its efforts at conversion. These policies escalated further under the last two Tsars, Alexander III and Nicholas II, as part of the reactionary policies which both of these rulers pursued, alienating the elites emerging amongst the minority peoples.[10]

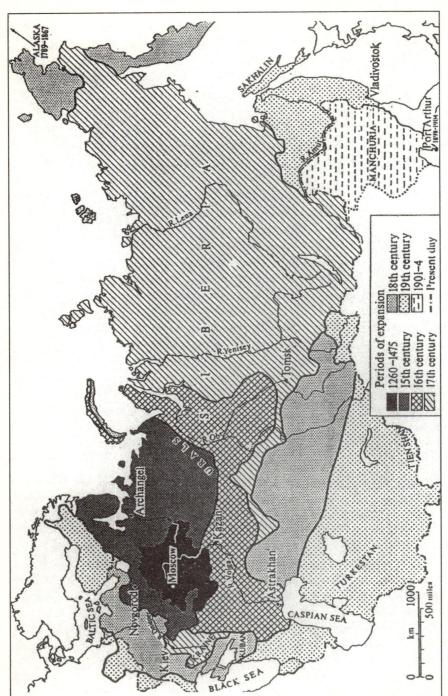

ALASKA
1789–1867

SAKHALIN

Vladivostok

Port Arthur
1898–1904

MANCHURIA

R.Lena

S I B E R I A

R.Yenisey

Tomsk

Periods of expansion

			18th century
1260–1475		19th century
15th century		1901–4
16th century		Present day
17th century		

TIEN SHAN

R.Ob

U R A L S

Archangel

Kazan

R.Volga

Astrakhan

TURKESTAN

Moscow

Novgorod

CASPIAN SEA

Kiev

UKRAINE

R.Kuban

km   1000

500 miles

BALTIC SEA

0

BLACK SEA

10. Expansion from Moscow, 1260–1904

The Bolsheviks made the most of the divisions caused by attempted Russification and realised their potential for their cause before they seized power. Nevertheless, the issue was forced upon them to a considerable extent by the existence of secessionist movements in various parts of the Russian Empire, some of them Social Democratic, which wished to escape Russian control. In 1913 Lenin published his important text on this issue entitled *The Right of Nations to Self-Determination*, in which he declared that every nation had the right to separate from Russia and create its own independent state. But he did not promise self-rule to every movement wishing to obtain independence. When the Bolsheviks seized power he said they would introduce a policy of national equality which would guarantee each nation the right to use its own language. However, as the ultimate aim of all Marxists was the elimination of national differences, the policy to be pursued would eventually lead to centralisation.

The ethnic development of the early years of post-Tsarist Russia proceeded along the lines set out by Lenin. The importance which the Bolsheviks gave to minorities is indicated by the fact that on 8 November, the day after they seized power, Stalin became Commissar for Nationalities with the task of solving a 'troublesome problem', while Lenin became the Chairman of the Council of People's Commissars. They committed the new state to supporting self-determination, even to the extent of the formation of independent states, so that by the end of 1918 the Soviet government had recognised thirteen new states. The main practical reason for this policy lay in the fact that counter-revolutionary forces, which refused to accept secession, were almost entirely in control of non-Russian areas. As the Red Army began to take over the Russian borderlands, it snuffed out many of the independent states which had developed in these areas, offering them, instead, incorporation into the Union of Soviet Socialist Republics, established in 1922 and formalised in 1924.

In 1922 four republics had existed, consisting of Russia, the Ukraine, Belorussia and Transcaucasia; by 1925 two new ones had developed in the form of Uzbekhistan and Kazakhstan. Transcaucasia and Russia were federal republics with their own autonomous regions. In addition, there also existed autonomous republics, while the dispersed peoples of the Soviet Union also had representation in the All-Union Congress of Soviets. The Union republics retained the right to secede. Each Soviet Socialist Republic (SSR) had its own flag, national anthem, legislature and government. While the SSRs decided upon some fields of policy, others, notably defence and foreign policy, were controlled centrally.

Despite the apparent autonomy which existed, the Communist Party acted as a centralising force, throwing the concept of a federal state into doubt. The Politburo and Central Committee enjoyed supreme authority over all other institutions. However, during the inter-war years the numbers of local Communist Party officials from the native populations increased. The central government had a progressive attitude towards local languages and cultures, some of which Soviet influence made literary for the first time.

All citizens of the Soviet Union became victims of Stalin, including the nationalities. The Ukrainians fared worse than most, enduring famine and social cleansing, in the attempt to eliminate kulaks (peasants who owned too much land). The constitution of 1936 had limited benefit for the nationalities. It increased the number of SSRs to eleven, consisting of the RSFSR, the Ukraine, Belorussia, Armenia, Georgia, Azerbaijan, and the Kazakh, Kirghiz, Tadzhik, Turkmen and Uzbekh republics. Smaller nationalities found representation in autonomous republics, autonomous regions and national areas. A total of fifty-one groupings had some form of official recognition. One of the two chambers of the supreme Soviet, the Soviet of the Nationalities, represented the above groupings.

Against this we need to set the vicious policies which Stalin pursued against some nationalities, which amounted to genocide. These brutal measures went together with an increasing Russification. Stalin believed that his regime should identify with the majority population, whose support he needed in the drive towards industrialisation. This meant a glorification of Russian culture and language. In addition, Russians replaced members of the local populations in control of the administration of the various levels of government. This culminated in purges in the late 1930s when large numbers of people were either executed, committed suicide or disappeared. The terror stretched to affect even minor local officials. Nations especially affected included Azerbaijan, Belorussia, Georgia, Kazakhstan, Kirghizia, Tadzhikistan, Turkmenia and Uzbekhistan. During the Second World War Balkars, Chechens, Crimean Tatars, Ingushis, Kalmyks, Karachians, Meshketians and Volga Germans all faced deportation for alleged treason. A more subtle method employed for lessening the ethnic cohesion amongst particular nations consisted of the importation of outside populations, especially Russians, into particular regions, although this process was also a consequence of the industrialisation of the lands on the Soviet periphery. This happened particularly in the central Asian republics, where 1,700,000 new settlers emigrated to Kirghizia, Tadzhikistan, Turkmenia and Uzbekhistan between 1926 and 1939.[11]

The Second World War resulted in a further expansion of Soviet territory, making up for some of the losses of the early days of the Revolution. These had included Estonia, Finland, Latvia, Lithuania and the Polish territories, as well as Bessarabia, which went to Rumania. Under the Nazi-Soviet Non-Aggression Pact of 1939, these fell into Stalin's sphere of influence, a fact

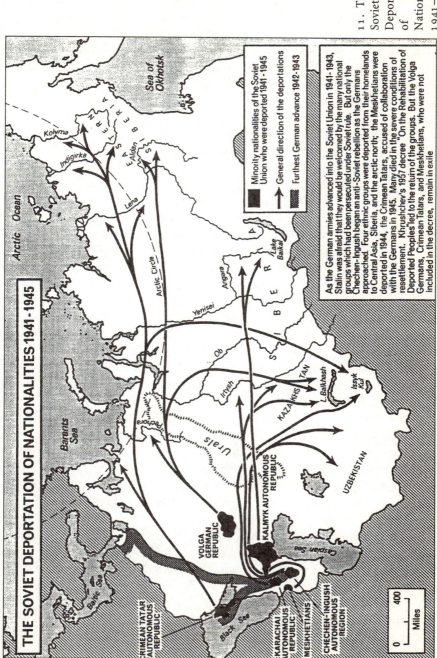

THE SOVIET DEPORTATION OF NATIONALITIES 1941 - 1945

11. The Soviet Deportation of Nationalities 1941−1945

Minority nationalities of the Soviet Union who were deported 1941-1945

General direction of the deportations

Furthest German advance 1942-1943

As the German armies advanced into the Soviet Union in 1941-1943, Stalin was afraid that they would be welcomed by the many national groups which had been persecuted under Soviet rule. But only the Chechen-Ingush began an anti-Soviet rebellion as the Germans approached. Four ethnic groups were deported from their homelands to Central Asia, Siberia, and the arctic north; the Meskhetians were deported in 1944, the Crimean Tatars, accused of collaboration with the Germans in 1945. Many died in the severe conditions of resettlement. Khrushchev's 1957 decree "On the Rehabilitation of Deported Peoples" led to the return of the groups. But the Volga Germans, Crimean Tatars, and Meskhetians, who were not included in the decree, remain in exile

Arctic Ocean

Sea of Okhotsk

Barents Sea

Baltic Sea

Black Sea

Caspian Sea

Kolyma

Indigirka

Lena

Aldan

Arctic Circle

Yenisei

Angara

Lake Baikal

Ob

Irtysh

Urals

Pechora

SIBERIA

KAZAKHSTAN

L. Balkhash

Issyk Kul

UZBEKISTAN

VOLGA GERMAN REPUBLIC

KALMYK AUTONOMOUS REPUBLIC

CRIMEAN TATAR AUTONOMOUS REPUBLIC

KARACHAI AUTONOMOUS REPUBLIC

MESKHETIANS

CHECHEN-INGUSH AUTONOMOUS REGION

0   400
Miles

which he used to his advantage. In July 1940 the Red Army occupied the three Baltic states, which joined the USSR as Union Republics; a status they retained until the collapse of the Soviet Union, in which they played a major role. Also in the summer of 1940 Stalin, by agreement with the Nazis, annexed Bessarabia and Bukovina from Rumania to establish the Moldavian SSR. In addition, the Soviet Union seized about a tenth of the territory of Finland to establish the Karelo-Finnish SSR. Although these new acquisitions fell to the Nazis during their invasion of the Soviet Union, the Red Army regained them once the Germans were expelled. At the end of the Second World War, sixteen Union Republics existed. By the early 1950s, in the Soviet population of two hundred million, about seventy million consisted of Russians, followed, in order of size, by Ukrainians and Belorussians.[12]

Inevitably, this meant that Russians played the major role in the control of the USSR in the last few decades of its existence, even though the other groupings did not face the sort of exclusion characteristic of many western states. Language represented one of the most significant identifiers of Russian dominance, as it became by far the most important form of communication, with only small numbers of people unable to use it, even though large percentages could use other tongues. In 1970 a total of 58.6 per cent of Soviet citizens classed Russian as their native tongue,[13] while the 1989 census revealed that 48.1 per cent of Soviet citizens claimed Russian as their second language.[14] Economically, Russia also became dominant, even though some of its neighbours, notably the Baltic Republics and the Ukraine, had higher standards of living. Nevertheless, the relationship of Russia and the Soviet periphery resembled colonialism, with the centre having the greatest choice of the raw materials available.[15]

In other ways, the individual republics did well for themselves, notably by developing their own cultures, encompassing native literature, theatre, music and museums.[16] However, this culture inevitably led to the development of national pride, which the Soviet authorities hoped they could control within their federal structure. This remained the case for much of the post-war period, partly as a result of the nightmare of Stalinism, as well as further repression after 1945.

Following the advent of Mikhail Gorbachev in 1985, with his policies of liberalisation, the individual nationalities took the message to its logical conclusion so that, by the early 1990s, the Soviet Union no longer existed. Nevertheless, what has followed in what was its centre, Russia, has led to equally complex ethnic problems, because only the peripheral areas, which had their own Republics, became fully independent.[17]

Of the individual peripheral peoples within the Russian Empire and the USSR, the Ukrainians have a history at least as old as the Russians with

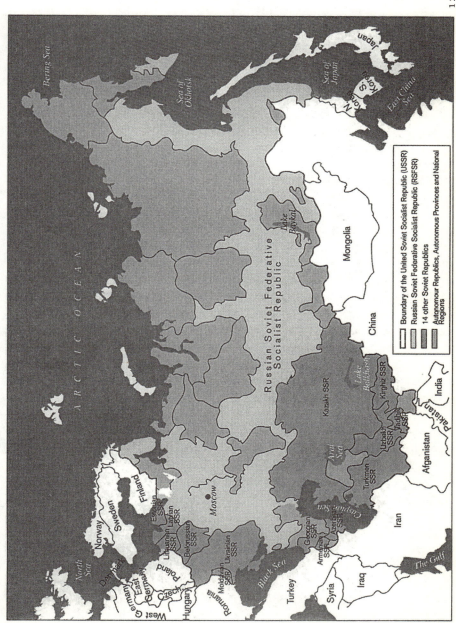

12. The USSR

whom their development has been intertwined. One author, referring to the post-Soviet period, has described the relationship between the two countries as resembling a fairy tale about two quarrelsome brothers.[18] The countries have the same historical roots in the form of ninth-century Kievan Rus, but they had begun to distinguish themselves from each other by the fourteenth century. This was due to the Ukraine's closer connection with Europe. Under Polish and Lithuanian rule, the establishment of the Uniate Church at the end of the sixteenth century caused a schism in the local population, many of whom remained Orthodox. At the same time the existence of Cossacks, frontiersmen, also differentiated Ukrainians from Russians. In 1667 Poland and Russia divided the Ukraine between them. The partitions of Poland at the end of the eighteenth century brought the rest of the Ukraine under Russian rule, with the exception of Galicia, which went to Austria. Russian expansion southwards allowed the settlement of Ukrainians to the north of the Black Sea during the eighteenth century.

Ukrainian nationalism, distinguishing itself from Russia, began to develop during the nineteenth century and gave birth to a literary language based upon peasant dialects. Orthodox priests played a role in this process and the seminaries in Kiev and Poltava became hotbeds of Ukrainian nationalist and revolutionary socialist agitation prior to the Revolution.[19] The Tsarist authorities had little time for the concept of a Ukrainian identity from the time of Catherine II onwards. The nineteenth-century Tsars, in keeping with their generally repressive attitudes towards nationalities, made efforts to suppress the growth of Ukrainian nationalism, most notably by prohibiting the printing of Ukrainian texts between 1876 and 1905, a ban which was only partially lifted after 1905. Consequently, Ukrainian intellectual nationalism developed more freely in Austria, where political parties and periodicals and newspapers existed by the outbreak of the First World War.

After the February Revolution of 1917 the newly established National Council declared full independence. Although Lenin initially accepted a separate non-Communist Ukraine, there followed a war which lasted between 1918 and 1920, during which time the Central Powers, the Allies and Poland all invaded the country. The war ended with the Bolshevik conquest of the Ukraine. The territory became one of the founder members of the USSR in 1922.

During the 1920s the Soviet government tolerated a Ukrainisation pro-gramme which would de-Russify Ukrainian language and culture, but Stalinism changed all of this: Ukrainians suffered as much as any other national group from the ruthless repression of the dictator, enduring a combination of collectivisation, dekulakisation, suppression of the Uniate Church, the murder of Ukrainian nationalists and the purging of local party functionaries at the end of the 1930s. Finally, when, in accordance with the Nazi-Soviet Pact, the Soviet Union invaded the western Ukraine, which had remained part of Poland at the end of the First World War, as many as 1,250,000 people faced deportation, imprisonment or execution to add to the millions who had already perished.[20]

Their experiences during the 1930s led some Ukrainians to welcome the Nazi invaders as liberators, although the Germans pursued equally repressive policies. The Ukrainian Insurgent Army came into existence in 1942, declaring war upon both Nazis and Communists. It inevitably faced reprisals once the Soviets regained control of the Ukraine, a process which continued into the late 1940s, as guerilla operations did not cease when the war ended.

Throughout the history of the Soviet Union the Ukraine remained the second most important republic after Russia, reflecting its land mass, its population, its economic resources, its culture and its identity as separate to Russia. This led to the rebirth of nationalism, which began to resurface after the death of Stalin: it strengthened in the 1960s but faced repression during the early 1980s. Under Gorbachev in the second half of that decade it rose once again. The Ukraine emerged as an independent state by the end of 1991.[21]

The Baltic nationalities, like the Ukrainians a periphery taken over by the centre, represented some of the sharpest thorns in the side of the Soviet Union. The reasons for this lie in the short period of time that they formed part of the USSR, the lateness of their incorporation into the state and their previous existence as nation states. The origins of the Baltic populations lie partly in the Finno-Ugrian migration to this area, which occurred from Central Asia before the first millennium BC, although intermixing with Slavs and Germans, as well as old established Balts, has certainly taken place.

The first Lithuanian state came into existence in the thirteenth century under Mindaugas. This king accepted Christianity, although this was reversed by his successors until 1386 when the country joined with Poland in a monarchical union. Significantly, no Lithuanian literary language developed during the medieval period. Under the Treaty of Lublin of 1569 Lithuania surrendered much of its autonomy to a strengthened Polish monarchy. Lithuanian did not begin to develop as a literary language until the early eighteenth century at the University of Königsberg, and its territory fell under Russian rule as a result of the third partition of Poland in 1795.

The national revival of the nineteenth century involved a growth of Lithuanian as a literary language and manifested itself politically in the participation of Lithuanians in the Polish revolt against Russian rule in 1863, but this was followed by a period of attempted Russification. Nevertheless, by the start of the twentieth century, nationalist movements existed; and during the 1905 revolution the Assembly of Vilnius demanded autonomy for Lithuania.

Following the outbreak of the First World War, the Germans occupied Lithuania at the end of 1915 and remained there until 1918, establishing a state council in September 1917. Between 1917 and 1920 Lithuania experienced Germans, Bolsheviks and Poles as occupying forces. The country declared independence in 1920 and quickly received recognition from the League of Nations and the Soviet Union. [22]

The incorporation of Lithuania within the Soviet Union did not kill off the idea of an independent state, a concept fired by two issues in particular. First, the strength of the Lithuanian economy, one of the most successful within the USSR. [23] Secondly, an influx of Russians, who made up 9.3 per cent of the population in 1989 and whose presence led to the rise of xenophobic anti-Russian and anti-Soviet sentiments. [24] Lithuania, along with the other Baltic states, became one of the most vociferous campaigners for secession from the USSR in the last days of Gorbachev, but, when it gained independence, it had a serious minority problem of its own in the presence of a large number of Russians, who received less than equal treatment as symbols of the previous five decades of Soviet rule. [25]

Estonia and Latvia represent some of the most artificial of nation states amongst all of the manufactured ethnicities of Europe. The histories of the two countries are inextricably linked. Finno-Ugrian peoples arrived in Estonia up to 5000 years ago, but they were followed into that area by Balts who moved from further east, who also make up the bulk of the population of Latvia. Neither area had a history of state organisation until the thirteenth century, when the two countries became the constituent parts of Livonia, ruled by the Teutonic Knights with an economy controlled by Hanseatic merchants. Nationalist historians of the two countries work on the concept that the medieval 'indigenous' peoples of Livonia, whoever they may have been, were ruled by foreign occupying powers. Livonia collapsed and fell to Swedish and Polish rulers during the sixteenth century but, due to the expansion of Russia into the area through conquest and Polish partitions, the Tsars had control of the entire region by the end of the eighteenth century.

The Latvian and Estonian languages began to spread in their literary forms during the course of the seventeenth century and their further expansion played an instrumental role in the development of concepts of nationhood in late Tsarist Russia. The economic basis for the spread of nationhood consisted of the ending of serfdom, which had taken place in Latvia and Estonia by 1819. This allowed the development of small independent farms whose owners educated their sons; and, in the long run, a movement to the cities. Overall, the economic and educational changes meant the emergence of a bourgeoisie which focused its dislike upon foreign, particularly German landlords, who had retained economic power in the agricultural sector since the Livonian state of the middle ages. During the 1905 Revolution attacks took place on both German and Russian targets. However, at the start of the twentieth century, any concept of an ethnically pure population in the Baltic states proved absurd. In 1913 Riga, in Latvia, had a Latvian population of 42 per cent although, significantly from the point of view of the spread of ideas, this had increased from 24 per cent in 1867. [26]

Both Latvia and Estonia emerged as nation states at the end of the First World War. Before finally achieving complete independence they too, like the Lithuanians, had to fight off both German and Soviet invasions. The Second World War meant incorporation into the Soviet Union, although the years of Nazi occupation, 1941–44, resulted in the elimination of the long-standing Jewish population in the area. The large-scale immigration of Russians in the post-war period led to further xenophobic resentment.

The post-war history of both Lativia and Estonia closely resembles that of Lithuania. Both had succesful economies within the Soviet system, under-going rapid industrialisation. Both witnessed large influxes of Russians and both were vociferous in their desire to obtain independence from the Soviet Union. Once again, neither has regarded its residual Russian minorities favourably during the 1990s. [27]

Belorussia, another peripheral area bordering the Baltic states, is again a completely artificial creation, with historical developments which link it to these three Baltic states. The earliest recorded inhabitants consisted of Balts. Slavs arrived in the area during the sixth century and the national myth, portrayed as history, suggests that 'the Belorussian people' developed by a mixing of Balts and Slavs, with the latter becoming the dominant grouping. In common with the Baltic states, the area came under various types of medieval domination, which must have further affected this alleged purity. By the fourteenth century the area had fallen into the kingdom of Poland and Lithuania. One of the main myth-makers of Belorussian history, in his attempts to draw a continuity, claims that a literary language, used in the Lithuanian kingdom, had developed during the sixteenth century, used by the Lithuanian state. By the end of the eighteenth century the territory of present-day Belorussia had gone the way of the entire kingdom of Poland by falling under Russian control.

The birth of a Belorussian nationalism was a problematic process because of the diversity of the population typical of this part of Europe, which included Belorussians, Jews, Lithuanians, Poles, Russians and Ukrainians. In the 1897 imperial census 74.6 per cent of the population in the areas designated as Belorussian gave Belorussian as their native language. Yet literacy was not widespread amongst Belorussian speakers, who remained underrepresented in the educated classes. Nevertheless, during the nineteenth century, publications appeared in Belorussian and by the beginning of the twentieth century an anti-Polish and anti-Russian political movement had surfaced.

By the time of the 1917 Revolution and the collapse of the Tsarist Empire, the Belorussian middle classes and their ideology, nationalism, had not developed sufficiently to convince either the local masses or external powers of the right of the country to statehood. An independent Belorussian republic declared in 1918 was quickly overrun by Soviet forces. In 1919, as a concession to nationalism within the country, the Belorussian SSR came into existence, although its boundaries were subsequently changed several times. Belorussian national consciousness developed during the 1920s under the new order. But, in common with the whole of the Soviet Union, Belorussian intellectuals suffered under Stalinism, as did the Autocephalous Belorussian Orthodox Church, established in 1923 and destroyed in 1937, although the Belorussians got off relatively lightly in comparison with other ethnic groupings in the Soviet Union.

Belorussia gained independence at the death of the USSR, but nationalism remained relatively dormant here in the last years of the old order, particularly in comparison with the neighbouring Baltic republics. One of the core issues mobilising Belorussian independence was the Chernobyl disaster of 1986. Although the nuclear power station was situated in the Ukraine, the meltdown also seriously affected Belorussia. [28]

Of the other peripheral Soviet peoples west of the Urals, the Georgians have one of the oldest traditions of statehood, dating back to antiquity. A Georgian kingdom developed from the eleventh to the thirteenth centuries, falling to the Mongols and eventually the Ottoman Turks and Persians. The Russian advance southward brought the whole of Georgia into the Tsarist empire at the start of the nineteenth century.

Despite repression, national consciousness took off during the nineteenth century, initially as a cultural and intellectual movement, subsequently developing into a political one. By 1900, the most influential political movement was the Marxist Third Group, in which Stalin obtained his political education. The Mensheviks actually declared independence at the end of the First World War, although by 1921 Georgia had fallen to the Red Army, becoming part of the Transcaucasian Republic in 1922, along with Armenia and Azerbaijan. All three obtained self-standing republic status under the 1936 constitution and all three still have serious ethnic problems. In the case of Georgia, the 1989 census revealed that, out of Georgia's 5,400,000 inhabitants, 8 per cent were Armenians, 6 per cent Russian, 6 per cent Azerbaijani, 3 per cent Ossetian and 6 per cent Abhzians, together with 392,000 Adzhanans, an Islamic ethnic Georgian group. This complexity of minorities exploded into ethnic violence during the 1990s when Georgia became an independent state and the different groupings strove for autonomy. [29]

Other significant geographically marginalised European groups within the Soviet Union included Moldavians and Poles. The former, who lived in an Autonomous Soviet Socialist Republic within the Ukrainian SSR, bordered Rumania. During the Second World War territory annexed from Rumania led to the formation of the Moldavian SSR, which gained independence after the collapse of the USSR. Throughout its existence, Moldavia has had a significant Ukrainian minority. [30] The Polish minority of the Soviet Union, which totalled over one million for much of the twentieth century, [31] lived mostly in areas of the Soviet Republics bordering Poland. Polish autonomous republics were formed in the Ukraine and Belorussia in 1925 but abolished during the Stalinist repression of the 1930s. Nevertheless, an improvement took place in their position, especially with the advent of Perestroika.

As is the case elsewhere, the nationalities which became republics in the Soviet Union were fortunate in their geographical location. Historical traditions proved crucial in the case of groupings such as Georgians, while the development of a bourgeoisie, accompanied by the growth of literacy, played a fundamental role in the emergence of the Baltic republics, which seized their chance when the Russian Empire collapsed. One can imagine circumstances in which Lithuania, Estonia and Latvia might never have emerged, but remained as a remnant minority never to reach nationhood. This might have happened with Belorussia, but the creation of an SSR with this name guaranteed the development of a Belorussian nation state. There was little doubt that all of the Soviet Republics would emerge as fully-fledged independent states, in the western sense, if and when the Soviet Union collapsed.

Just as much of a certainty was the presence of minorities. None of the states which succeeded the Soviet Empire has anything remotely resembling ethnic homogeneity. The arch stretching from the Baltic to the Black Sea contains a hotchpotch of ethnic groups, including so-called Lithuanians, Latvians, Estonians, Belorussians, Ukrainians, Russians, Moldavians, Jews and Gypsies. A similar complexity existed in the Caucasus, where Armenians, Azerbaijanis and Georgians simply make up the largest groups.

Victims of Unification

Many European states have come into existence since the fifteenth century due to the unification of previously existing political entities, a process which accelerated after 1800. Inevitably, one power within the new structure has had a greater influence than the others; meaning that, in the same way in which expanding states have taken over peripheries, so has the dominant grouping in the newly created states.

One minor example of such a situation is provided by the Netherlands, where there is a group called the West Frisians, residing in the province of Friesland and numbering up to 400,000 speakers there, as well as a further 300,000 in other parts of Holland. Although the province joined the Netherlands in 1648, a West Frisian ethnicity and political consciousness survives into the twentieth century. In contrast to many other ethnic conflicts in Europe that in Holland remains insignificant, due to the relative closeness of Dutch and West Frisian and to the fact that there is no major religious cleavage. [32]

The French state was also initially created by a unification process, although it subsequently expanded to incorporate peripheral areas. In 1415 the kingdom of France was divided into three parts, the one being English, the other Burgundian, and the third organised around Poitiers and Bourges. However, by the end of the fifteenth century the three parts were unified. Four major languages were spoken in medieval France: Basque, Breton, Flemish and French, with the *langue d'oil* in the north, and the *langue d'oc* in the south, both of which were subject to a number of regional variations and to a multitude of local dialects, meaning that people from one part of the country had difficulty in understanding those from another. The church, universities and monarchy used the ancient lingua franca, Latin. [33] In the middle of the nineteenth century 20 per cent of 'Frenchmen' could still not speak French, while one in five communes did not have French as the language of everyday use. [34]

As in the Dutch case, and in contrast to other states formed through a process of unification, particularly Spain and Yugoslavia, internal ethnic issues in France have not led to serious conflict in the modern period. The explanation of this lies in two apparently contradictory developments in French history. First, French monarchs pursued greater and more direct centralisation during the sixteenth and seventeenth centuries, affecting, for instance, law, language and religion. This centralising process continued with the French Revolution and Napoleon. Yet French governments through the ages have appeared to offer something in return, in the form of an advanced system of local government and, after the Revolution, the concept of equality. Both of these objects came at a price. In the first place, local government was at least in part an attempt to impose the will of the centre, while equality could not be achieved without sacrifice. The assimilationist Jacobin tradition in modern French history, characteristic of liberal democracies, demanded

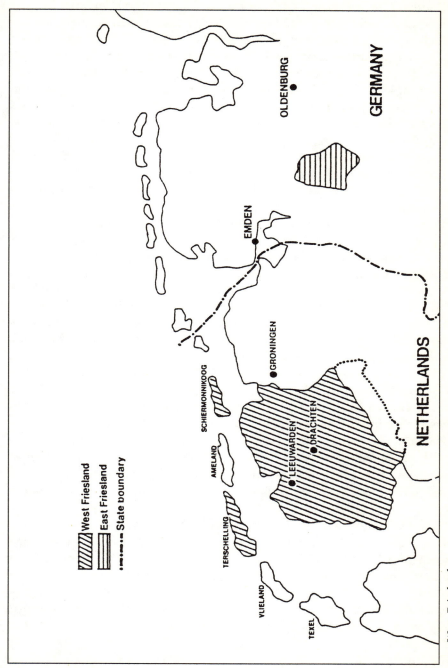

13. West Friesland

the souls of those who desired the reward. For equality grant me your identity. Those unprepared to make the sacrifice have remained marginalised, an issue which has particularly surfaced with post-war newcomers to France.

Certain pre-modern groups have maintained something of an ethnicity distinct from that created by the medieval monarchs and modern politicians. The most important of these consist of Bretons and Corsicans. In addition, several other remnant minority languages are spoken in the French regions. The most significant and self-confident groupings, the Bretons and Corsicans, have the characteristics of peripheral minorities both in their geographical relation to the centre and in the fact that they have faced incorporation into an already existing state.

The origins of Brittany lie in the movement of Celts into the area from Devon and Cornwall during the sixth century. By the ninth century a Breton monarchy developed in the region. This lasted until 1531, when Brittany joined France under an Act of Union. The national revival of the late nineteenth century had, as its economic base, dislocation in fishing and farming, as well as problems created by overpopulation; notably by scarcity of land. Cultural associations had developed from the 1830s but political nationalism took off at the turn of the century. Breton nationalism faced discredit and sanctions at the end of the Second World War, because of collaboration with the Nazis, but resurfaced by the 1960s due to the continued existence of unfavourable economic conditions and the survival of the Breton language. [35]

Corsica was ruled by Italian states from Roman times until it passed into the hands of the French in 1768, after only two decades of independence. As in the case of Brittany, separatist movements have developed during the twentieth century. The other minorities in France, all peripheral, include the Alsatians, who speak German and French: Alsace has, during the course of its history, switched between German and French rule. In addition, Flemish is spoken on the border between France and Belgium, while Catalan and Basque are local languages spilling over from the major concentrations of these people in Spain. [36]

The history of the Spanish state began in the late fifteenth century when Ferdinand, heir to the kingdom of Aragon, married Isabella of Castile in 1469, which shortly after resulted in the union of these two kingdoms, quickly followed by the annexation of Granada in 1492 and Navarre in 1515. The following centuries of Spanish history witnessed several episodes of savage repression which successfully expelled the Jews and attempted to suppress any traces of consciousness amongst the regions which had existed before the unification of the late fifteenth century. [37] Nevertheless, in two major cases, the Catalans and Basques, as well in Galicia, this centralising policy

14. Geographic Location of Minority Languages in France

Catalonia, in north-eastern Spain, was an important force in the political history of the Iberian peninsula during the middle ages, especially after it merged with the neighbouring kingdom of Aragon. Sixteenth-century attempts at centralisation and increased taxation caused resentment leading to a revolt in 1640. Although during the eighteenth century the Catalans lost their own laws and self-government, Catalan nationalism was born in the late nineteenth century; this was driven by a distinct linguistic and political heritage, as well as by the more immediate factor of the economic progress of Catalonia in contrast to the areas of Spain which controlled more political power. At the 1907 general elections, nationalists won forty-one of the forty-four seats on offer in Catalonia.[38] The issue of Catalonian self-rule reached centre stage in Spanish politics in the period of the Second Republic and the

Civil War during the 1930s, when the area was granted autonomy only to
face ruthless repression from General Franco; this failed, however, to wipe
out the independence movement which resurfaced in the later years of the
Franco regime. The Catalans managed to regain some autonomy in the new
republic which followed the death of Franco.

The opponents of Franco during the Civil War included the Basques,
whose history has similarities with that of the Catalans. One significant
difference lies in the origin of the Basques, as indicated in their language.
They represent, along with the Finns, the only grouping in western Europe
which does not use an Indo-European tongue.[39] Also in contrast to the
Catalans, a medieval Basque state seems never to have existed. Nevertheless,
the Basques were guaranteed their ancient local rights called *fueros* which
lasted, in a diluted form, until the French Revolution on the French side of
the border and into the 1870s in Spain.

The similarities with Catalonia begin in the nineteenth century, as the
Basque region also stood out as a major area of industrialisation within Spain.
Most authorities on the subject lay stress on one particular consequence of
industrialisation as the basis for the growth of Basque nationalism in the
form of the immigration of workers from other parts of Spain. This gave rise
to a native reaction led by members of the local bourgeoisie, who resented
the fact that much of the industrialisation which took place in the area was
financed by external funding and non-Basque entrepreneurs. The main group
which emerged, the Partida Nacionalista Vasca (PNV), most closely resembles
many of the racist anti-immigrant groupings which have developed an appeal
to some members of the working classes in post-war Europe. The middle-class
leaders of this nationalist grouping attempted to win over the Basque peasantry. The nationalists stressed the distinctiveness of the Basques in terms of
their religion, language and regional rights. In 1918 the PNV obtained seven
out of twenty seats in a general election.[40]

The 1920s witnessed an explosion of Basque culture in the form of music,
theatres and dance. By the beginning of the Second Republic the nationalist
movement saw itself as one great family tied by blood, culture, shared
interests and destiny.[41] The Basques obtained a statute of autonomy from
the Popular Front government in 1936 in return for supporting it, but faced
defeat by Franco's forces by the end of 1937. Thousands of nationalists were
killed or imprisoned and the military governor of San Sebastian issued an
order prohibiting the use of Euskera, the Basque language,[42] although by the
end of the Second World War activity had begun amongst nationalists again.

This led to the development of several nationalistic groupings by the end
of the 1960s. The most infamous of these, because of its readiness to use
violence, was ETA, an organisation which continued to exist and carry out

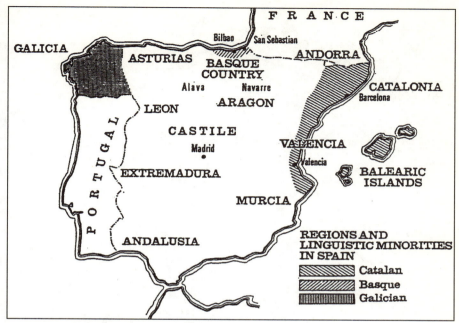

15. Location of Minorities in Spain

killings after the death of Franco. This was despite the granting of autonomy to the region under the 1978 constitution, which was not, however, regarded as having gone far enough. [43]

The third national grouping in Spain consists of the Galicians, who live to the north of Portugal and seem to be of Celtic origin, with their own distinctive language. A regionalist movement did not develop in this area until the Second Republic because industrialisation had never occurred there, which meant that the region was integrated into the rest of the Spanish social, economic and political system. Again, in contrast to Catalonia and the Basque land, nationalists have remained weak here since the 1940s. [44]

Italy, like Spain but much later, came into existence as a consequence of unification, but it has few serious ethnic problems. However, several minority languages survived from the medieval period beyond Italian unification in 1870. Three of these, Greek, Croatian and Albanian, originated in migrations into southern Italy from the Balkans dating back, in the first of these cases, to the sixth century, although both Greek and Croatian are now dying out. Up to 80,000 people speak Albanian; Franco-Provençal is spoken on the border with France; and Ladin, which predates Italian, is spoken in three northern Italian provinces, Bolzano, Trento and Belluno. Occitan and Piedmontese are spoken in Piedmont and Friulian in north-eastern Italy, while

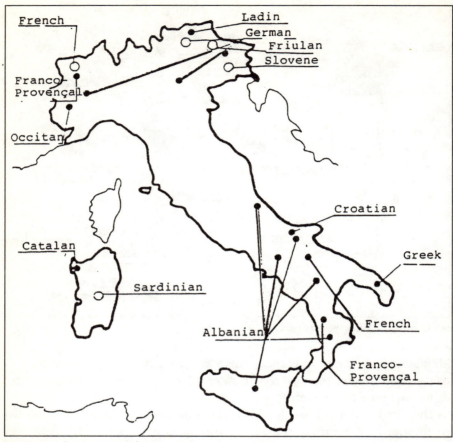

16. Geographic Location of Minority Languages in Italy

most people in Sardinia speak their own language. In nearly all cases, however, the speakers of the above and other languages have a native command
of Italian. [45]

Despite the existence of territories with German rulers for over a thousand
years, the first German nation state only came into existence in 1871. Apart
from the dispersed Jews and Gypsies, and the survival of regional dialects
throughout Germany, the most distinctive localised minorities in the new
state consisted of Danes and Lusatian Sorbs. The former were essentially
remnants from changes in the border with Denmark (which also created a
German minority on the Danish side of the boundary) because, in the age
before nationalism, Schleswig and Holstein contained a mixture of Danish
and German speakers. The Danish-German border, established at the end

of the First World War, has meant the survival of a Danish-speaking population in Germany of about 50,000. [46]

The history of the Lusatian Sorbs is more complicated. They are a Slav group which lived in their current homeland before the eastward movement of Germans. Some authorities see Lusatia, situated next to south-eastern Germany's borders with Poland and Czechoslovakia, as part of the original homeland of the Slavs, from the third millennium BC. [47] Others believe that Slavs arrived in Lusatia during the sixth and seventh centuries AD. [48] Whatever the true position, Germans did not move into the area until the tenth century and, since 1300, Lusatia has been subject to some sort of Germanic control, with German rulers settling their own subjects in the area.

The age of nationalism gave a boost to the Sorbs with cultural organisations and student societies developing in the early nineteenth century. The newly-created German state viewed the group as a threat in the late nineteenth century, although national organisations continued to survive. The Nazis denied the existence of a Sorb minority and placed some of its leaders in concentration camps. At the end of the Second World War a Sorbian National Committee in Prague demanded independence, but this idea disappeared after the Communist takeover of that country in February 1948. The German Democratic Republic recognised the Sorbs as an independent minority, which meant that they developed a rich ethnicity revolving around numerous cultural activities. Nevertheless, the free market of the Federal Republic, the collapse of the economy of the area and the less ethnically conscious policies of the new regime have had a negative effect on the Sorbs. [49]

Czechoslovakia was one of the most artificial of nation states, created at the end of the First World War through the unification of Czech and Slovak areas. The original Slavonic Czech and Slovak tribes appear to have arrived in the present areas of Czechoslovakia during the sixth century. While the Czechs inhabited Moravia and Bohemia in the west, the Slovaks lived in the east in Slovakia. The first Moravian state developed in the ninth century, followed by Bohemia, ruled by a native dynasty from the tenth until the fourteenth centuries. From the twelfth century until the Thirty Years War (1618–48), it maintained autonomy within the Holy Roman Empire ruled by the Habsburgs. After defeat at the Battle of the White Mountain in 1620, the Czech-speaking lands fell under direct Habsburg control. The nobility was exiled, Bohemia was declared an Austrian hereditary kingdom, German gained an equal footing with Czech and Catholicism replaced the Hussite religion which had been the state faith since the early fifteenth century. In contrast, the Slovaks did not establish a medieval kingdom, falling under Hungarian rule from the tenth century, and played no role in administering their own lands.

Czech nationalists regard the seventeenth and eighteenth centuries as an 'Age of Darkness',[50] ended by the national revival of the nineteenth century. The abolition of serfdom in the eighteenth century allowed the agricultural population to move into the cities, a process aided by the fact that the Czech lands became the most industrially advanced area of the Habsburg Empire. These developments allowed the spread of nationalism both through the rise of an educated bourgeoisie and through the new ideas spread amongst the working classes in the cities. In the early nineteenth century Czech language publications had become widespread. By this time a Slovak national consciousness, distinguishing itself from the Hungarian rulers of the country, had developed with the beginning of publications in the Slovak language.

The Czech national movement surfaced during the 1848 revolutions against European autocracy but was suppressed in the reaction against them. For the rest of the nineteenth century, and at the beginning of the twentieth, Czech nationalist ideas spread, helped by continuing industrialisation, which created a working class wanting independence from the Habsburgs. An artistic movement also developed. In it the composers Friedrich Smetana, who composed a cycle of six symphonic poems called *Má Vlast* (My Father-land) between 1872 and 1879, and Antonín Dvořák became leading figures.

The First World War played a determining role in the foundation of Czechoslovakia. The new state came into existence at its conclusion. The Czechs and Slovaks were unenthusiastic about fighting on the side of a German power against a Slavonic one in the east. The union of the two peoples became a reality under the influence of three academics who campaigned for the creation of a Czechoslovak state in America and gained Allied support for the concept. These consisted of two Czechs, Tomáš Masaryk and Eduard Beneš, and a Slovak, Milan Štefánik.

The artificiality of the new Czechoslovak state was best indicated by the ethnic composition of its population, which created serious problems. In the first place the number of Czechs in 1921 was far greater than Slovaks at 6,796,343 and 1,967,870 respectively. Together they made up just under two-thirds of the population. The rest consisted of just over three million Germans, as well as 744,621 Hungarians, 461,449 Ruthenians, 180,504 Jews and 75,987 Poles.[51] Aware of this situation, the constitution of the new state guaranteed the linguistic and political rights of minorities.

The largest of the minority groupings, the Slovaks, was an unequal partner from the early days of the new republic. Apart from the fact that Czechs outnumbered them by three to one, Slovakia was economically weaker. Slovak nationalists did not feel that they had gained the sort of autonomy promised to them in 1918, while Czechs dominated the central administration of the new state. Consequently a Slovak People's Party demanded greater autonomy, an aim achieved by the passage of legislation to this end, most notably in 1938 (at a time the state was being devoured by the Nazis). Negotiations between Beneš and Stalin during the Second World War ensured the rebirth of Czechoslovakia at the end of the conflict, ignoring the wishes of the Slovak Communist Party.

An uneasy alliance between the Czechs and Slovaks lasted until the 1990s, when the two peoples split apart relatively amicably, in the context of events elsewhere in eastern Europe, to form their own new nation states. Part of the reason for the 'Velvet Divorce' lay in the similarity between the Czechs and Slovaks in both linguistic and religious terms. Furthermore, much intermarriage had also occurred. In addition, while the Czech lands were more industrially advanced during the early history of Czechoslovakia, by the 1990s Slovakia had come quite close to a par with its neighbour. [52]

During its period of existence, Yugoslavia was one of the most artificial and consequently the most complicated states in Europe. Apart from the substantial minorities of Bosnian Muslims, Croats, Montenegrins, Serbs and Slovenes, the country had several regions, Macedonia, Voyvodina and Kosovo, with an almost impenetrable complexity of minority problems revolving around differences in religion and language. While all the ethnic distinctions have been exaggerated by nationalists, they can back up their claims by pointing to the varying histories of the different peoples within the Balkans, some of whom had their own states before the Ottoman conquest.

The common origins of the Yugoslav peoples lie in the Slav migrations into the area which took place after the fall of the Roman Empire, although even in these migrations differences existed in the groups who moved into the region. While the exact date of settlement of the different groupings is open to dispute, the seventh century is accepted as a starting point for the history of Slav settlement in the area. Slovenes represent one of the earliest arrivals into the area, converting to Christianity in the eighth century. The various empires, notably the Serb Empire and the long-lasting Habsburg Empire, which have controlled the region in which they lived and now live, have determined their fate.

Serbs, numerically are the largest of the Yugoslav peoples, first arrived in the mountainous heartland of the Balkans from Bohemia at the request of the Byzantine Emperor Heraclius I at the start of the seventh century. Their conversion to Christianity occurred in the ninth century and in the thirteenth century St Sava founded the Serbian Orthodox Church. Although Serb states had existed before the twelfth century, the reigns of Stephen I (1168–96) and his son Stephen II (1196–1227), of the Nemanjia dynasty, represented a major period of consolidation in the development of the medieval Serb state. This reached its height under Stephan Dušan (1331–55), but the kingdom subsequently disintegrated under the claims of competing nobles and the advance of the Turks. The symbolic victory over the Turks at Kosovo, on 28 June 1389, did not immediately destroy the Serb state which lasted for another fifty years. Under the period of Ottoman rule the Serbian Orthodox Church remained the representative institution within the millet system. One territory within the medieval Serbian kingdom, Montenegro, managed to maintain autonomy throughout the history of the Ottoman Empire.

The second largest group in Yugoslavia, the Croats, distinguish themselves from the Serbs by religion and by geographical concentration. Another Slav group by origin, they moved towards the Dalmatian coast from the seventh until the tenth century. Tomislav established the first Croat kingdom in 924. Although he changed his religious allegiance from Constantinople to Rome, the process did not reach completion until the reign of Zvonimir (1075–89). From the twelfth until the early nineteenth century Croatia fell under the control of Hungarians, Ottomans and Venetians, finally becoming part of the Austrian Empire after the Congress of Vienna in 1815.

During the nineteenth century nationalists could point to the religious and political history of Croats and Serbs in their attempts to manufacture states to succeed the Ottoman Empire. Serbia became the first to gain independence from the Turks after a series of revolts, receiving formal recognition in 1815 and full independence in 1817, after which large-scale expansion took place as the Ottoman Empire collapsed. By the outbreak of the First World War, sparked off by Serbian nationalist claims over Bosnia, the country resembled its present-day shape. Other areas of what was to become Yugoslavia simply gained a degree of autonomy from Austria-Hungary, notably Bosnia-Herzegovina and Croatia. [53]

The development of the South Slav (Yugoslav) idea occurred during the nineteenth century and had the support of both Croats and Serbs. For the former, the backing of the Serbs was a useful tool against Austria-Hungary. The Croatian Illyrian movement, led primarily by urban elites, and reaching its height during the first half of the nineteenth century, stressed the similarities of the South Slav peoples, who could be united by linguistic uniformity. Serb nationalists, while also stressing linguistic similarities, had their own political agenda. This aimed at uniting the South Slav peoples under their own leadership. By the end of the nineteenth century two distinct concepts of Yugoslavia existed, as recognised by George Schöpflin: 'the Croat Illyrianism, which sought to include all the South Slavs while recognising some of the differences among them, and the Serbian version, which was purely linguistic and ignored cultural, religious and historical factors'. [54]

The First World War resulted in the formation of the Yugoslav Committee by the end of 1914. This grouping issued the fourteen point Corfu Declaration on 20 July 1917, which aimed at the formation of a state of Serbs, Croats and Slovenes. The idea became a reality because members of the group living in London managed to persuade the Allies. With the defeat of Austria-Hungary, the newly created Yugoslav National Committee became the de facto government of the South Slav lands by the end of 1918, establishing the kingdom of the Serbs, Croats and Slovenes. Montenegro and Bosnia-Herzegovina also joined the new state, known as Yugoslavia.

The artificiality of the newly-created Yugoslavia meant that it had a large number of minority problems. The 1931 census listed seven groups of over a million people, although the largest, the Serbo-Croats at 10,731,000, included Serbians, Croatians, Bosnians, Montenegrins and Macedonians. In addition to Germans, Gypsies and Jews, the smaller minorities included 468,000 Hungarians, [55] who found themselves in the new state because the Serbians happened to be on the right side during the Great War and therefore received favoured treatment when it came to deciding boundaries. The area in which most of them lived, the Voyvodina, had the greatest ethnic diversity of any region of a comparable size in the whole of Europe, due mainly to the fact that Hungarian and Habsburg monarchs had imported a large variety of minorities into this region at various times from the fourteenth to the eighteenth centuries when it formed a boundary with the Ottoman Empire. At the end of the Second World War it had an extremely diverse ethnic structure in which the Serbs made up 50.6 per cent (841,246) and the Hungarians 25.8 per cent (248,932) of the population. [56]

The most significant problem in inter-war Yugoslavia, which resulted in several constitutional crises and threatened the continued existence of the new state (as it was to throughout the history of Yugoslavia), revolved around the relationship between Serbia and the rest of the Yugoslav peoples, especially the Croats, the second largest minority, who made up about a quarter of the population compared with the Serbs who made up about 43 per cent. [57] Ethnic conflict exploded into genocide during the Second World War, when the Croatians, siding with the occupying Nazis, who gave them their own state, had the upper hand. 1,750,000 Yugoslavs – almost 11 per cent of the population – died during the war. Of these more than half were killed by other Yugoslavs. Serbs made up about 350,000 of those murdered. [58] In turn, the Serbians also carried out similar atrocities against Croats and were again the dominant grouping in the Communist Party which came to power after the war.

The catastrophe of the 1990s had a number of elements. A series of post-war constitutions had attempted to create a federal system in which each of the republics maintained a considerable degree of control. However, Marshal Tito had great difficulty in keeping all sides equally happy. But he did ultimately succeed in his aim, even if this meant the use of force, as happened during the Croat Spring of 1971. One of the most intractable problems lay in the economic differences between the regions. Slovenia and Croatia, the richest republics, resented the fact that redistribution of wealth within Yugoslavia meant that they lost out to the benefit of the poorer Muslim areas.

The death of Tito in 1980 signalled the end of the Federal State of Yugoslavia, even though it lasted for another decade. Unfortunately, none of the constitutional structures could control the nationalism of the individual peoples, especially that of the Slovenes and Croats, which essentially fed off hatred towards the Serbs, as well as dislike of the poorer republics. This in turn

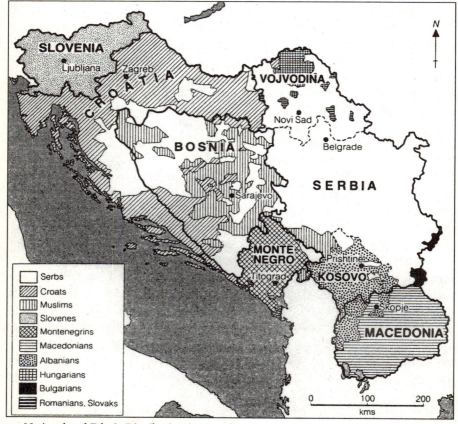

17. National and Ethnic Distribution in Yugoslavia

fuelled Serb nationalism. Consequently, deep distrust marked the relationship between the Serbs and their neighbours by the beginning of the 1990s.

In 1991 the Slovenes and Croats had developed enough self-confidence to declare themselves independent states, which caused a reaction from the Serbs, under Slobodan Milosevic, who also controlled the army. In many ways the Yugoslav War, like the whole history of Yugoslavia, revolved around the axis of Serb and Croat resentment, even though it sucked in Bosnia. While much of the international attention focused upon this nominally Muslim republic, especially from the summer of 1992, much of the fighting and ethnic cleansing involved the Croats and Serbs eliminating the populations of their mutual enemies. [59]

The peoples of Yugoslavia, with their own religions, predate the arrival of nineteenth and twentieth century nationalism. Nevertheless, the new ideology of nationalism and those who controlled it in the modern age destroyed the ethnic tolerance which had characterised the Ottoman period and its millet system. The post-Yugoslav War situation in Croatia in particular is completely artifical, as the new state has gone through a process of virtually complete and perfect ethnic cleansing, leaving an ethnically pure population in which any extreme nationalist could take pride. Perhaps all true nationalists desire such clarity.

Border Groupings

Similar to minorities on the periphery of European nation states are border groupings; peoples who found themselves living on the edge of the newly-created states which emerged during the nineteenth and twentieth centuries, especially those which grew out of the Ottoman and Habsburg Empires. The artificiality of the borders of the new states meant that they inevitably spread over, and ignored, areas where peoples had evolved historically. Several of the states created out of the Habsburg and Ottoman Empires subsequently had bits added and chopped off, which often worsened the situation for the border peoples. Once again, economic factors, and the rise of nationalism and ethnic consciousness in opposition to it, determined the evolution of states and border minorities; as did, above all in this case, the concerns of the Great Powers.

The borders of Finland which emerged during the nineteenth and twentieth centuries meant that minorities evolved on either side of them. The intertwined nature of Swedish and Finnish history, whereby the Swedes ruled the latter for seven centuries until Sweden ceded Finland to Russia in 1809, means that Swedes live in Finland, while Finns also find themselves in Sweden. Three concentrations of Swedes reside in Finland: on the south

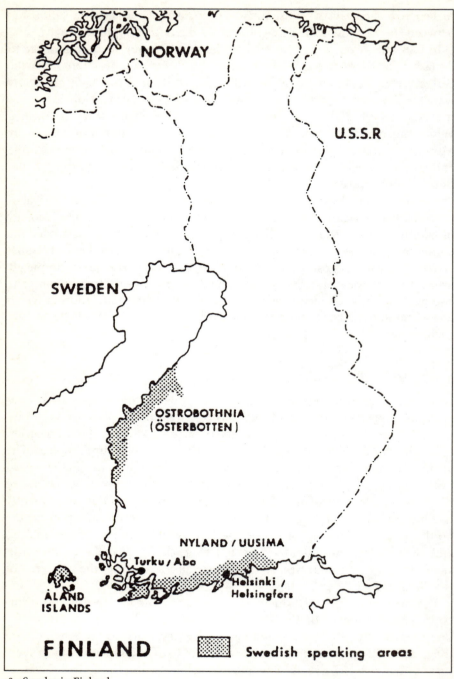

18. Swedes in Finland

coast, stretching for about fifty miles from Turku eastward beyond Helsinki; on the west coast around Ostrobothnia; and in the Åland Islands. The first two of these groups essentially represent a remnant of Swedish-language speakers within the country, as Swedish was the literary means of communication until the nineteenth century, when Finnish began to undergo standardisation at the same time as Swedish nationalism developed. The Åland Islands, on the other hand, were granted to Finland by the League of Nations in 1921. [60]

The communities of Finns in Norway and Sweden remain tiny. In the former, the Kvens, as they are known, live in the far north, where they settled from the end of the middle ages. The Finns in Sweden reside in the Torne Valley along the boundary between Sweden and Finland. Their existence here is due to the border established in 1809 between the two countries, which left the Finnish speakers on the wrong side of the border. [61] Only a few thousand Finnish speakers survive in these areas, [62] although since the Second World War economic immigration has brought in hundreds of thousands of Finns into Sweden.

One of the most significant minority problems in Italy lies in the border region with Slovenia, around Trieste, which contained a Slovene minority of 25,582 according to the 1961 census, although the true figure may have been closer to 40,000. Trieste has a complicated history and the ethnic difficulties which exist essentially lie in the mixed Slovene and Italian population on both sides of the border between Italy and Slovenia, which developed during the centuries of Habsburg control. The area also contained Germans and Croats. As a reward for joining the First World War on the winning side, the Italians gained Trieste and surrounding areas under the Treaty of Rapallo of 1920. During the inter-war years Mussolini pursued a repressive policy involving the dismissal of Slovenes and Croats from employment, as well as the changing of place names to Italian, with over 100,000 Croats and Slovenes emigrating. The region became a focus of violence during the Second World War and a contested region immediately after the end of the conflict, which did not reach a resolution until partition occurred in 1954. [63]

In view of the vast area of central and eastern Europe controlled by the Habsburg Empire from the middle ages until the twentieth century, it is surprising that there are not more minorities in twentieth-century Austria. The reason for this lies in the near perfection of the carving up process which reduced the Austro-Hungarian Empire to its core German-speaking areas at the end of the First World War, so that bits of the old empire went to all and sundry, including Czechoslovakia, Poland, Rumania and Yugoslavia. Likewise, Hungary was also cut down to size, although in this case the post-war settlement created as many problems as it solved.

Even the new Austria is not ethnically perfect. The two most significant minorities consists of the Croats in Burgenland and the Slovenes of Carinthia. The former territory forms the boundary between Austria and Hungary. About 100,000 Croats moved into this underpopulated area during the sixteenth century, encouraged by local Hungarian rulers. Some of the population was subsequently assimilated into the surrounding Germans. While during the nineteenth century others migrated, amongst those who remained a national consciousness developed after 1800. They received protection under the Treaty of St-Germain of 1920, which decided Austrian borders at the end of the First World War. The minority faced persecution under the Nazis but 30,599 survived into the 1950s, although ethnic consciousness has further declined since that time. [64]

The Slovenes of Carinthia are situated on the border with Slovenia. They are a Slavic grouping which moved into the eastern Alps during the sixth and seventh centuries, subsequently followed by Germans. This meant that by 1846 there were 120,000 Slovenes and 198,000 Germans in the area. [65] In 1848 the Carinthian Slovenes wanted to unite with their 'brethren' further afield to create a united Slovenia. Although the majority of Slovenes voted to join the newly-created Yugoslavia, under a plebiscite held in accordance with the Treaty of St-Germain, Carinthia as a whole opted to join Austria due to a further increase in the proportion of German-speakers. This was caused by Slovene migration out of the area, industrialisation within it and the spread of the German language, as education in that language increased. Despite repressive policies pursued by the Nazis, and continued pressure to assimilate after the Second World War, about 50,000 people still spoke Windisch, the Carinthian dialect of Slovene, during the 1980s. [66]

The presence of a Hungarian minority in Czechoslovakia resulted principally from the fact that the latter gained a mixed area of Hungarians and Slovaks at the expense of the defeated Austro-Hungarian Empire by the Treaty of Trianon of 1920. Tens or even hundreds of thousands of Hungarians left Czechoslovakia during the inter-war years, which meant the disappearance of about 200 villages with a Hungarian population. [67]

The Hungarians, like the Sudeten Germans, became scapegoats for the death of Czechoslovakia. During the Second World War Beneš had decided upon an exchange of populations between Hungary and Czechoslovakia. This was a rather lopsided affair as 200,000 Slovaks lived in Hungary compared with the 600,000 Hungarians in Slovakia. [68] As both countries remained within the Soviet sphere of influence, exchange occurred on a limited scale, involving 90,000 Slovakians departing from Hungary and 70,000 Hungarians leaving Slovakia. [69] Some Hungarians who remained were declared to be Slovaks, while others were transferred to the border with Hungary. The first

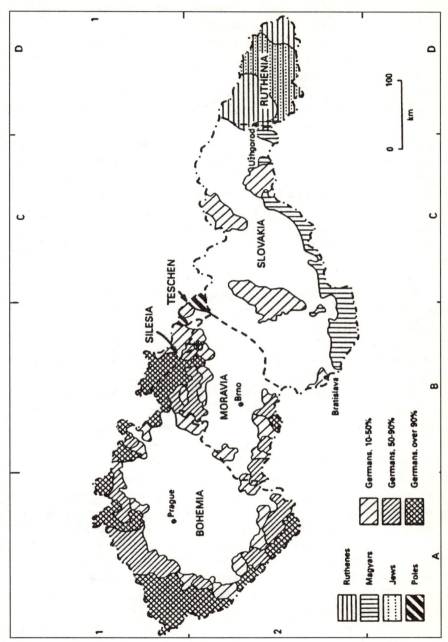

19. Ethnic Composition of Inter-War Czechoslovakia

action affected 327,000 people and the second 44,000. Consequently, just 190,000 official Hungarians lived in Czechoslovakia in 1948, although this figure had increased to 579,717 by 1980.[70]

The Ukrainian, or more accurately Ruthenian, population of Czechoslovakia lived in its easternmost province, Subcarpathian Ruthenia, which was incorporated into the state after the First World War with the agreement of the leader of the Ruthenians in the United States, Grigory Satkovic. The Soviets occupied the territory in 1944 and it joined the Ukrainian SSR in June of the following year. There still remained 58,000 Ruthenians in Czechoslovakia in 1967, concentrated in the north-eastern corner of east Slovakia; although this figure also includes Russians.[71] Finally, the presence of Poles in Czechoslovakia resulted from the annexation of the Teschen territory on the border with Poland, which had belonged to Bohemia from the fourteenth century. The Poles took this area over after the dissolution of Czechoslovakia, but it was regained at the end of the Second World War. In 1980 their total numbers stood at 67,923, concentrated overwhelmingly in the Czech Republic.[72]

Poland was another state created at the end of the First World War, using parts of the three collapsed central and east European empires, Austria-Hungary, Germany and Russia, which had partitioned the medieval Polish state during the eighteenth century. Along with Italy and Germany, Poland was perhaps the most symbolic nationalist cause, embodying a demand for self-determination, during the nineteenth century. A Polish state, which changed during the course of time, had existed since the tenth century, when one particular Slavonic tribe settled near the modern city of Poznan. The recreation of Poland became certain during the First World War when the American President, Woodrow Wilson, made this Allied policy as the thirteenth of his fourteen points for the post-war order in January 1918.

The new Polish state had severe ethnic problems. In 1931 only 68.9 per cent of its people, 21,993,444 out of a total population of 31,985,779, were Polish speakers.[73] Several of the minorities counted millions of people. Apart from Jews and Germans, these consisted of Ruthenes or Ukrainians, the largest minority of all at nearly four million; Belorussians, with more than a million; and, much smaller at less than 100,000, Lithuanians, Russians and Czechs.[74]

The largest of these groups, the Ukrainians, lived in the south east of the country, on the border with the Ukrainian Soviet Socialist Republic, while the Belorussians were concentrated in the north east of Poland. Of the other minorities, the Lithuanians were situated in the province of Vilna, a source of conflict between Lithuania, Poland and Russia.[75]

The Second World War and its aftermath had a dramatic impact upon the situation. The Nazi-Soviet Non-Agression Pact of 1939 meant that most of the Ukrainians, Belorussians and Lithuanians fell into the eastern part of the country taken over by the Soviet Union. Eventually they all came under Nazi rule, as the German army advanced eastward, and suffered as 'sub-humans' in the Nazi racial hierarchy. Most of the Polish minority problems were solved at the end of the Second World War by moving the Polish border further westwards. While Poland took over East Prussia and Silesia, which had formerly belonged to Germany, and expelled most of the Germans from these territories, the Soviet Union took control of most of the areas with Ukrainian, Lithuanian and Belorussian minorities. Finally, Poles left in these areas moved westward, while minorities from those groups that still found themselves within the new Polish boundaries were forced to move eastward. Consequently, Poland became one of the most ethnically homogeneous states in Europe, with non-Polish minorities making up just 1.5 per cent of the population by 1950.[76]

Even so, by 1975 these groupings made up a total of 704,000 people,[77] the most significant of whom consisted of Belorussians and Ukrainians, both of whom had guaranteed rights and their own ethnic organisations, as well as advanced school systems. Both of these groups numbered over 100,000 members after the end of the Second World War.[78] The Ukrainians divide further, with a sub-group called Lemkos. The Czechs and Slovaks who have remained within Poland have also maintained an ethnic identity since the Second World War, although this has proved more difficult because of their smaller numbers.[79]

The existence of minorities in Rumania is very closely connected with its good fortune, in territorial terms, in gaining Transylvania from Hungary. Rumania's destiny has been shaped by experiences both within the Ottoman and Habsburg Empires, even though, like many of the other contemporary states in central and eastern Europe, it has a history which predates these two empires. Although some nationalists have suggested connections with the pre-Roman Dacians and the Romans, the reality is that much intermixing has taken place.

The principalities of Moldavia and Wallachia developed during the fourteenth century and joined together to form the Rumanian kingdom. Despite defeat by the Turks, they retained a privileged position within the Ottoman Empire. In the early nineteenth century a Rumanian national movement emerged. Bourgeois nationalists had a brief victory in the 1848 Revolution but, as in other parts of central and eastern Europe, faced repression in the following year. The formation of a Rumanian state became closely tied to international diplomacy on the lower Danube, as Britain, France and Russia all regarded a new state in the area as advantageous. The 1856 Treaty of Paris recognised the right of Moldavia and Wallachia to become self-governing and they united in 1861. The new state subsequently gained Dobrudja and southern Bessarabia, which gave it a Black Sea coast.[80]

Until the First World War Rumania remained an ethnically homogeneous state, but this completely changed as a result of territorial gains at the end of the First World War which doubled its size and population. The Allies viewed Rumania especially favourably because it was 'bordered by two defeated states, Hungary and Bulgaria, and two untouchables, Hungary and Russia'.[81] The territories gained consisted of the Banat and Transylvania from Hungary; northern Bukovina from Austria; and Bessarabia from Russia. Only 70.8 per cent of the population of Greater Rumania consisted of Rumanians, the rest being made up of Hungarians, who numbered 1,426,000, making up 8.6 per cent of the population, as well as seven other groupings with numbers in excess of 150,000: Germans, Jews, Russians, Ruthenes/Ukrainians, Bulgars, Gypsies and Turks.[82] In addition, there were another nine groupings varying in size from 4670 to 105,750,[83] which means that inter-war Rumania had an ethnic complexity comparable to the Soviet Union and Yugoslavia.

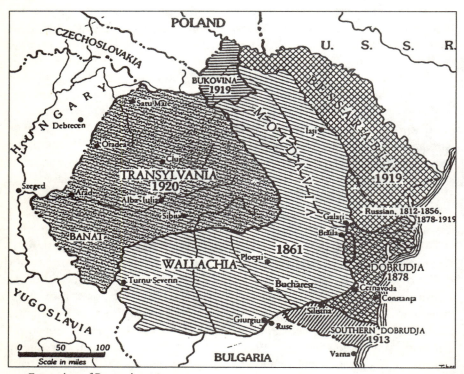

20. Expansion of Rumania, 1861–1920

The presence of the Hungarian minority in Rumania was essentially the result of the transfer of Transylvania from Hungary to Rumania under the Treaty of Trianon. This area had been much contested by the two states since at least the mid nineteenth century. In 1848 the Transylvanian Diet, controlled by Hungarian nobility, had associated itself with the kingdom of Hungary which it eventually joined in 1867. In 1910, out of a population of 5,263,282, Rumanians made up 53.8 per cent, Hungarians 31.7 per cent and Germans 10.6 per cent,[84] mainly due to the immigration of these groups into the area during the middle ages encouraged by Hungarian rulers. In an age of nation states the area therefore had an insoluble minority problem. If Hungary had obtained Transylvania this would have created an even greater difficulty, as Hungarians would not have been the largest grouping. Partition was out of the question because Hungarians were concentrated in the east and west, while Rumanians mostly lived in the middle. Ethnic cleansing represented the only 'rational' solution, but this was in an age before the concept had become fashionable. Nevertheless, between 1920 and 1924 about 197,000 Hungarians did actually leave, due to expulsion as well as voluntary movement, while Rumanians moved into the area.[85] Around two million Hungarians still lived in Rumania at the time of Ceaçescu's fall, making up about 10 per cent of the population, although they had faced much persecution during his rule which attempted to create a unitary Rumanian culture.[86]

Apart from Hungarians, Germans, Gypsies and Jews, the other minorities which inhabited inter-war Rumania declined due to the fact that at the end of the Second World War Rumania lost Bessarabia and northern Bukovina, with their large Russian, Ruthenian and Ukrainian populations, to the Soviet Union, while Bulgaria obtained southern Dobrudja, which contained its own speakers. Consequently, the number of minorities outside the four main groups fell from 1,800,000, 10 per cent of the population, to 250,000, or 1.5 per cent of the population,[87] divided between twelve groupings, although there exist further tiny minorities.[88]

The Greek minority in Albania also found itself present in that state due to artificial boundaries. Greece represents one of the nation states which claims the longest existence, drawing links with antiquity. Nevertheless, in the past 2000 years enormous changes have taken place in the region, something stressed by Greek historiography. The most important was the existence of the Byzantine Empire, which lasted from the fourth to the fifteenth century and whose most important legacy was the Greek Orthodox religion, the key determinant, along with language, in modern Greek ethnicity. During its period of existence Byzantium extended to encompass southern Italy, Anatolia and much of the Balkans but went into terminal decline from the eleventh century, falling victim to the various Slav states which rose in the area and, ultimately, to the Ottoman Empire, although Constantinople itself survived until 1453.

Under the *Tourkokratia*,[89] the Greeks fared better than many of the other Balkan minorities, primarily because of the status of members of the Greek Orthodox Church as the most favoured Christian group. The genesis of Greek nationalism during the eighteenth and early nineteenth centuries had several roots, including the growth of a Greek commercial class and, linked with this grouping, the revival of interest in ancient Greece with a move away from stressing Byzantium and its religion. The armed struggle for Greek independence which began in 1821 led to the creation of the first Greek state in 1832, which expanded northwards and into the Aegean by 1947.[90] Its main minority problems of Turks, Macedonians, Bulgarians and Vlachs were solved by policies of assimilation and population exchange, leaving one of the most homogeneous of populations of any post-war European nation state. According to the 1951 census 7,297,878 of the entire population of Greece of 7,632,801 consisted of people having Greek as their mother tongue,[91] although these figures would be hotly disputed by the supporters of Turks, Macedonians and Vlachs.

Greek minorities remained in several neighbouring countries, the most significant of which are Albania and Turkey. The Greeks who live in Albania represent a classic border minority in an area inhabited by Greeks since antiquity, subsequently adopting Greek Orthodox Christianity during the Byzantine Empire. However, by the start of the twentieth century, northern Epirus, the Greek Albanian boundary, had developed a mixed population of Greeks and Albanians and was disputed by their respected mother countries. The original border settled in 1912 has remained stable since that time, despite several Greek attempts to move it further northwards. In 1923, under pressure from the Great Powers, Greece accepted the boundary on condition that its minority received protection, agreed under the Corfu Protocol. The precise number of Greeks in southern Albania at any one time is difficult to establish: present estimates vary between 40,000 and 400,000.[92]

Macedonians represent a minority which found itself on the borders between Albania, Bulgaria, Greece and Yugoslavia by the early post-war period. They are one of the most complex and dubious of European ethnic groups, whose existence as Macedonians is partly as an administrative geographical grouping. The issue causes considerable tension amongst those who see themselves as Macedonian and amongst the states who house this grouping and deny its existence.

Historically, it is possible to return to antiquity. Macedonia was the birthplace of one of the most famous of ancient Greeks, Alexander the Great, although the people who lived in the area were regarded as distinct by the

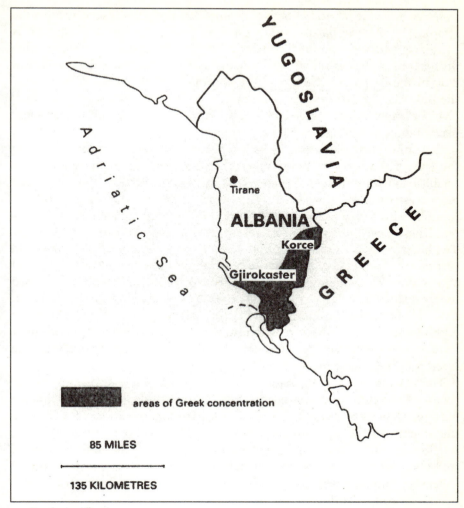

21. Greeks in Albania

Athenians. Nevertheless, numerous groupings have migrated into the region since the fourth century BC, the most important of which were the Slavs and Bulgarians at the end of the first Millennium. Before the conquest of the area by the Ottoman Empire at the end of the fourteenth century, parts of Macedonia were controlled by Byzantium, Bulgaria and Serbia.

The issue of Macedonia did not begin to surface until the second half of the nineteenth century, initially as a territorial dispute between the Greek state to the south, which was expanding northwards, and the newly-created Bulgaria, hostile to the already existing Greece and claiming all Macedonians as its own people, although Serbia also quickly laid territorial claims to the region. The area was partitioned by the three powers during the Balkan Wars of 1912–13 which ended the Ottoman Empire in Europe. In addition, a tiny proportion of the region went to Albania as a result of these developments. Due to the boundary changes at the end of the First World War, notably the Bulgarian loss of western Thrace to Greece, transfers of population took place between Bulgaria and Greece reducing Greek speakers in Bulgaria and Slavophones in Greece.

The concept of Macedonians as a separate grouping became an issue at the end of the Second World War, when the republic of Macedonia was established within the new Yugoslavia. It was given a literary language, based on a western Bulgarian dialect,[93] its own Orthodox Church in a socialist republic with a very substantial Muslim minority, and its history was rewritten. These developments caused resentment in both Bulgaria and Greece. The latter refused to recognise Macedonians as a distinct ethnic group and carried out further deportations of Slavophones at the end of the Second World War. The issue surfaced again after the republic of Macedonia gained independence in 1992. The Greek state feared the destabilising potential on its own Macedonian minority, whose numbers are under dispute. Bulgaria and Albania have also been reluctant to recognise Macedonians within their borders as distinct ethnic groups, although the issue has not caused the same level of hostility as it has within Greece.[94]

The origins of the Bulgarians lie in Asia, from where they moved into their present heartland around the fifth century and then mixed with the Slav populations of the area. The first Bulgarian Empire, which existed from the seventh to the eleventh century, adopted Orthodox Christianity as its religion, as well as devising its own Slavonic alphabet. This empire ended in 1018 after defeat by Byzantium. At the end of the twelfth century a second Bulgarian Empire developed, but by the end of the fourteenth century this had fallen to the Turks.

The first traces of a national revival occurred in the seventeenth and eighteenth centuries through Catholic and Orthodox monks who wrote histories of Bulgaria. Bulgarians also began to gain political encouragement from the declining Ottoman Empire during the late eighteenth century. By the 1830s a Bulgarian cultural revival had occurred with the spread of Bulgarian as a literary language and the development of poetry. The economic basis for this consisted of a movement of Bulgarians into towns; the establishment of Bulgarian merchant houses; and an increase in the prosperity of cotton farmers, due to demand for their crop in western Europe.

The development of Bulgaria into a nation state became a reality in the second half of the nineteenth century. The first major step was the creation of a Bulgarian Orthodox Church, separate from the Greek one and recognised by the Turks in 1870. In the same year a Bulgarian Revolutionary Committee was established which led the revolt against Ottoman rule in 1876. The ruthless suppression of this uprising by the Turks backfired, as it increased Bulgarian self-belief and brought the Bulgarians onto the world stage and to the attention of the Great Powers. In 1878 modern Bulgaria came into existence, although nominally still under the control of the Sultan and not obtaining full independence until 1908. Its boundaries have remained fairly stable since then, except for the loss of western Thrace to Greece at the end of the First World War. This resulted in population exchanges which meant a fall in the number of Greeks within the country from 58,518 in 1893 to just 8265 by 1965. [95]

Outsiders in the Interior

The history of the territory now covered by Belgium is extremely complicated and any attempt to draw a straight line between the modern Belgian state and the period before the nineteenth century is hazardous. Before 1800 the region had fallen, at various times, under the control of Spanish, Dutch, French and German states. The major events in the process towards Belgian independence include the fact that most of Belgium did not form part of the original United Provinces in the seventeenth century, drifting into Austrian Habsburg rule in 1713. The development of the concept of an independent Belgium began to solidify during the French Revolutionary and Napoleonic Wars, when the region escaped from Austrian rule to fall to the French. This had a positive effect on the economy of the region, as well as introducing revolutionary principles and confirming French as the literary language. The attempt by the Great Powers at the Congress of Vienna in 1815 to attach the Southern Netherlands to the already existing Northern Dutch state ultimately failed. The ruling French-speaking elites had no desire to join the Dutch-speaking state to the north and therefore established an independent Belgian state in 1830 after a revolution in Brussels, something the Great Powers finally accepted in 1839.

As the newly-created state ignored the Flemish-speakers within its borders, these developed a movement primarily rebelling against the lack of recognition given to their language. The basis of the movement rested upon a rising educated and industrial Flemish-speaking class. Its members had achieved many of their aims by the end of the nineteenth century. In 1898 both Flemish and French were recognised as official languages, although Flemish remained marginal in some areas of life such as the army. During the First World War a small Flemish independence movement developed, encouraged by the Germans, who pursued a similar policy during the Second World War as a divide and rule tactic. By the inter-war years Flemish nationalists had become a major force in the Belgian political scene.

Ethnicity has remained a central issue in Belgian politics since 1945. All of the major parties, Christian Democrats, Liberals and Socialists, have separate parties in Flanders and Wallonia. Both Flemish and Walloon nationalism have taken off. The major organisations in the former category have included the Volksunie during the 1960s and 1970s and the extremist Vlaams Blok during the 1980s and 1990s. The most successful grouping of the Franco-phones has been the Rassemblement Wallon, founded in 1968. The effect of the rising nationalism has been to turn Belgium into a federal state, through a series of constitutional reforms implemented in 1970, 1980 and 1992. These changes have managed to control ethnic hatred so that Belgium, with a long liberal democratic tradition, has remained mainly free from the violence and serious conflict characteristic of many European states with similar divided populations. [96]

Switzerland should be one of the European states with the greatest ethnic problems because of the distinct groupings that exist within it. Nevertheless, its historical evolution has meant that the separate communities have moulded together, essentially against external aggressors, to form one of the most unified and stable states in Europe. The concept of excluded and persecuted minorities in the Swiss case consequently proves problematic. The history of Switzerland began in the late thirteenth and early fourteenth century, when three areas separated themselves from Habsburg control. Since that time the country has gradually expanded in stages as peripheral areas have joined the three original cantons. Although beginning as a Germanic group, it has subsequently expanded to include French and Italian speakers. The country also recognises Raeto-Romantsch. The state works through a complex local government system and the representation of each of the minority languages in the political system.

The majority language is German, spoken by 63.6 per cent of the population as its mother tongue in 1990. Within this figure we have to recognise the existence of distinct dialects spoken by limited numbers of people in small areas, as well as a common Swiss German used on a national scale. The number of French speakers fell from 22.6 per cent in 1850 to 18 per cent by the 1970s, due to a lower fertility rate amongst this section of the population. The importance of Italian has increased since the Second World War because of the immigration of large numbers of Italian workers into the country to add to the 5 per cent of Italian speakers concentrated mostly in the canton of Ticino. Finally, about 50,000 people speak Raeto-Romantsch, less than 1 per cent of the population. This language dates back to antiquity and was raised to the status of Switzerland's fourth language in 1938 following a campaign by a group called the Lia Rumantscha, which feared for its survival. [97]

Bulgaria contains a group within its borders called the Vlachs, one of the least conscious of minorities within Europe and also one which finds itself concentrated in several Balkan states. Unlike many of the border groupings, the Vlachs cannot appeal to any neighbouring nation state. In many ways they are therefore completely unique and perhaps most closely resemble the dispersed peoples. Nevertheless, in the sense that they find themselves situated within the heart of individual nation states, they also resemble minorities in Belgium, Switzerland and Turkey.

The Vlachs live in several Balkan states in minuscule numbers, although their total may be several hundred thousand. The fact that they have no nation state to protect them means that they have tended to be ignored. The main strand of their ethnicity consists of a common language, related to Rumanian. There do not appear to have been Vlach kingdoms in the past, but the Vlachs enjoyed administrative autonomy under the Ottoman Empire. The boundaries drawn up by the nation states created after the fall of the Ottoman Empire meant that they were divided up between several of these political entities. They have different names in these various states, as their historian has pointed out: 'Known in general by themselves as Aroumanians, by the Greeks as Koutzovlachs, by the Yugoslavs as Cincars, and by the Romanians as Macedo-Romanians, and in particular groups by a whole host of names, they are best called Vlachs.' [98]

One of the most significant concentrations lies in the Greek mainland away from the sea. During the nineteenth century many Vlachs made a living as shepherds, migrating with their herds when the seasons changed. Industrialisation and the growth of transportation has had a negative impact on the Vlachs in Greece. Both developments have affected the isolation of the communities: their members increasingly adopt Greek as their language when they move into the cities or when Greek-speakers come into contact with them. In addition, the Greek state is reluctant to recognise their existence. Until 1945 Rumania displayed concern for the interests of the Vlachs, because of a belief in common ancestry, which meant the existence of Vlach-speaking schools and churches, but this interest diminished after 1945. There is much dispute about their numbers in Greece. The 1951 Greek census gave a figure of 39,855. [99]

Outside Greece, one of the main official Vlach populations lives in the republic of Macedonia, many of its members having migrated there during the eighteenth and nineteenth centuries. The major settlements are in west Macedonia, with perhaps 30,000 people in 1900, [100] although another significant, nomadic, community developed in eastern Macedonia. By 1981 the

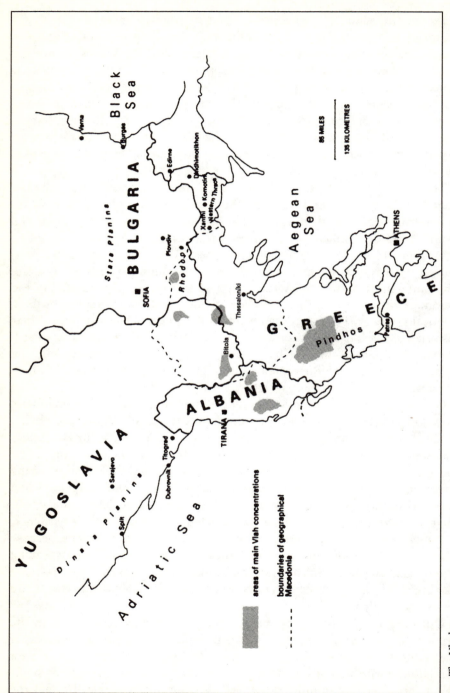

Black Sea

Vienna
Burgas

BULGARIA

Stara Planina

Edirne
Didhimotikhon

Xanthi Komotini
Western Thrace

Plovdiv

Rhodopi

SOFIA

Aegean Sea

Thessaloniki

GREECE

Bitola

Pindhos

ATHENS

Patras

ALBANIA

TIRANA

YUGOSLAVIA

Sarajevo

Dinara Planina

Split

Dubrovnik
Titograd

Adriatic Sea

85 MILES

135 KILOMETRES

areas of main Vlah concentrations

boundaries of geographical
Macedonia

22. The Vlachs

number of Vlachs in Macedonia had fallen to 6392. [101] According to a statement made at the European Parliament in November 1985, a total of 400,000
Vlachs live in Bulgaria, [102] although this seems a gross exaggeration, as the
country probably has one of smallest totals of Vlachs in the Balkans. [103] As
many as 80,000 Vlachs may also live in Albania. Having suffered some
persecution under the Hoxha regime, a Vlach association came into existence
in 1990 and held a congress two years later. [104]

The Turkish state which emerged at the collapse of the Ottoman Empire
contained several minorities within its interior. In an attempt to move
towards a homogeneous population the Turkish state, which has passed
through varying phases of dictatorship and democracy, has used any means
possible, including genocide and deportation, to eliminate the Armenians,
Greeks and Kurds remaining within Anatolia.

The presence of Greeks within Turkey was mostly a legacy of the Byzantine
Empire, although some of the communities traced their origins back to
antiquity. The major areas of concentration after 1912 included the Aegean
coast, around Smyrna; the islands of Imbros and Tenedos, which are located
just off the Dardanelles; and Constantinople. The first of these settlements
was also the first to face elimination. Smyrna itself contained more Greeks
than Athens and in 1919 Greece invaded the Turkish Aegean coast around
the city in an expedition that had almost reached Ankara by 1921. There then
followed a catastrophic defeat, which involved the murder of 30,000 Greeks
in Smyrna by Turkish forces and the escape of approximately 850,000 with
the withdrawing Greek forces. There still remained about 200,000 Greeks in
Asia Minor, who faced deportation to the Greek mainland under the Treaty
of Lausanne of 1923. This arranged for the exchange of populations between
Greece and Turkey, thus ending a 2500 year history of Greek settlement in
Anatolia. [105]

Exempted from the population exchange were Constantinople and the
islands of Imbros and Tenedos. The islands, which had populations of less
than ten thousand before 1914, were mostly inhabited by Greeks and have
remained under Turkish rule since then – except for a brief period after
the end of the First World War. Immediately after the Greco-Turkish War,
the Turkish government tried to abolish the Greek language on the islands,
although it subsequently eased its intolerant attitude. Nevertheless, the population of Greeks declined with the deterioration of Greek-Turkish relations
over the Cyprus issue from the 1950s. [106]

The Greek population of Constantinople, whose presence in the city is
inextricably linked with its status as the capital of the Byzantine Empire and
the centre of Greek Orthodox Church, has also declined over the course of
the twentieth century. During the nineteenth century the Greek population

of the city increased as it underwent an urban expansion, so that by 1914 about a quarter of a million Greeks lived in Constantinople. By this time the community supported over one hundred schools. However, by 1923 the Greek population had declined to about 100,000. The issue of the Greek community in Constantinople exploded during the dispute over Cyprus in the 1950s, since when further large-scale emigration has taken place, leaving just 5000 Greeks in 1988, many of them functionaries of the Greek Orthodox patriarchate. [107]

The plight of the Greeks in twentieth-century Turkey has been relatively bearable compared with that of the Armenians, whose fate as victims in twentieth-century Europe is second only to the Jews in the sense that they became victims of a genocide. As a people living in eastern Anatolia, they pre-date the Turks by at least 1500 years. They have had their own church since the fourth century and their own literary language since the fifth. Their history has been bloody partly because of their location in a crossing-point between east and west.

In the nineteenth century the Armenians experienced a national reawaken-ing, helped by the commercial accumen of many of them; but, because of their location in the Turkish heartland, they could not secure the inde-pendence granted to the Balkan states. At the end of the nineteenth and beginning of the twentieth century the Armenians became victims of regular massacres, culminating in the genocide of the First World War launched by the revolutionary Young Turk government. This process killed up to one million Armenians, while one million more may have migrated, particularly to Syria, France, the USA and what was to become Soviet Armenia. Despite the offence it causes, Turkish governments continue to deny that the mas-sacre of Armenians took place. [108] About 40,000 to 50,000 Armenians still live in Turkey, 10,000 of them in Istanbul. [109]

The Kurds have similarities to the Armenians in their area of concentration within eastern Anatolia and in the fact that they have stretched over the artificial boundaries of this region into Iran, Iraq, Syria and the USSR. They most resemble the Vlachs in the sense that they have never possessed their own nation state but have been present as long as many of the groups in their region which have succeeded in creating their own political units. Nevertheless, they are much more numerous than the Vlachs, totalling over 16,000,000 according to one, extreme, estimate in 1980. Of these, 8,455,000 live in Turkey, where they make up 19 per cent of the population. [110]

Theories about their origin suggest that they may have been present since as long ago as the fourth century BC. The Arab invasions of the area converted them to Islam during the seventh century. Today most of them are Sunni Muslims. They speak at least three different dialects, according to the area

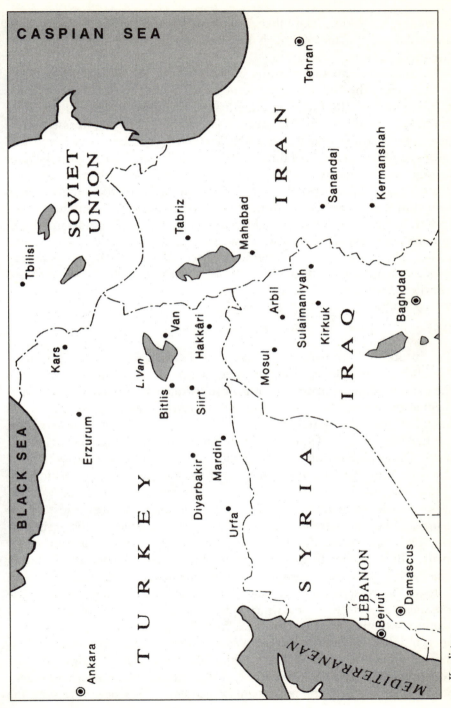

23. Kurdistan

in which they reside. The other characteristic of the group is its nomadic and tribal way of life, although this has been breaking down during the twentieth century.

In common with many forms of nationalism, the Kurdish variety developed from the late nineteenth century. The short-lived Treaty of Sèvres of 1920, imposed by the Allies on Turkey, attempted to grant a degree of autonomy to the Kurds. However, this collapsed after the reassertion of power by Mustafa Kemal, while the Treaty of Lausanne, which replaced Sèvres, made no mention of the Kurds. There followed three major rebellions in 1925, 1930–31 and 1937, all of which resulted in savage repression.

Since 1945, the history of the Kurds in Turkey has followed a similar pattern to that of the pre-war years. In the first place, nationalism resurfaced at the end of the 1950s and has never subsided since that time. The most important grouping consists of the Marxist PKK, established in 1978 and using violent tactics. The Turkish state has pursued extremely repressive policies against its Kurdish opponents throughout the post-war years, which have included imprisonment, murder and torture. [111]

Why Do Localised Minorities Exist?

The European continent clearly has a detailed mosaic of peoples. While many find themselves residing in nation states which regard them as members of the correct ethnic ingroup, millions of individuals live in states which view them as outsiders. The evolution of this pattern of majorities and minorities has taken place over hundreds of years, speeded up during the industrial age.

After the collapse of the Roman Empire political control in Europe remained primitive in most of the continent for hundreds of years. During this time, until the crystallisation of medieval state structures in the form of feudal kingship, city states and the Habsburg and Ottoman Empires (processes which intensified from around the eleventh century), most of the peoples of Europe, later to emerge as ethnic and national groups during the nineteenth and twentieth centuries, moved into their present areas of settlement. The centuries from the sixth to the fourteenth were those during which some of the greatest population movements occurred within European history. The reasons for such ease of mobility is partially explained by the looseness of political control which existed on the continent, which allowed people from other parts of Europe or further afield to move into new areas, often uninhabited, as they wished. With the development of medieval kingship this became more difficult, although clearly such a form of state development could not exercise the sort of political control which a modern nation state can over the movement of peoples. It was nevertheless in the years between the collapse of the Roman Empire and the crystallisation of the medieval state structures that many of the linguistic and religious patterns of European peoples developed.

The process of minority creation began, in the British case, in the Dark Ages and the movement of Angles, Jutes and Saxons into England. Britain represents one of the classic cases in which minority populations have come into existence through the expansion of a central dominant population into distant areas, inhabited by people who have different ethnic characteristics, but over which the dominant population eventually gains control. In this sense the minorities remain distant and marginalised in both geographical and ethnic terms.

State creation through unification also has a long history, dating back to the medieval period in the Spanish and French cases, although such processes have more commonly characterised the modern era. Minority creation is again part and parcel of such a situation because not all of the populations in the areas which find themselves within the new states will have the ethnic characteristics of the dominant populations.

The emergence of new states during the nineteenth and twentieth centuries from the dying Ottoman and Habsburg Empire also led to the development of minorities. Unlike the loose control which existed in the old imperial systems, the new nation states exercised greater authority over their ethnically deviant populations, confirming their minority status. The majority of the outgroups which developed in the political structures which emerged from the Habsburg and Ottoman Empires found themselves on the borders of the new states: the new boundaries displayed little concern for the settlement patterns which had emerged in Europe during the previous 1500 years. The strength of armies and the attitude of the Great Powers, rather than the wishes of local populations, determined such developments.

Other minorities, for a variety of reasons, have found themselves deeper within the heart of particular nation states which emerged during the nineteenth and twentieth centuries. In the case of the Vlachs, their lack of national consciousness and dispersal meant that they emerged as a minority within the various Balkan states which developed during the nineteenth and twentieth centuries. The minorities which exist in Turkey, on the other hand, found themselves present within the Anatolian heartland after the rest of the Ottoman Empire had withered away, while the minorities of Belgium and Switzerland emerged as linguistic groupings in states which split away from neighbouring controlling powers.

The four different categorisations of localised minorities overlap with each other. Geographical location plays a part in the existence of minorities within all of the above categories. If a group has different ethnic characteristics from the controlling population, especially in terms of language and religion, the further away it is situated from the centre of a particular nation state, the more likely it is to be a minority.

While the process of minority creation has taken hundreds of years on the European continent as a whole, changes since the eighteenth century have bought about minority creation from the Atlantic to the Urals. The most important reason for this lies in the emergence of nationalism and of nation states with a tight control over the populations that live within their fixed borders. The emergence of peoples into nation states is a fairly random process, but the dominant population always has something which links its members together, most commonly language. From this develops a literary culture, usually consequent upon the rise of the bourgeoisie, although in some eastern European cases religion has played a leading role in the process. Once a culture has crystallised, a nationalist movement can emerge from it. The leaders of the new political ideology and movement, concerned with creating a national market for their goods, work towards building nation states; an aim which was easier with support from the Great Powers, as was the case throughout central and eastern Europe during the nineteenth and twentieth centuries. However, no state in Europe has an ethnically homo-geneous population, no matter how long or short the period of its evolution, because the drawing of lines, called national borders, upon maps cannot eradicate thousands of years of settlement patterns in particular locations. Nationalism leads to the development of ethnicity within particular states during the modern era because the attempt at closer control, both political and cultural, means that those sections of the population which do not have dominant ethnic characteristics react against the attempts at standardisation.

4

Post-War Arrivals

The Nature of Post-War European Migration

Migration has played a central role in the development of all geographical areas and all peoples during the entire course of European history. The evolution of settlement patterns on the continent which had crystallised by the nineteenth century rested upon the influx of peoples who had made their way into and across Europe during the course of thousands of years. The peoples who had moved towards and within Europe did so both for economic reasons and as a result of political persecution.

European population movements have not been a constant and steady process but, instead, have gone through a series of phases. During some periods, notably the second half of the first millennium, the first great age of migration, people streamed throughout Europe, establishing the territories in which they have been based until the present. Stability of population, however, then characterised the history of Europe until the nineteenth century. This is not to say of course that individual movements, often on a large scale, did not take place in the intervening centuries; they clearly did. By the early modern period, after this first great age, the development of states made this process more difficult. In the centuries immediately following the collapse of the western Roman Empire large tracts of land remained open for settlement; as one group vacated a particular area, another people moved into it.

The nineteenth century saw the beginning of one of great ages of mass migration in human history, an era which has continued until the present and which is inextricably linked with the major developments which have moulded the modern world. The population explosion is the most fundamental change of all, representing the basis upon which all other elements of modern society rest. Since the end of the eighteenth century the number of people in the world has increased from about seven hundred million to a figure of around six thousand million in the 1990s. This has made migration far more likely because of the pressure it creates upon land use.

Population growth in itself does not inevitably lead to emigration, as the examples of twentieth-century rural India and China indicate. A second necessary element characteristic of modern society consists of industrialisation. For capitalists, in theory, the more people the better; both because of the potential market they represent and, just as important, the labour supply they make available. In industrial society labour power represents a central commodity, as important as capital and machinery. For industrialisation to take place a surplus population has to be available. This is either imported from the locality, from another area of the nation state or, if necessary, from beyond its boundaries.

The European countries which industrialised during the nineteenth century generally used their own citizens in the process. After 1945 western Europe entered a period when population began to stabilise, just at the time when economic growth entered one of its longest and most spectacular phases, lasting for three decades. European industrialists and their governments therefore made efforts to import as much of the commodity of labour as required from whichever supply seemed most appropriate to the interests of a particular nation state.

Technology, more specifically its application to transport, has also made population movement easier. Before the advent of canals, modern road building technology, railways and steamships, movement of people over any sort of distance was a hazardous and laborious process. Trains, steamships, and during the twentieth century cars and aeroplanes, have meant that human beings can travel over distances of all ranges extremely quickly.

The political changes which have characterised modern European history have also played a central role in population movements throughout the continent, especially during the twentieth century. The modern omnipotent state has controlled migration in various ways. In the first place, twentieth-century wars and their aftermaths have proved crucial in redistributing Europe's population, most notably the two world wars and, on a smaller scale, the conflict in Yugoslavia. Great Power diplomacy played a role in such processes, supporting the redrawing of national boundaries. In other cases, of course, people simply fled for their own safety – whether or not a threat actually existed to them. An equally malign practice involved the singling out of individuals who held views contrary to those of the ruling regime and persecuting them, meaning that emigration became attractive to them, providing they could find a state which would accept them.

The spread of government control has also played a determining role in immigration flows into post-war Europe. States have developed policy on every aspect of the territory and peoples over which they have control: from their health and economic security to the incomes which they earn and the houses in which they live. The number of foreigners allowed into any particular nation state rests upon a series of things, above all the continued well-being of those people already resident within its boundaries. The state, concerned about its survival, is influenced by big business, looking to its profits, and the media, interested in its circulation and viewing figures. These factors collectively determine the level of immigration within a particular nation state. A simple policy develops, running as follows: 'If we need foreign labourers we will import them from wherever is easiest and most appropriate. As long as they are beneficial to our own citizens, with the birthright, we will continue to import them but once they start to threaten these indigenous citizens we will stop the flow of immigration.' By the end of the twentieth century, immigration policy in most western European states has reached a stage in which the restriction of immigration to as few as possible has become orthodoxy, because of the perceived threat which newcomers would pose to the economic well-being of those already living within the artificially created boundaries. Immigration policy represents one of the clearest indications of racism in western Europe, giving benefits to those who hold the birthright and virtually denying the existence of those who live outside its boundaries. The modern state works in much the same way as the industrial system which supports it – profit and loss. Of course, political practicality also plays a role: by focusing on the difference of outsiders the unity of the insiders can be further strengthened.

The history of international population movements in post-war Europe falls comfortably, though not perfectly, into three phases, which illustrate the above processes in action. European states did not all experience the three phases at exactly the same time. The years since 1945 have witnessed migration in Europe on a scale never seen before; during this period hundreds of millions of people have moved into and across Europe.

The first of the three phases covers the years immediately following the end of the Second World War, when population movements particularly affected the areas which the Nazis had controlled. The tens of millions of people on the move included victims of Nazism, in the form of foreign workers used by the German economy and former inmates of the camp system; German expellees from the victorious and vindictive regimes which followed the defeat of the Nazis; and victims of Stalinism, attempting to escape from that particular system of totalitarianism, but in many cases forced back by the agreements of the Allies at the end of the war. In fact Allied policy at the end of the war played a major role in the refugee crisis of the immediate post-war years. Several European states, notably Britain and France, used the opportunities presented by this mass of wandering people to import them into their economies to help in the reconstruction process, while Germany gratefully accepted the expellees from the east for the same reason.

The refugee crisis had died down by the end of the 1940s, although the movement of East Germans into the Federal Republic continued for another decade. The second phase of European migration essentially represented the search for labour supplies to act as fodder for the expansion of the European economies which took place until the early 1970s. While initially most importing states made use of the surplus population of their neighbours, they subsequently cast their nets far and wide. Those countries with colonies, notably Britain, France and the Netherlands, made use of supplies of labour from those areas. Other European states used, instead, the European periphery, especially the Mediterranean edges of the continent, Spain, Italy, Greece, Yugoslavia and Turkey. Push factors had a secondary role in this second phase of migration because the determining issue in causing population movement consisted of the initiative of business and industry in the receiving state. However, in many countries, such as Turkey and Italy, the government of the sending society actually pursued a policy of exporting people as part of a solution to domestic overpopulation and underdevelopment. Tens of millions of people moved into western Europe during this period, which finally ended in the mid 1970s.

Eastern Europe and the Soviet Union do not easily fit into this second phase. If the Stalinist take-overs had not occurred, eastern Europe would have provided much of the labour for the German economic boom, as it had during the first half of the twentieth century. Many of the eastern European countries which industrialised after 1945 did so for the first time, which meant that they had their own surplus labour to utilise for the purpose and therefore had no need to import any manpower from abroad. A few exceptions exist to this rule, most notably the German Democratic Republic, although the numbers of people brought in remained tiny compared with the millions who moved into the capitalist west. Nevertheless, a considerable amount of movement took place between the different Soviet republics during the period of post-war economic expansion, initially consisting mainly of Russians moving to industrialising areas such as the Baltic states and the Ukraine. Subsequently, some of the Muslim populations started to move away from their relatively underdeveloped areas towards Russia, acting as a surplus labour supply.

The third phase of post-war European migration, which again did not apply equally to every European state, involved, initially at least, two contradictory developments in the form of the bolting of doors by the western European industrial democracies to migrants from all over the world, just at the time when the number of people who actually wished to move towards the wealthy parts of western Europe actually increased. Britain first introduced controls upon post-war immigration in 1962, following an economic downturn and a racist anti-immigration campaign supported by politicians and the press. Since that time the British state has regularly tightened its controls on the amount of immigration, to the extent that virtually no member of the human race can enter the country permanently unless they can prove a connection with a person, preferably one with a white skin, already residing within Britain. All other European states have followed Britain's lead, although few have implemented such draconian controls.

Push factors played a more important role at the start of the final phase of post-war European migration, especially in the form of political pressure. Before the late 1980s these factors consisted of the increasing persecution practised by military regimes and eastern European Stalinist governments. Yet numbers remained small until the collapse of Communism. This had two contradictory effects. In the first place it released an economic migration of those who suffered because of the end of the certainties provided by Communist economics and were destroyed by the arrival of free market policies. These people moved towards Germany, the first rich country reached by westward-moving east Europeans. Upon arrival they had encouragement on entering the country. Either they could find work within the black economy, which grew significantly, or they could present themselves as asylum-seekers. In most cases the reasons why they fled from their land of origin consisted of a combination of political and economic factors. Their claims therefore represented reality, as it has proved difficult to separate the economic causes of migration from the political ones, whatever the legalistic policy makers might like us to believe.

The political crises caused by the death of Communism, more specifically the revival of nationalism, were the main political factors which led to emigration out of eastern Europe. Epitomised by the war in Yugoslavia, similar ethnic hatred surfaced elsewhere in Europe, including Rumania, leading to population flows on both a local and trans-European basis. In the Yugoslav case, refugees moved from one republic to another, during the implementation of the policy of ethnic cleansing, while others made their way to western Europe.

The last phase of post-war European migration has two other characteristics. First, many of the countries on the Mediterranean periphery which previously experienced emigration now find themselves acting as importers of migrants from eastern Europe and north Africa. At the same time, the fact that the EU allows internal free movement of labour has meant that its nationals can move in whichever direction they wish.

Whenever and wherever migration has taken place in post-war Europe, migrants, immigrants and refugees always find themselves as outsiders, minorities in their new surroundings. The state, media, their employment conditions and geographical concentration make this a certainty, even in cases where the newcomers consist of people who have had some previous connection with their new land of settlement.

The Post-War Refugee Crisis

The number of refugees created by the Second World War and its aftermath ran to tens of millions, leading to a situation in which Europe choked with refugees.[1] The exact number of refugees created by the Second World War in Europe is probably impossible to establish, although the United Nations and the Allied Powers tried to keep track. The most widely accepted estimate puts the figure at thirty million, covering the entire period 1939–47, with a movement of about twenty-five million after 1945.[2]

The countless individuals who found themselves on the move in the immediate aftermath of Nazi Europe can be divided into a series of groups. The easiest to distinguish consisted of the westward-moving ethnic Germans expelled from states temporarily occupied by the Nazis. Between eight and ten million workers forced to labour for the Nazi War economy made up the second category, consisting mostly of Soviet citizens, as well as Poles and nationals of western states, notably France. A small number of Jewish survivors of the camp system constituted a third category. A fourth group was made up of over a million Balts, Belorussians, Poles and Ukrainians moving westward with German troops away from Stalinism. Collectively, all of the members of the above categories made up a larger group known as displaced persons (DPs). To these, can be added two further categories. First, Soviet citizens who returned to their homes after the German army withdrew; and, secondly, the victims of post-war boundary changes in central and eastern Europe.

While the principal responsibility for the immediate post-war refugee crisis must lie with the Nazis, the nation states which defeated or survived the Third Reich also played a major role in the population movements which took place. Most directly, the Allied powers agreed the boundaries of the new European continent, which they realised (but accepted) meant a vast amount of population redistribution. In addition, the western powers also sanctioned the repatriation of hundreds of thousands of non-Russian Soviet citizens, even though they knew that many would be returning to their deaths, as this process formed part of the carving up of post-war Europe into Soviet and American spheres of influence. More positively, the UN put much work into rehousing displaced persons, through the United Nations Relief and

Rehabilitation Administration (UNRRA) and the International Refugee Organisation (IRO).[3] Finally, some western European states also realised the labour potential of millions of people, some of whom did not wish to return home, and accepted tens of thousands of them to help in their reconstruction processes, sometimes scouring the camps to find suitably acceptable individuals.

Germany represented the European focus from which much of the refugee activity took place, with foreign workers used by the Nazi economic war machine flooding out of the country, and ethnic Germans moving towards it. The latter migratory wave continued until the early 1960s, when most of those entering the Federal Republic consisted of citizens of East Germany. This willingness to take in Germans from the east partly rested upon the German need for manpower to rebuild the wasteland left by Allied bombing in 1945. Furthermore, some Jewish victims of the Nazis also moved out of Germany, having in many cases moved there after the end of the war from Poland, the location of the Final Solution, but also from further away.

Foreign workers had played a key role in the Nazi economic machine during the Second World War, fulfilling Hitler's ideology, outlined in *Mein Kampf*, which dictated that in the thousand year Reich Germans would form a master race ruling over the Slav peoples of the east, who would provide the industrial fodder for the German economy. More than five million foreign workers laboured for the Nazis for much of the conflict: by the end of 1944 one in every five labourers employed in the Reich was a foreigner. At this time, including prisoners of war, 7,615,970 non-Germans, primarily from the Soviet Union, Poland and to a lesser extent France, worked for the Nazis in both the armaments industry and agriculture in degrading conditions.[4]

By 1945, as a consequence of the destruction caused by Allied bombing, foreign workers and prisoners of war had begun to wander aimlessly around German cities without food or shelter. But their fate had been sealed by the Yalta Treaty of February 1945, signed by Stalin, Churchill and Roosevelt, which provided for the repatriation of civilians and prisoners of war on both sides after liberation. Most of the Soviet DPs went home voluntarily, totalling about 5,000,000 by March 1946, although some were forced to return. Those who resisted included Ukrainians and citizens of the Baltic states swallowed up by the Soviet Union at the start of the war. Some Poles also displayed a reluctance to move back home, partly due to political changes in the country, which had fallen under Soviet influence, and partly due to the circulation of anti-repatriation propaganda in the camps in which they found themselves. From 1946, new solutions had to be found for these reluctant Soviets and Poles, including emigration to western states, mostly outside Europe, who accepted willing manpower.

Liberated Jews made a significant proportion of the DPs who found themselves in Germany. Upon their release, about 50,000 Jews were situated upon
the territory of pre-war German borders, although, within a few weeks,
because of the high death rate, this figure fell to just 30,000.[5] By 1947 the
number of Jews in Germany had grown to about 200,000,[6] originating mostly
in Poland. Because of their experiences during the Second World War, and
the continuing existence of hostility towards them and the activities of
Zionists, very few had any desire to remain in Europe. Not surprisingly, the
vast majority made their way to the newly-created Jewish state of Israel.

In place of the Jewish and non-Jewish DPs came the ethnic Germans
expelled from the east European countries which had experienced Nazi
occupation. They entered a country devastated by years of Allied bombing
in which over 50 per cent of the housing in the big cities had been destroyed,
industrial production stood at zero and about 40 per cent of the population
was on the move.

While ultimate blame for this situation may lie with the Nazis, the vindictive policies of the Allies made it a reality. Apart from the saturation
bombing employed in the west,[7] the invading Soviet armies in the east had
driven out millions of Germans because of the brutal policies which they
had pursued. The expulsion received a legal basis at the Potsdam Conference
of July and August 1945 involving Truman, Stalin and Churchill (replaced
during the meeting by Clement Attlee because of the Labour Party general
election victory). When the leaders of Britain, the USA and the USSR met
to decide the fate of Europe, the issues they resolved included the Polish
border and the fate of the Germans in eastern Europe. Article 13 of the
Potsdam Protocol declared that:

> The three Governments having considered the question in all its aspects, recognize
> that the transfer to Germany of German populations, or elements thereof, re-
> maining in Poland, Czechoslovakia and Hungary will have to be undertaken.
> They agree that any transfers that take place should be effected in an orderly and
> humane manner.[8]

There also followed German exiles from Rumania and Yugoslavia and a
further movement of Germans from the eastern, Soviet-controlled sector of
Germany to the zones controlled by Britain, France and the USA which
formed the Federal Republic of Germany in 1949.

Enormous numbers of Germans from the east moved into the Federal
Republic during the first decade of its existence. The census of May 1946
gave a figure of nine million expellees in the four occupied zones.[9] By 1950,
out of a total population in the Federal Republic of 50,800,000, 7,900,000
consisted of refugees and victims of expulsion and resettlement. Another

1,600,000 were refugees from the German Democratic Republic (GDR), meaning that almost one in five citizens of West Germany was some sort of refugee.[10] From September 1949 until the construction of the Berlin Wall, in August 1961, at least 2,700,000 people moved out of the GDR into the Federal Republic,[11] so that by 1960 German refugees accounted for 23.8 per cent of the population of the Federal Republic.[12]

Political and economic push and pull factors explain the massive movement from east to west. The refugees felt attracted to the greater freedom apparent in a western liberal democracy in which there also existed greater potential to progress economically. The Federal Republic welcomed the refugees with open arms. Under Article 116 of the Federal Constitution anyone who could demonstrate German ethnic origin could enter the newly-created state. Economically the labour power of the newcomers, from the GDR and further afield, played a significant role in the beginnings of the German economic miracle. After the Berlin Wall went up, industry and state in the Federal Republic searched desperately for supplies of people in southern Europe.

The GDR and Austria also attracted ethnic Germans from further east. In 1966 approximately 3,500,000 expellees lived in the GDR.[13] The number who made their way to Austria totalled about half a million, which in 1955 made up about 10 per cent of the population. Austria had some difficulties absorbing the newcomers, although it began to recruit foreign workers at about the same time as the Federal Republic of Germany during the early 1960s.[14]

The dire social and economic circumstances facing Germany in the early post-war years meant that some emigration took place, mostly to beyond Europe.[15] In addition, over 180,000 Germans made their way to other European states,[16] usually through an agreement with the occupying powers in Germany during the late 1940s. Again the need for labour in the receiving countries played a central role in this process.

France took the largest amount of German labour. As well as importing about 31,000 Germans escaping from the desperate conditions of their country in the late 1940s,[17] the French state made arrangements to keep some of the 719,840 German prisoners of war held on its soil at the end of 1945.[18] Those who wished to remain, a total of 110,496, working mostly in agriculture and mining, received the status of German free workers.[19] Britain retained about 15,000 German prisoners of war who chose to stay because of economic opportunities. The need for labour also led to the importation of over 90,000 displaced persons from the European continent, more than 10 per cent of whom consisted of Germans.[20] Several other west European states, including Belgium, Norway and Sweden, imported German labour for the same reasons as Britain and France.

Apart from Germany, the Soviet Union represented the other major focus of post-war refugee movement, because of repatriation, deportation and boundary changes. In nearly all cases a certain amount of force played a role in the redistribution of population, often with consent from the western Allies. Because of the prospect of returning to Stalin's Russia, some individuals made a successful effort to find employment in the west, where the need for labour helped their plight.

As a result of the Second World War the Soviet Union had suffered massive destruction, something which lay at the bottom of its desire to see the repatriation of displaced persons. Clearly, the able-bodied who had borne arms suffered the heaviest casualties. Reconstruction required every fit Soviet citizen, including those abroad. [21] The vast majority of Soviet citizens went home voluntarily. Those who did not, like most refugees in all situations, wished to remain outside their country for a combination of political and economic reasons. Balts did not wish to return to a bestial and murderous reign of terror in their states, which had recently been taken over by Stalin. [22] Other Soviet citizens had even more to fear from returning, as they had fought against their state. Up to 10 per cent of German prisoners brought to Britain consisted of Russians. [23]

Some Soviet DPs, having spent several years in camps situated throughout central Europe, looking to the west for salvation, were eventually able to secure employment in western European states. Britain acted as one of the main destinations, taking in a total of 91,151 'European Volunteer Workers' for employment in a restricted range of industries with a shortage of labour, such as the National Health Service, farming, coal mining and textile production. Interviewers from the Ministry of Labour went to the continental camps to make sure that they only recruited people in good health. [24] Other European states which took in smaller numbers of Soviet and other central European DPs included France, Belgium and the Netherlands.

As a result of the Second World War Britain also accepted about 145,000 Poles, consisting of troops (and some of their dependants) who had formed the part of the Polish army which had fought with the British forces, as well as the small number of people who had made up the Polish government in exile in London, none of whom wished to return home. Like the DPs, they provided a source of labour for the recovering British economy. One of those finally making their way to Britain consisted of Creslaw, a victim of both Nazi and Soviet forces, who claimed that he eventually found himself amongst the latter in France:

> I told them I was a Russian. I told them where I came from in Russia, I spoke Russian. I was given plenty of food, cigarettes, plenty to drink. I stayed there

about three weeks, after that I saw two Americans and a Polish officer, they said 'any Polish people step forward'. Only I stepped forward and everybody looked at me because I had said I was Russian. So I went back and joined the Polish Army in France. I joined the army and from there, there were a lot of us, it took two big ships to transport us to England. [25]

Significant population movements also affected Italy at the end of the Second World War. The change in the location of the border with Yugoslavia in February 1947 gave the latter an Italian population of 900,000, of whom 300,000 left for Italy. [26] The movement began during the war and continued into the early 1950s, when international agreements finally settled the border between Italy and Yugoslavia. At the end of the war Italy also contained refugees, made homeless by fighting within its borders, whose numbers ran into tens of thousands. Furthermore, the country also took in people of Italian nationality, repatriated from Tunisia, Egypt, Libya and other parts of Africa. Finally, in 1960, Italy also housed a further 18,500 foreign refugees living in various camps. [27]

Population movements also took place in Yugoslavia, where several types of refugee developed, including returning forced labourers used by the Nazi economy, Chetniks who had fought on the side of the Nazi-backed Croatian army, and anti-Communist Serbs and Slovenes. Over 100,000 within the last three groups fled to Italy and Austria and, subsequently, further afield with the assistance of the IRO, refusing to return to Yugoslavia. [28]

During the late 1940s and 1950s, refugees began to disappear as a phenomenon specifically affecting Europe, so that, with the exception of Germany, only three significant population movements took place for political reasons. First, over 100,000 people left Greece as a result of the civil war between Communist forces and their opponents which ravaged the country between 1946 and 1948, resulting in the defeat of the former. The exiles made their way to destinations which included Bulgaria, Czechoslovakia, Hungary, Poland, Rumania and Soviet Union. The largest number, including 25,000 Macedonians, moved to Yugoslavia. [29]

In the early 1950s Turks faced expulsion from Bulgaria when the new Eastern Bloc regime pursued a policy of 're-educating' the Turkish minority, which involved direct control of Turkish schools and mosques. A programme of collectivisation in the late 1940s caused further resentment. [30] In 1949 a total of 24,332 Turks left Bulgaria and went to Turkey, [31] followed by a further 154,393 during 1950 and 1951. [32]

The other major refugee movement of the 1950s, from Hungary in 1956, received far more publicity, partly because it served as a stick with which to beat the USSR. The spark for the migration was the Soviet suppression of the revolt against Communist rule at the end of October 1956, which involved

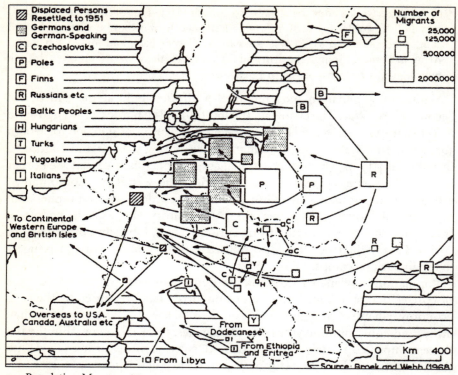

24. Population Movements, 1944–51

the use of the Red Army. The uprising lasted for less than two weeks and by
the beginning of November the Soviet forces had restored order. The 780
refugees who crossed the border into Austria in October increased to 113,820
by the end of the following month. In all, by the spring of 1957 about 180,000
people had fled to Austria, while a further 20,000 moved south into Yugoslavia. They received assistance from UNHCR and western governments, as
well as from the local population. Of those who made their way to Austria,
only 19,000 still remained within the country by the start of 1958. The rest
had divided equally to make their way to other European destinations and
locations further away. Within the European continent France, Germany and
Switzerland took in more than 10,000 each, while the United Kingdom
accepted 20,690. Similarly, by January 1958 only 675 Hungarians remained
in Yugoslavia. The refugees as a whole included large numbers of professionals
and miners. [33]

Most of those who migrated during this first phase of post-war population
movements have not formed long-lasting ethnic communities, due to the

often limited difference from the majority grouping in the countries to which they moved. In the case, for instance, of ethnic Germans moving to the Federal Republic of Germany, the German Democratic Republic or Austria, or of Bulgarian Turks moving to Turkey, the similarities clearly outweighed the differences. Nevertheless, the newcomers could not suddenly transplant themselves and forget about everything they had left behind. The process of adjustment could last for decades.[34] Those migrants who moved from one nation state to another as a foreign population often had an additional set of problems, revolving especially around language. In the long run many of these people, such as the Germans and Poles in Britain, have almost (but not quite) disappeared, still forming ethnic communities with their own organisations.[35]

The Age of Labour Migration

The second phase of post-war population movement on the European continent is the longest lasting and the one which may have affected the largest number of people, either moving into the continent or across it. For the first time since the arrival of the Gypsies and Turks, almost one thousand years previously, the period from the late 1940s witnessed large numbers of newcomers from beyond the European continent, moving from Asia, the West Indies and Africa. But there was also an equally large amount of migration across Europe. Tens of millions of people were involved. Because of the level of their ethnic and economic difference from the dominant groupings, as well as the attitudes of dominant nation states towards them, the immigrants of the 1950s and 1960s developed into ethnic minorities.

An overall theoretical perspective explaining these mass movements needs to focus on a series of levels of causation, pointing to economic, demographic and political factors, although the three remain inextricably linked. Certainly, most commentators have pointed to the requirement for labour of the European economies in the first few decades after the end of the Second World War, sparked off initially by the need to rebuild the devastated European continent, a process not completed until the 1960s in the case of the states, such as Germany, which had suffered the most seriously. The population movement was controlled to a large extent by business and the state using labour agreements with sending countries, although in Britain the recruiting process was not so formal. When it came to restricting the movement of population, however, the state became heavily involved throughout western Europe, using immigration controls together with nationality laws. In all cases of large-scale migration, immigrants moved from poorer states. These could be located anywhere because of the number of poor countries existing throughout the world compared with the fabulously wealthy west European states. In all cases the recruiters displayed some concern for the compatibility of the newcomers with the native population. As well as these macro-level determining factors, decisions to move also acted on an individual level. Human beings faced a traumatic experience when moving, for example, from a Cypriot village to an area of inner London. For this reason, patterns of chain migration developed in many cases, whereby people from particular families or locations migrated to a city in western Europe already inhabited by their friends or relatives in an attempt to lessen the impact of moving abroad. After the imposition of controls on movement, family reunification represented the main type of migration into western Europe.

Returning to the macro scale, there is no doubt that those states most directly affected by the Second World War had a need for labour in the first few decades after its end, because of two fundamental, and fairly obvious, problems caused by it, which working together created almost a double demand for labour. The first was the loss of population, which may have totalled forty million people. The second consisted of the damage caused by the Second World War. Destruction of cities, industrial installations and transport facilities due to bombing occurred throughout the European continent, meaning an enormous demand for labour to rebuild a devastated Europe.

The phase of economic growth in Europe went well beyond the reconstruction period which ended by the 1960s at the latest. The period between 1945 and the economic crisis of the early 1970s witnessed the most rapid and sustained expansion in recorded history, with world capitalist output doubling in the sixteen years from 1952 to 1968 alone.[36] Growth in Europe gathered momentum more quickly than in any other part of the world. Between 1950 and 1970 European gross domestic product increased by an average of about 5.5 per cent per annum, while industrial production increased at an annual average of 7.1 per cent.[37] The boom had a variety of causes, including increasing investment, productivity and mechanisation, as well as more direct state intervention in the economies of western Europe in an attempt to prevent a repetition of the depression which had devastated the European economy during the inter-war years.

Britain was the state which had one of the strongest desires for labour in the first two decades after the end of the Second World War, experiencing an average annual growth rate of 2.7 per cent between 1953 and 1961. Just as important, the large-scale unemployment of the inter-war years, which had stood at over 10 per cent for most of two decades, had fallen to an average of 1.7 per cent for the UK as a whole during the course of the

1950s.[38] Germany, meanwhile, had annual economic growth rates ranging from 2.9 per cent to as high as 9 per cent between 1960 and 1966, falling back in 1966–67 and rising to between 3 and 8 per cent between 1968 and 1973.[39]

The need for foreign labour also requires further explanation. Demographically, Europe could not produce enough people, despite increasing productivity, to sustain the scale of economic growth taking place. The natural growth rate of northern and western European populations lagged behind that of those on the south and east of the continent, as well as that of areas outside Europe. By 1970 virtually the whole of Europe had entered a phase of low population growth. Obviously, this meant a slow rate of increase for the indigenous labour force, which had declined to 0.6 per cent per annum in the continent as a whole by 1970,[40] although regional variations certainly existed.

Concerns about demographic growth rates played a particularly significant role in the French case, as they had done historically within that state. As well as continued declining birthrates, which had characterised the country since the nineteenth century, France also lost a further 600,000 people during the war. De Gaulle, along with mainstream French opinion, believed that France would need to import millions of people in order to maintain her status as a great power. Part of the process involved a clear assimilation of the newcomers aided by a new Nationality Code of 1945 which emphasised *jus solis* (nationality according to place of birth) in French citizenship.[41]

The combination of rapid economic growth and slow natural population increase only partially explains the process of labour importation. We also need to consider the fact that manpower shortages tended to exist in particular sectors of the economy, generally occupations at the lower end of the social scale, including engineering, building, public works, transport, textiles, hotels, catering and clothing. This situation was intensified by the increasing well-being, education and social expectations of the native populations of western European states, which meant that they wished to move towards employment higher up on the social scale. The contractual system used by most western European states, whereby a system of pure importation took place, added to the profitability of the workers moving into these states. Theoretically, the short-term contracts they received meant that they would return home once they had fulfilled their economic function. Entering western European states as single young men and women at the lower end of the social scale, they lived in poor accommodation and incurred no social costs, such as education and health care, for their children. This situation changed because of the social mobility of some of the immigrants and, more importantly, subsequent reunification with their families in the countries to which they had moved. In addition, deportation did not generally take place, although the decline of economic growth from the 1970s, and the onset of mass unemployment, meant labour importation stopped. By this time the development of a media and right wing led public opinion facilitated this process.

All these served as the pull factors in the post-war European migratory process. On the push side, in the countries of emigration a different series of factors existed, although we need to stress that the labour needs and recruiting policies of western European states far outweighed all other factors: north-western Europe was spoilt for choice in the number and range of countries and areas of the world to which it could turn.

The societies and economies of the sending countries faced problems of unemployment, poverty and underdevelopment. Two basic characteristics of these areas contrasted directly with the situation in northern and western Europe. First, they had high rates of natural population increase. Secondly, the sending countries had low rates of per capita income. The two factors worked together so that a situation directly opposite to the one in western Europe existed, with too many people and not enough work: in other words an oversupply of labour and consequent unemployment and poverty. The economies of the sending countries had undergone a lesser degree of industrialisation and urbanisation, meaning that the surplus population on the land could not be absorbed. Needless to say, technological advance and capital investment had also not developed to the same extent as within highly industrialised states.

Turkey, one of the main sources of labour supply for western Europe from the late 1950s, sending over two million workers abroad, possessed all of the above characteristics. This country has had one of the highest birth rates in the world since 1945, peaking at forty-four per thousand in 1960. In 1972 the country had a population of 36,500,000, which had increased to 55,000,000 by the end of the 1980s, when it was growing by one million a year. This rapid population growth resulted in the presence of a large number of children, dependants who could not play a full role in economy. In the early 1970s about 40 per cent of the population was under fifteen, about twice the figure in industrial societies. However, between 1960 and 1970 Turkey's labour force only grew by about 1.9 per cent per annum. Economic growth, although it took place on a scale comparable with the rest of Europe, did not expand quickly enough to keep pace with the population explosion, so that high rates of unemployment developed, which may have reached about five million in the early 1970s. A final element which constitutes a push factor, almost as important as the willingness of European states to import labour, was the readiness of Turkish governments to export their population as part of a planned economic strategy. The effects of emigration were both to ease unemployment and, just as importantly, to bring back foreign currency to the country in the form of remittances to families. [42]

Other states which have lost population have had similar characteristics to Turkey. Yugoslavia had a primarily agricultural population during the early post-war decades, with limited opportunities for urban employment. The pull of higher wages in the west, especially within the Federal Republic of Germany, proved the fundamental attraction. In 1969 Yugoslav migrants in Germany could earn 318 per cent more than they would have done if they had remained at home. To this we need to add further factors causing movement, such as chain migration, as migrants came from particular parts of Yugoslavia; and the role of the Yugoslav state, the only east European regime to allow and even encourage emigration on a large scale. [43]

Further examples of characteristic sending societies include Algeria, Morocco and Tunisia. During the 1960s population grew three times faster in the southern and eastern rim of the Mediterranean than it did in north-western Europe. France's readiness to accept workers during the 1960s and its proximity proved fundamental for migration. [44] Elsewhere, of those countries which sent people to Britain, the 1967 per capita gross national product was $125 in Pakistan, $250 in Jamaica but, in comparison, $1977 in the United Kingdom. [45]

Once again the readiness of Britain to accept people from these states (a decade before the above statistics), because of the British need for labour and the imperial connection, served as the central factor in migration from Pakistan, Jamaica and other parts of the Commonwealth and Empire. To reiterate the point once more, push factors existed throughout the globe, but migration between the 1950s and 1970s was initiated and continued by the desire of the western economies for labour.

The various north-western European states which imported labour followed similar patterns in the sense that they initially utilised the nearest available supplies of people with acceptable ethnic characteristics. Once such supplies had dried up, all states then tended to look further afield, in the case of Britain and France towards their colonies; and in the case of the rest of Europe towards countries on the European periphery which wished to offload surplus population.

Italy, especially its southern portion, represented one source which several European states initially utilised. A high birth rate and an inefficient agricultural system in the south acted as the push factors sending people abroad. In addition, Italian migration had begun on a large scale to many European locations before 1945, which meant that a tradition of movement to particular locations already existed.

Britain, for instance, used Italy in the immediate post-war years. Although an Italian community had always existed in the country, it increased significantly after the Second World War, with a large influx during the 1950s resulting in a peak of 103,500 Italian born persons in Britain in 1971. [46] Ireland represented a more traditional source of immigrants into Britain, as millions of people had crossed the Irish Sea to help in the industrialisation of England, Wales and Scotland during the nineteenth and the early twentieth centuries. Clearly geographical proximity proved of crucial importance in this process, as did the fact that no restrictions existed on the movement of the Irish to Britain. Most of the immigrants consisted of people with a rural background born in Eire on tiny farms providing few economic opportunities. This meant that 60 per cent of children born in Ireland in 1956 could expect to emigrate to either Britain or the USA. By 1971 a total of 957,830 persons born in Ireland lived in Great Britain, making up 2 per cent of the total population, [47] and representing the largest immigrant minority in the country. Although largely invisible, because of similarities with the British in terms of language and appearance, they faced much hostility during times of IRA activity and developed their own ethnic organisations.

The French state began systematically to import labour from neighbouring countries immediately after the expulsion of the German army, establishing the *Office National d'Immigration* (ONI) in November 1945. This recruited directly in the countries of emigration by spreading propaganda, issuing employment contracts and negotiating migration agreements with foreign governments. Employers would inform the ONI of their labour needs and would not have contact with immigrants until they turned up for work.

The ONI initially utilised the traditional source of French immigrants in the form of Italy. This fitted in with the wishes of assimilationists, as Italians could disappear into French culture much more easily than many other groups. The large-scale movement of Italians started in 1946. By 1965, 525,000 had migrated to France, making up one half of all immigrants between 1946 and 1965. [48] However, the proportion of Italians amongst immigrants began to decline from 1956 and by the end of the 1950s Italy began to dry up as a source of labour for the French economy. This was because of a growth in the Italian economy, especially in the north, which could absorb unemployed people from the rural southern economy, and because of the agreement signed between the Italian and West German states in 1955 allowing Italian migration to that particular destination.

By the mid 1960s the ONI had signed agreements with several other nearby states to provide labour for the French economy. The most important of these were Spain and Portugal. Spaniards initially became the main alternative source of labour to the Italians but, like the Italians before them, they began to move more towards West Germany. The Portuguese became the largest European minority in France, totalling 649,714 in 1990, [49] by which time many Spaniards and Italians had left. Many of the Spaniards and Portuguese had originally moved to France in order to escape political repression and consequently had to enter the country illegally.

West Germany is a country of immigration *par excellence*, which by 1989 contained eighteen million people, or more than one-third of its total population of sixty-one million, obtained through immigration since the end of the Second World War. [50] However, only about five million of these consisted of foreigners, the rest being ethnic Germans. The history of the movement of these two groups into the Federal Republic is inextricably linked, as the West German government did not begin to import non-German labour on a large scale until the availability of ethnic Germans began to dry up during the 1950s, coming to a halt in 1961 with the construction of the Berlin Wall.

In the early post-war years Belgium and Luxembourg also imported at significant levels from nearby states. In fact, these two countries have had some of the highest proportions of foreigners amongst their population. By the second half of the 1960s foreign workers made up to 30 per cent of the population of Luxembourg, mostly consisting of Italians, Spaniards and Portuguese working in manufacturing and construction. [51] Italy represented the main country of origin of immigrants into early post-war Belgium, the rest coming from France, Germany, Greece and Spain to work mostly in coal mining and the steel industry.

In common with the rest of Europe, Switzerland experienced a post-war economic boom and entered into negotiations with neighbouring states for the importation of labour after 1945. The Swiss state pursued a policy of issuing permits on a short-term basis, usually for a year, as well as others for shorter periods, although these were renewable, while longer-term residence permits could also be obtained. In addition, other workers lived abroad and simply crossed the Swiss border on a daily basis. In the immediate post-war period the most important sources of migration, after Italy which dominated the statistics, consisted of Germany, France and Austria. Switzerland subsequently signed agreements with Spain, Turkey, Portugal and Yugoslavia, although only the first of these provided numbers reaching 100,000 and surpassing the number of Germans working in the country.

In 1961 Italians made up 71.5 per cent of aliens with work permits in Switzerland. For most of the post-war period they have formed the majority of foreigners in the country, although by 1981 their proportion had fallen to below 50 per cent. Several explanations offer themselves for the scale of Italian migration to Switzerland. Geographical proximity is obvious but needs to be stressed, especially when combined with the relative economic prosperity within the two states and the willingness of their governments to transfer population. People moved from all parts of Italy towards Switzerland, although those with southern origins gradually became more important than those from the north. The migrants either moved to a job when they had not had one before or moved to one where they could obtain higher pay. [52]

In Scandinavia, Sweden imported large numbers of Finns, as well as some Norwegians and Danes, in the early post-war period. This was assisted by the common Nordic labour market, allowing free movement between Scandinavian states, which came into existence in July 1954. Sweden became a net importer of population from the 1940s, due to a variety of factors. These included its neutrality during the Second World War and its emergence from the conflict relatively unscathed, which meant that significant numbers of refugees moved towards the country both during and after the conflict from neighbouring Baltic and Scandinavian states. In addition, Sweden also had a dramatically declining birth rate, which became more significant for immigration when combined with the high rate of growth in the Swedish economy during the 1940s, continuing into the 1970s.

Migration from Finland to Sweden occurred throughout the first three decades after the end of the Second World War, driven primarily by economic factors and resembling Irish migration to Britain, not only in terms of the freedom of movement but also because Finland has historically acted as a supply of surplus labour to Sweden, serving the same role that Ireland has for Britain. To continue the comparison further, the movement has consisted of a migration from rural to urban areas with many of the people originating from the Swedish-speaking population of Finland. Although a significant amount of return migration has taken place, Finns accounted for 42.9 per cent of foreigners in Sweden in 1980. Another 14 per cent consisted of immigrants from other Scandinavian countries, but this immigration has taken place on a much smaller scale. [53]

After initially recruiting primarily from neighbouring countries, most European states found that their economies continued to experience significant economic growth rates while the nearby areas from which they harvested labour could not provide the necessary further crop. Consequently, from as early as the 1950s, state and industry began to look further afield for more fodder to fuel western economic expansion.

Britain and France turned to their colonial possessions, past and present. The former differs from many European states in the sense that it recruited unofficially, with a lack of state or business involvement or of direct recruitment. However, the British Nationality Act of 1948 confirmed the willingness of the Labour government to allow citizens of the Empire and Commonwealth to move to Britain because, despite the creation of a distinction between citizens of the United Kingdom and its colonies and those who were citizens of the Commonwealth, both had the right to reside and work within Britain. Nevertheless, throughout the 1950s, under pressure from the press, right-wing MPs and some Labour supporters, Labour and Conservative governments preferred to see the entry of Europeans, who would not create racial problems on British soil. [54]

Although most colonial immigrants who made their way to Britain came from the Caribbean and specific areas of India, Pakistan and Africa, one colony within Europe which provided a significant number of immigrants was Cyprus, so that between 1951 and 1971 the number of Cypriots, both Greek and Turkish, in Britain increased from 10,343 to 72,665. [55] The reasons for this growth are the same as those which have caused people to move from other parts of the globe in the form of a population surplus reaching maturity in the 1950s; a lack of economic opportunities in an overwhelmingly agrarian economy; and the emergence even at the local village level of the concept of England as a land of economic opportunity. The latter process essentially developed through personal correspondence with relatives, leading to chain migration, so that a significant percentage of the inhabitants of some villages, such a Lympia, progressed to London. Others, such as Mitseron, lost virtually none of their people. Chain migration played a crucial role in the case of villages such as the former: remaining in a village when siblings had already left represented a nightmare, tantamount to defeat, a feeling of being left behind. [56]

The arrival of the *Empire Windrush* in Tilbury docks, carrying 492 passengers from Kingston, Jamaica, is regarded as the symbolic beginning of the process of Caribbean immigration to Britain, although, in fact, some West Indians already lived within the country, acting, in some cases, as the first link in a chain. By 1971 a total of 264,905 residents of Britain originated from the Caribbean. [57] People moved from Guyana, on the South American mainland; from a variety of larger islands, including Jamaica, Trinidad, Barbados; and from small islands such as Nevis, which developed a chain to Leicester. Some firms directly recruited labour, including British Rail, as one migrant recalled:

> In 1960 I was in charge of the Barbados police canteen. British Rail were recruiting in the West Indies at the time, and my superintendent said it would be a good experience to spend two years overseas before returning to train as an officer. So I went through the recruitment stages at the Barbados Labour Office, you had to take a test, write an essay on why you wanted to go to England and what you intended to do. Then there was a medical, and they checked that you didn't have a criminal record. At the end I was given a contract as a guard on the trains. They gave you a loan. You had to repay your fare over a period of years. [58]

For the overwhelming majority, migration remained informal. It was fuelled by the image of Britain as the mother country of West Indians, passed on though the British education system, and by the knowledge of greater economic opportunities in Britain. The movement of West Indians to Britain, in common with numerous other migratory flows, developed into what can be described as a social movement. [59]

By 1971 a total of 127,565 people born in Pakistan lived in Britain. [60] Some of these people already resided in the country at the end of the Second World War, but migration on a large scale took off in the late 1950s, particularly from the hill districts in the west and east of the country, in a new nation state with poor land, limited industrialisation and a consequent surplus of labour. The construction of the Mangla Dam in the Mirpur district in the early 1960s resulted in the displacement of 100,000 people, some of whom eventually made their way to Britain using the government compensation they had received. A pattern of chain migration also developed whereby those already present in the new country of settlement sent money back to help their relatives pay for their journey. Pakistani migration represents an instance of an initial male population of working age preceding wives and children who followed during the course of the 1960s and into the 1970s. [61]

Migration from India to Britain was a complicated process because of the ethnic differences within the country, meaning that we cannot possibly speak of Indians and that we have to recognise the varying geographical and religious divisions within the country. The main source of the migration lay in the Punjab and Gujarat in the north and west of India respectively. The partition of the former province in 1947, between the newly created states of India and Pakistan, caused massive population movements, a small proportion of whom made their way to Britain. Some Sikhs who migrated had planned economic motives for their movement. Although they had land in the Punjab, they hoped to accumulate capital and return home with it to improve their economic position.

Outside major sources of Imperial and Commonwealth immigration, other already established minorities, such as West Africans and Chinese, the latter from Hong Kong, Singapore and Malaysia as well as China, also made their way to Britain. Much of the increase of Africans consisted of people entering as students, continuing a tradition established over the previous century. [62] The influx of the Chinese has much to do with the growth of restaurants, although significant numbers of Chinese were in Britain as students or nurses. In the 1990 census 156,938 people described themselves as ethnically Chinese. [63]

By the end of the 1950s, immigration into France also began to come more and more from areas which had colonial connections with the country. Africa represented the most important of these, having sent immigrants to France from the nineteenth century. The number of Africans began to increase in the first decade after the war when people born in colonies, both north and south of the Sahara, could enter France. As these territories gained independence they signed agreements with the ONI in order to provide labour. For instance, Morocco and Tunisia, which became independent in 1956, signed treaties in 1963, as did Mali and Mauritania in the same year. Algeria, with a historical tradition of sending migrants to France, [64] has provided the largest number of African immigrants into France since the end of the Second World War, a figure reaching a total of 614,207 in 1990, [65] although this figure excludes 850,000 white French Algerians who returned to France after Algeria gained independence in 1962. [66] The Evian Agreement signed upon Algerian independence allowed freedom of population movement between the two states. A third group from Algeria consisted of Harkis – Muslims who had fought on the side of the French.

Immigrants have also made their way to France from the Caribbean, with the state playing a direct role in this process. Very few people had actually moved away from the French Caribbean in the first decade and a half after the end of the war. However, by the early 1960s, Guadeloupe, Martinique and French Guyana, which are still part of Metropolitan France, began to experience a population expansion at the same time as French economic growth was continuing apace. State recruitment, carried out from 1962, had several advantages. These included the fact that the newcomers were potentially more assimilable, having been educated in the French system. As French citizens, they could also work in the 'civil service', which does not employ foreigners; although this term applied to areas as diverse as the health service and the post office. Encouraging migration from the Caribbean also meant that the French government could point to a solution to the economic and demographic problems of its territories in the Caribbean. By 1982 a total of 282,300 people living in France had been born in its Caribbean possessions, about half of them having moved due to migration directly sponsored by the state. [67]

In Germany, the drying up of ethnic Germans as fodder for the economy by the early 1960s coincided with other developments which increased the need for employees, notably continued economic expansion, a decrease in the retirement age and a reduction in the working week. The economic need for immigrants is indicated by continued reconstruction, a task that was still not completed by the 1960s. Before that decade, due to the availability of ethnic Germans, the Federal Republic recruited only a small number of foreigners. [68] In 1955 only 80,000 foreigners lived in West Germany. [69] By this time, however, government, employers' organisations and trade unions had agreed upon the need to allow foreign workers to enter Germany because of labour shortages.

The German method of foreign recruitment closely resembled that of France, in the sense that it involved the signing of contracts with states which had workers to spare. Unlike either France or Britain, Germany did not have any colonies and therefore, after the drying up of ethnic Germans, turned to the European periphery. Germany signed her first contract with Italy in 1955, followed by others with Spain and Greece in 1960, Turkey in 1961, Morocco in 1963, Portugal in 1964, Tunisia in 1965 and Yugoslavia in 1968.

The Federal Labour Office (Bundesanstalt für Arbeit or BfA) established almost 400 recruitment offices in these countries. German firms who required labour would apply to the BfA and pay a fee. The offices in the various states in southern Europe and north Africa would interview potential migrants, screen them for political and criminal records, carry out medical examinations, issue contracts and transport them to the destination in which they had agreed to work. They obtained a work permit which initially lasted for one year but could then be renewed.

As a result, the 95,000 aliens present in Germany in 1956 increased to 1,300,000 by 1966. After a decline following recession in 1966–67, when many workers returned home, the figure reached 2,595,000 in 1973, when their share of the labour force stood at 11.9 per cent.[70] The most substantial total came from Turkey: from 1968 until 1973 an average of 97,053 Turkish workers moved into Germany each year, their numbers increasing from 123,386 in January 1968 to 599,000 in December 1973. This represents only a fraction of those who wanted to move. By September 1971 over 1,200,000 Turks had registered with local Turkish labour bureaus for employment in the Federal Republic. The second largest number of foreign workers in the Federal Republic in 1973 was provided by Yugoslavia, at 513,000, followed by Italy, with 423,000. Spain, Portugal and Greece sent smaller numbers. During the following two decades Turkey pulled far ahead of all the other states in numbers of foreigners and their dependants in the Federal Republic.[71]

Until 1961 more people left the Netherlands than moved into the country. It began to face a labour shortage by the mid 1950s, which became more serious during the early 1960s, as the country experienced economic growth rates comparable to the rest of Europe. The government therefore went the same way as Germany and began to import workers from the European periphery. It signed recruitment agreements with Italy in 1960, Spain in 1961, Portugal in 1963, Turkey in 1964, Greece in 1966, Morocco in 1969 and Yugoslavia and Tunisia in 1970. In 1973 the Netherlands contained 282,361 aliens, making up just 2.11 per cent of the population, compared with

6.65 per cent in Germany and 7.7 in France.[72] After family reunification, by far the largest immigrant minorities in Holland consisted of Turks and Moroccans.[73]

Like Britain and France, the Netherlands also exploited its colonies, especially its West Indian possessions of Surinam and the Dutch Antilles, from where a certain amount of migration had occurred since the middle of the nineteenth century. In 1954 the inhabitants of these areas gained full citizenship rights, guaranteeing their freedom to move to the mainland. Between the 1950s and the early 1970s Dutch companies carried out labour recruitment in Surinam and the Antilles, although the numbers of people obtained in this way remained small, totalling no more than a few hundred in the former and about 3000 in the latter. Nevertheless, a few thousand people moved from Surinam to the Netherlands every year throughout the 1960s, mostly of working-class origin, as part of a chain migration. The push factors were those characteristic of British and French islands in the Caribbean in the form of a high birth rate, a relatively low standard of living and poor educational and health provision, contrasting with the economic attractions of Holland.

Migration from Surinam to the Netherlands really took off during the early 1970s. Although this happened against the background of a deterioration of the Surinamese economy, the main reason for the movement lay in an impending change in the political relationship between Surinam and Holland, which happened in November 1975 when the former obtained independence. This meant that citizens from Surinam lost their right to settle in the Netherlands, unless they already lived in the country. Consequently, just before this change took place, the numbers of Surinamese migrating shot up from 15,674 in 1974 to 36,537 in 1975. Overall, the Surinamese population in the Netherlands increased from about 30,000 in 1970 to about 140,000 by 1980.[74]

Like the Netherlands, Austria sent significant numbers of people abroad during the 1940s and 1950s, mostly to West Germany and Switzerland, because it possessed a relatively slow growing economy with a limited industrial base and a high unemployment rate. The situation began to change in the late 1950s and early 1960s due, on the one hand, to an increasing economic growth rate and, on the other, to a lengthening of the education period and improved pension provision for the indigenous population.

The Austrian government, on advice from industrialists and trade unionists, followed the pattern of other western European states by signing bilateral migration agreements and establishing recruitment offices in states on the European periphery: Spain, Turkey, Yugoslavia and Tunisia. Nevertheless, no more than a limited amount of labour importation took place during the

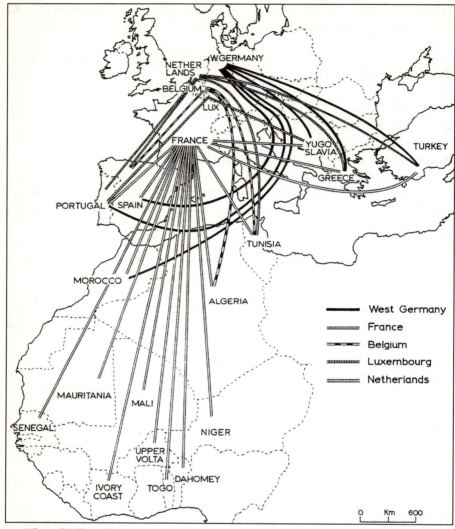

25. Bilateral Labour Recruitment Agreements Existing in 1974

1960s. Only the economic boom of the early 1970s resulted in large-scale immigration, with official recruitment combining with uncontrolled entry so that the number of foreign workers had increased to 226,800 by 1973, making up 8.7 per cent of total employment. [75]

Sweden began to import labour beyond its immediate periphery from as early as 1947, but had limited success: only about 12,000 non-Nordic immigrants entered the country during the 1950s, making up 5 per cent of the total of all newcomers. The situation changed during the 1960s and early 1970s, when Yugoslavia, Turkey and Greece became significant contributors to labour immigration into Sweden. Yugoslavia contributed the largest number, totalling around 40,000 by the early 1980s. Most moved during the 1960s, with their families, to work in the construction industry. Turkey sent about 20,000 people to Sweden from the 1960s, about a quarter of them from around the city of Kulu in central Anatolia, in a classic case of chain migration. This was sparked off by recruitment by Swedish firms during the 1960s and continued by the development of positive images of Sweden in the region, as information about it filtered back from people already in the country. Movement to Sweden became a dream or an epidemic. One non-migrant stated that: 'If it were possible not a soul would remain here.'[76]

Like Sweden, Norway witnessed a certain amount of immigration during and immediately after the end of the Second World War, but had a limited necessity to import workers during the following two decades, when most of the foreigners present in the country consisted either of citizens of the other Nordic countries or of other western states. An increase in newcomers from other parts of the world occurred during the late 1960s and early 1970s, mostly as a result of the growth of the North Sea oil industry. Pakistanis represented the largest group, moving towards Norway because of the impossibility of entering Britain, which would have been their first choice because it already had Pakistani communities.[77] Denmark and Finland resemble Norway, with little international migration taking place into them.

By the middle of the 1970s the major importers of labour throughout Europe had begun to cut down the number of people they imported. Britain led the way in this process. Hostility to the influx of immigrants from British Imperial possessions began with the landing of the *Empire Windrush* and affected all sections of British society from Cabinet level to workers involved in industries employing newcomers. The government did not publicly express its opposition to immigration until the late 1950s. Then it was persuaded by a slight economic downturn and the Nottingham and Notting Hill riots against West Indians in 1958, a classic example of a state giving in to right-wing opinion, which was to characterise the European, and especially British, response to immigration control. There duly followed the first piece of post-war British legislation restricting immigration from former imperial territories in the Commonwealth Immigrants Act of 1962. This made entry into Britain subject to the issue of a voucher to people in occupations in which Britain needed foreign workers. Although 30,130 vouchers were issued in 1963, this fell to just 2290 in 1972, when the scheme ended.

In the meantime, the British state had passed several other pieces of legislation in an attempt to stop the entry of non-whites into the country.

The cause of the increasing control lay in concern about the entry of East African Asians, who had moved to Africa from India when Britain controlled both areas during the nineteenth century. During the 1960s and early 1970s several of the newly-created African states pursued policies of Africanisation, aimed at limiting the economic and political power of Asians and, ultimately, resulting in their expulsion. As many held British passports, they made their way to Britain, as the 1962 Act did not prevent British passport-holders from entering the country. The Labour government obligingly gave in to the press. Enoch Powell, the anti-immigration Conservative MP, made a series of inflammatory speeches, most famously in Walsall in April 1968, when he declared:

> As I look ahead, I am filled with foreboding. Like the Roman, I seem to see 'the River Tiber foaming with much blood'. The tragic and intractable phenomenon which we watch with horror on the other side of the Atlantic, but which there is interwoven with the history of the States itself, is coming upon us here by our own volition and our own neglect. [78]

There followed the Commonwealth Immigrants Act of 1968 which imposed controls upon holders of British passports, unless they, or at least one parent or grandparent, had been born, adopted or naturalised in the UK. The measure clearly discriminated in favour of white people living in the Commonwealth. There then followed the Immigration Act of 1971, imposing yet further controls upon entry. Nevertheless, despite these measures, as many as 155,000 East African Asians entered Britain between 1965 and 1981. [79] By the early 1970s Britain had moved away from its *laissez-faire* immigration policy of the 1940s to a Dark Age of obsessive control which would infect much of Europe.

The French state began to limit the numbers of immigrants from Algeria during the 1960s. The two countries signed agreements over this issue in 1964, 1968 and 1971. By the early 1970s overt hostility had developed against the immigrants, manifesting itself most obviously in the form of racist murders and growing support amongst extreme right-wing groupings. This coincided with the oil crisis of 1974, the economic recession consequent upon it and a decline in the demand for unskilled labour. All of these factors combined in the decision to ban the arrival of new foreign workers in 1974, as France also entered an age of restrictions upon immigration which even involved an ultimately unsuccessful attempt to prevent family reunification.

The mid 1970s also represented a major turning point in the migration of foreign workers into Germany. As a result of the recession caused by the oil crisis of 1973, the government immediately banned the recruitment of foreign workers. The recession and a consequent rise in unemployment, which has continued for decades, coincided in the 1970s and 1980s with the entry into the labour market of large numbers of people born during the baby boom of 1955–66. Politicians were also displeased at the fact that so-called 'guest workers' tended not only to remain for long periods, but also brought over their families to Germany, consequently adding to social costs within the economy. [80] Fears about the threat of foreigners to German employment and culture had also begun to circulate by this time, so that one foreign worker in 1974 could declare:

> I quickly noticed that, as a foreigner in Germany, I am a second or third class citizen and not a normal person: compared with Germans, foreign workers are treated badly. [81]

Despite the stop on recruitment in 1973, the number of foreigners in Germany increased dramatically during the following two decades due mostly to the migration of dependants.

In Switzerland, concern about swamping by foreign cultures (*Überfremdung*) and overdependence upon foreign workers began to develop during the 1960s. Combined with an economic downturn, these perceptions led to reductions in the number of migrants in the country. A decrease first occurred in 1964 but, as in the case of the French and German cutbacks of 1966–67, the number of foreign workers hit new high levels by the early 1970s. However, because of the nature of work permits, the Swiss government managed to reduce the numbers quite easily so that over 300,000 immigrant and seasonal workers left the country between 1974 and 1977. [82]

Belgium halted the immigration of workers in August 1974, although family reunification continued. The foreign population rose from 716,000 in 1970 (7.2 per cent of the total) to 900,000 by the middle of the following decade (9 per cent), with Italians making up the largest grouping. [83] As a result of the 1973–74 recession Austria deported large numbers of foreign workers, whose total fell by 50,000 by 1976 and subsequently decreased even further. By 1983 only 145,300, 5.3 per cent of the working population, remained. The increasing participation of Austrian women and the arrival of the post-war baby boom generation on the labour market did not help the position of foreign workers. [84]

In the Eastern Bloc importation of labour did not take place in the same way as it did in western Europe, but a limited amount did occur, as the example of the German Democratic Republic illustrates. In fact, several groups of foreigners lived in this state during its existence from 1949 until 1990, including students, who came mostly but not exclusively from other Soviet Bloc countries, a situation which also existed in other states in eastern Europe, all of which had, for instance, a small number of Greek Cypriot students, who received financial assistance in contrast to the exorbitant fees being charged by western universities. The German Democratic Republic further served as home to refugees during its existence, especially those from eastern Europe, including during the late 1970s a small number of Soviet Jews and Rumanian Gypsies. The largest numbers of foreigners always consisted of Soviet troops and their families, who totalled 580,000 in 1990.

The second largest group in the GDR consisted of foreign workers, who began to move into the country in the late 1950s. The need for labour took place against the background of a haemorrhaging of population from the GDR and one of the healthiest economies in eastern Europe. From the 1950s until the 1980s East Germany primarily made use of workers from other Soviet Block countries, including Poland, Czechoslovakia, Hungary, Vietnam and Cuba, although importation also took place from Turkey during the 1970s. The recruitment process followed that of capitalist states in the sense that the GDR signed treaties with the countries from which they received labour and also offered employees short-term contracts. In contrast to West Germany, under the agreements the migrants received something in return in the form of assistance with their education. By 1990 about 250,000 foreign workers lived in the German Democratic Republic. [85]

Fortress Europe?

The final phase in the history of post-war migration, which runs from about the middle of the 1970s, is characterised by a number of contradictory developments within the continent as a whole. The main one is that, while all of the west European democracies have reduced the numbers of people they wish to admit, a large movement of refugees has developed, especially immediately after the death of Communist states in eastern Europe. To complicate the picture further, countries in southern Europe which sent out millions of people to help the economies of states further north, began to attract immigrants themselves; although ultimately, like their northern neighbours, they did not wish to see uncontrolled immigration into their territories. Finally, within the boundaries of the European Union, movement has become much easier as border controls have begun to disappear. At the same time, the southern and eastern boundaries of the EU have become more tightly controlled in an attempt to keep out economic and racial undesirables from eastern Europe and Africa, leading to the development of the concept of Fortress Europe, which countless people wish to enter but which is guarded like a medieval castle under siege from the infidel. Despite this, millions of people have moved into western Europe since the middle of the 1970s due both to family reunification and to the fact that all states have admitted a certain number of refugees, under the 1951 United Nations Geneva Convention on the Status of Refugees, although all have tried, especially in recent years, and in varying degrees, to discourage people.

Italy best illustrates the changing character of population movements in southern Europe, developing from a state which lost almost three million people due to emigration in the early post-war decades to one which had begun to attract immigrants by the middle of the 1970s. The total, including those present illegally and working in the black economy, may have reached 1,500,000 by the early 1990s.[86] The take-off phase in Italian immigration during the 1970s had a number of causes. These included the closing of borders by the traditional north European labour recruiting countries, which redirected much potential immigration to the south. The first people who entered the country fitted into three distinct groups consisting of maids from the Cape Verde Islands, Ethiopia, El Salvador and the Philippines, who obtained work permits and could not change their employment; 'border immigrants', including Tunisians and Yugoslavs, working in the construction industry; and political refugees from Latin America, Vietnam and Ethiopia.[87]

Hundreds of thousands, if not millions, of illegal immigrants have moved into Italy since the 1970s, working in an underground economy which may employ as many as five million people. People have migrated into the country via Sicily in the case of North Africans, Trieste in that of Yugoslavs and Apulia in that of Greeks. These illegal immigrants have tended to take on jobs rejected by Italians because they are insecure, unhealthy, poorly paid and do not have prospects of any sort.

With little experience of dealing with immigrants, and with virtually no specific immigration legislation, the Italian state took time to react but, by the 1990s, had developed a clear policy, influenced by rising xenophobia, as well as concern for the welfare of newcomers expressed by the Roman Catholic Church and left-wing parties. In 1986 Law 943, in common with practice in the rest of Europe, tied future admissions of foreign workers to labour market conditions, as well as allowing an amnesty to those already illegally within the country and punishing employers who hired or imported illegal workers. Those who declared themselves would have the same rights as legalised Italian workers. Nevertheless, because of the prospect of losing their employment altogether, to be replaced by other illegal immigrants, only a relatively small number actually made themselves known. Law 39 of 1989 was passed following continued right-wing hostility towards immigration, as well as pressure from other members of the EU to control the number of people entering Europe through southern Italy. It essentially extended the provisions of the 1986 law by allowing a further amnesty, granting more solid rights, recognised under international agreements, to immigrants; and by further regularising the entry of immigrants into the country.

In the early 1990s Italy found itself surrounded by three potential sources of migration: Yugoslavia's civil war; economic collapse in Albania; and the population explosion and unemployment in Africa.[88] The influx from Albania took place on a large scale and became a major issue in the international media. In 1991 the collapse of Albanian Communism and its political and economic consequences led to the arrival of 45,000 Albanians, with 20,000 entering in March, followed by a further 20,544 in the second week of August.

While the Italian state absorbed some of the newcomers into the country, and placed others in massive refugee camps, it did not process their cases properly under the 1951 Geneva Convention. It then repatriated large numbers of them and provided £27,400,000 to the Albanian state to prevent further migration to Italy. Perhaps no other incident signals the arrival of a north European style immigration policy in Italy than the Albanian débâcle, in which, significantly, the actions of the Italian state received support from the German and British governments. Six years later, in March 1997, following the virtual collapse of the Albanian state, Italy declared a state of emergency throughout the country until June 30 to cope with the influx of more than 10,000 refugees from Albania. The Italian government believed that criminal elements predominated amongst the exiles and made efforts to carry out deportations.[89] In the longer term, in view of the geographic and demographic situation of Italy (as the country has a typically low European birth rate together with continuing economic growth, as well as the size of the black economy), it seems likely that immigration, whether legal or illegal, will continue into the country on a significant scale.

Spain has several similarities to Italy. In the first place both countries experienced large-scale population loss during the first post-war decades and both experienced significant return migration during the 1970s. By this time some immigration had begun to take place into Spain, so that about 200,000 foreign residents lived in the country by 1980. Those who had entered the country by that time included about 1000 refugees from Laos and Vietnam, whom the Spanish government had agreed to accept at a conference in Geneva in 1979. During the 1980s, again like Italy, it experienced significant immigration, both regular and irregular, although on a smaller scale, arriving from South America, Asia and North Africa, particularly Morocco. By 1988 the official number of foreigners living in Spain totalled 484,334, the majority from other member states of the EU. This figure excluded an estimated 294,000 irregular immigrants working in the black economy. However, the Spanish government, as in the Italian case, declared amnesties in 1985–86 and 1991. The legislation of the latter year also imposed controls upon immigration, although this excluded citizens of Latin America of Hispanic origin who could live and work in Spain without a visa. [90]

Portugal also experienced large-scale emigration in the first post-war decades, continuing a long-standing historical tradition, but had reached a stage by the early 1990s where immigration and emigration almost neutralised each other. During the 1970s Portugal witnessed an influx of 700,000 people who returned as a result of the collapse of its African empire. [91] More recently, much of the immigration which has taken place has consisted of black Africans from the former Portuguese colonies of Angola, the Cape Verde Islands, Guinea-Bissau, Mozambique and São Tomé, with the newcomers working in the classic immigrant occupations of manufacturing and the service industry. By 1991 approximately 100,000 officially registered foreigners lived in Portugal. [92]

Since 1973 more people have entered Greece than have left it. Once again, the country also has large numbers of immigrants working in the black economy: in 1988 Greece had 184,000 officially registered foreigners within its boundaries, and perhaps 30,000 irregular ones. A range of groups have entered the country since the early 1970s due to a combination of demographic, economic, geographic and political factors. Demographically and economically, a combination of a scarcity of unskilled labour, caused by mass emigration and a fall in the birth rate, particularly pronounced during the 1980s, led to a demand for labour. The size of the black economy, which may account for about 30 per cent of GNP, makes it easy to employ foreigners without their being registered, especially in tourism and harvesting, which both tend to use people on a seasonal basis. About half of those working in the black economy consist of people from EU countries, North America and Australia. In the late 1980s, 50 per cent of registered immigrants came from western and former socialist European states, while the other 50 per cent arrived from the Third World, including Egypt, the Philippines, India, Pakistan and Iraq. The large size of the Greek merchant navy offers opportunities for foreign seamen to enter the country and move into other sectors of the economy, while the geographic position of Greece means that it has attracted people fleeing from both eastern Europe and the Middle East. The Polish community in Athens initially developed from refugees who fled the repression in their country during the 1980s, but, after the collapse of the old order, the group attracted economic migrants, especially male construction workers and female cleaners. The collapse of Communism also meant that Greek-speakers in the Soviet Union and Albania moved to Greece in the early 1990s. Between 1987 and the summer of 1991 approximately 30,000 Greeks from the Soviet Union entered Greece, while in 1990 and the first half of 1991 a total of 13,338 people moved from Albania. [93]

At the same time as immigration into southern Europe has increased, most north and west European states have made efforts to decrease the number of foreigners they allow into the country. This has proved more effective in some cases than others. Two of the strictest excluders of newcomers, especially in relation to their own population, are Britain and France. An explanation for the attitude of the former needs to take into account a variety of factors. In common with the rest of Europe, Britain experienced dramatic economic changes during the 1970s and early 1980s, the most visible impact of which consisted of a rise in unemployment to a peak of over three million. As industrial decline began to gain momentum and to display its consequences during the 1970s, support for the racist National Front also increased. Into this situation stepped Margaret Thatcher, elected leader of the Conservative Party in February 1975. In the second half of the 1970s she returned immigration and race to the centre of mainstream politics, claiming that Britain was in danger of being swamped by immigrants.

After its election victory of 1979 the Conservative Party introduced a series of measures which built upon the legislation of the 1960s and early 1970s, rather than indicating a radical departure. The British Nationality Act of 1981 was the most important measure, dividing British citizens into three categories in an attempt to prevent further non-white people living in still existing British possessions overseas from moving to Britain. [94] Since then the British state has taken measures to put off refugees. All in all, British policy has proved highly effective in keeping out immigrants and refugees from the 1970s. Between 1980 and 1988, 37,690 people applied for asylum in Britain, of whom 9057 received asylum or refugee status and 11,742 obtained exceptional leave to remain. [95] Immigration from former British colonies has also been cut right down since the 1960s, while the number of EU nationals has significantly increased. The non-Europeans who do manage to enter Britain often find themselves detained in prisons, indicating the criminalisation of immigration. One inmate of Wandsworth prison wrote to Amnesty International stating:

> Today is my birthday and I'm in such a hopeless situation I wish I was never born, and I did nothing to deserve it, I only wanted peace and to be free. This prison, without hope and faith to survive, is hell. Please help me. [96]

France has followed a similar path to Britain since the early 1970s, with mainstream politicians again being influenced by the wishes of extremists in the form of the Front National. As in the case of Britain, unemployment rose to new post-war heights during the 1980s while economic growth rates fell. Restrictions began during the 1970s. These included a short-lived attempt at preventing family migration and the implementation of a scheme in 1977 aimed at the repatriation of Africans, who received 10,000 francs if they left. In reality, Spaniards and Portuguese took more advantage of the offer, which only lasted until 1981. In 1983 the government of Pierre Mauroy reintroduced repatriation by offering financial incentives, imposed stricter border controls for people coming from North Africa, brought back limits on admitting dependants and started seeking out illegal immigrants again. Much of the other legislation of the 1980s focused upon French citizenship.

Despite the attempts by French governments since the early 1970s to reduce the number of foreigners passing through its borders, an increase in numbers has occurred because of, amongst other factors, family reunification and (especially during the late 1980s and early 1990s) an increase in asylum seekers. From a foreign population of 3,400,000 in 1975, the total had reached 3,700,000 in 1982 and 4,700,000 by 1988, representing 7 per cent of the population. The number of asylum applications rose from 7000 in 1981 to 80,000 in 1989, although the rejection rate also increased to 85 per cent by 1990.[97]

Some other states have shown a more liberal attitude towards immigrants than Britain and France, notably those in Scandinavia, although no country in northern or western Europe operates an open-door policy any longer. Nevertheless, in the case of Sweden, for instance, the halting of labour immigration during the 1970s was compensated by an increase in refugees.[98] During the 1980s Sweden continued to receive significant numbers of applications for asylum, which usually far exceeded the annual quota set by the Swedish parliament and, in proportion to the Swedish population, was far higher than the proportion received by Britain and France. In 1990 applications for asylum in Sweden totalled 29,400, of whom, keeping in line with the European situation as a whole, 34 per cent obtained asylum, 15 per cent were refused entry into Sweden and 50 per cent were denied residence permits. By 1990 Sweden had a foreign-born population of 790,000 people.[99] Although Finns still formed the largest single grouping, the proportion of people from outside Europe stood at 34 per cent in 1991, with Iranians representing the most substantial minority.[100]

Norway has also accepted significant numbers of refugees from outside Europe from the 1970s, including Chileans fleeing the military coup in 1973 and Vietnamese boat people picked up at sea by Norwegian ships, whose numbers had reached 5500 by 1986.[101] Iranians moved to Norway as a result of the 1979 revolution, more specifically members of the Bahai religious minority, businessmen and people who had married Norwegians. In many cases a chain migration of families developed. By 1991 Norway had a foreign population of 143,000, making up a low proportion of 3.4 per cent. A peak of asylum seekers was reached in 1987 when the figure totalled 8600. [102]

Denmark has one of the lowest foreign populations in the whole of Europe, just 2.2 per cent at the start of 1987, of whom 55,000 were from Scandinavia, western Europe and North America. Although most foreigners who had entered the country up to that time had done so for economic reasons, the early 1980s began to witness an increase in refugees, reaching a peak of 14,347 asylum applications in 1993. [103] Finland has an even lower proportion of immigrants in its population than Denmark and perhaps the lowest proportion in the whole of Europe. In 1986 the total number of foreigners in the country stood at just 17,269, making up a tiny 0.4 per cent of the population. [104] Even so, as in the case of all other western European states, Finland witnessed an increase in asylum applications during the early 1990s, in the case of Finland reaching 3634 in 1992. [105]

The states which accepted most refugees lay in central and eastern Europe, closest to the conflicts which followed the end of the Cold War and created millions of victims, although the European continent certainly did not become the vast refugee camp which it had been at the end of the Second World War. Neither did it, with a few exceptions, resemble some of the states throughout the globe which have experienced refugee influxes more recently due to conflicts on their doorstep. In 1986, for instance, Pakistan contained 2,500,000 refugees who had fled from the Afghan conflict. [106] The only parts of Europe which have witnessed such influxes since 1945 consist of those which have directly experienced conflict, such as the former Yugoslavia and parts of the former Soviet Union.

Significant numbers of refugees had actually begun to move towards Europe, especially Germany, before the end of the Cold War. They fled mostly from conflicts outside the continent, played out as part of the international division of the globe between the Soviet Union and its allies and the USA and its supporters in western Europe. Neither group of countries demonstrated much enthusiasm in dealing with the human consequences of the conflicts they had created. The second post-war international refugee crisis began to develop during the mid 1970s, with mass departures from American-backed conflict in Vietnam, Kampuchea and Laos, followed by movements caused by war and political change in Lebanon, Afghanistan, and several parts of Africa, including Zaire, Uganda, Namibia and South Africa; while, in South America, right-wing regimes and their intolerant policies caused refugee movements out of Chile and Argentina. The number of refugees in the world increased from 8,200,000 in 1980 to perhaps twenty million in 1992, although, throughout this period, unlike the immediate post-war years, the vast majority have remained outside Europe in the areas where conflict has taken place. Even during the 1980s most refugees in Europe originated within the continent. Those who have progressed to Europe from further afield have been aided by the globalisation of transportation and information. As we have seen, as the numbers of asylum seekers attempting to move to Europe increased, the European states augmented their efforts to keep them out. The most generous state during the 1980s was the Federal Republic of Germany, the destination of 47 per cent of asylum-seekers in Europe between 1984 and 1988, a total of 369,215 people, the most steady stream fleeing repression in Poland. [107]

The movement out of Poland represented an early sign of the political developments affecting eastern Europe as a whole from the 1980s and into the 1990s. The increasingly repressive Communist regimes of the former decade, which caused some emigration, were followed by more nationalistic governments leading to the rebirth of larger-scale migration in eastern Europe. Apart from Poland, Rumania and Bulgaria also experienced population loss during the 1980s. In the case of Rumania, most of those who left came from two of the largest minorities in the country, Germans and Hungarians. The migration occurred due to a combination of economic and political factors. An increasingly intolerant policy pursued by the Ceaçescu regime, aimed at homogenisation, left migration as one of the possible options for ethnic minorities. The deteriorating economic position of Rumania during the 1980s, caused by Ceaçescu's decision to pay off the country's $10 billion debt, further added to emigration pressure. Furthermore, as Rumania received 'Most Favoured Nation Status' in trade relations from the USA, as a reward for distancing herself from the Soviet Bloc, she had to allow emigration. During the 1980s an average of 12,000 ethnic Germans left the country every year bound for West Germany. Ethnic Hungarians could not emigrate in large numbers until the end of the 1980s, mostly proceeding towards Hungary, although others also went on to Austria and even Sweden. [108]

The late 1980s also witnessed an exodus of Turks from Bulgaria, the largest such movement since the early 1950s, although 113,193 people had followed this migratory path between 1968 and 1984. Like the movement of the early 1950s, that of 1989 took place against the background of a repression of the Turkish minority. This reached a peak in 1989 when the Bulgarian government asked the Turkish state to take in Bulgarian Turks, which resulted in 369,839 people fleeing across the border, although most of them actually returned shortly afterwards. [109]

By 1989 the political and economic processes which would cause large-scale migration within the European continent had been set in motion. While the end of Communist regimes and their replacement with more ethnically intolerant nationalist governments may represent a major motivation in causing migration, other preconditions, a combination of push and pull factors, already existed to make migration a possibility; especially in the case of movement from eastern to western Europe. The most important economic push factor in this case consisted of the devastation of the Communist economies caused by their attempt to adapt to economic policies practised by the west. In 1990 the output of all goods, excluding services, fell on average by 11 per cent in Central and Eastern Europe and by 4 per cent in the Soviet Union, while unemployment in Poland rose from 56,000 in early 1990 to two million by the end of 1991. [110] Elsewhere, 360,000 Czechs and two million Soviets were unemployed by the end of 1990. Throughout eastern Europe social security systems had difficulty in dealing with such levels of people without work. In contrast, while western Europe may have experienced a slight downturn in economic productivity during the early 1990s, it clearly did not face the seismic crisis occurring further east. Even before the collapse of Communism, GDP per capita in eastern Europe stood at one eighth the level in the rest of Europe and has declined even further. [111] Such a contrast of stark differences in the economic prosperity of east and west helped to send people towards the already existing mature capitalist economies. Yet such economic disparities do not automatically cause population movement, especially against a background of obsessive immigration control practised throughout western Europe, in which one of the only realistic possibilities of purely economic movement rests in illegal migration, so that as many as 150,000 illegal immigrants may have made their way to Germany in 1992. [112] Focusing upon Hamburg, an article in *Stern* revealed the story of Stefan, who slept in his car, queued up for a job by the harbour every morning and shaved once a week looking into a car wing-mirror. [113] Other population movements affecting eastern Europe have usually had a political motivation, whether it is racial persecution, the war in Yugoslavia or ethnic connections with Germany. Ultimately, most of the migrations caused by the collapse of Communism were determined by geographical factors: most people have moved to the nearest safe haven, in the hope that they would eventually return to what they saw as their home.

The political changes in the Soviet Union have been responsible for the largest number of European migrants and refugees during the 1990s, especially as a result of the emergence of new states which contained minorities left over from the Soviet years. For instance, at the death of the Soviet Union twenty-five million Russians found themselves in former republics outside Russia. By 1995 about two million of these people had moved to Russia, where they received assistance under legislation passed in June 1992, migrating in largest numbers from Tajikistan in central Asia, Georgia and

Azerbaijan. The reasons why they fled included the attempt to replace Soviet Russian institutions and dominance with that of the local population, leading to discrimination against the Russian population, as well as the deterioration of the economic position of the areas from which the Russians fled. [114]

Movement within the former Soviet Union also occurred from the areas where ethnic conflict developed, especially in the Caucasus. The war between Armenia and Azerbaijan over Nagorno-Karabakh may, by its seventh year in 1995, have displaced as many as 1,600,000 people. Two secessionist conflicts in Georgia also led to refugee movements. The war which began in 1989 for the independence of South Ossetia, in the centre of the country bordering Russia, created 120,000 refugees who fled to Russia by 1995. Conflict in Abkhazia, in the north west of the country, caused 80,000 people to flee to Russia and other CIS states by 1995. [115] Between 1992 and 1997 over three million people made their way to the Russian Federation from other states.

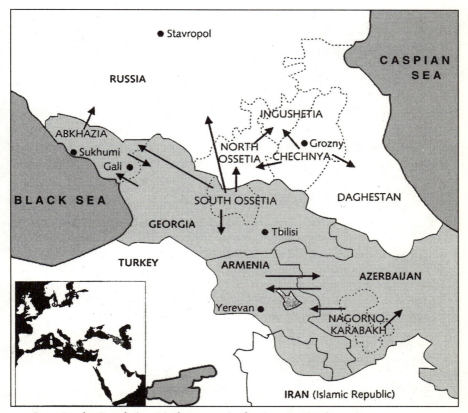

26. Cross-Border Population Displacements in the Caucasus Region

They consisted of ethnic Russians, refugees from conflict in the Caucasus, together with illegal immigrants and asylum seekers from Africa, Asia and the Middle East. [116]

Emigration from former Yugoslavia had begun to increase before the outbreak of the war there: the number of Yugoslavs abroad grew by 11 per cent between 1989 and 1990 to total 716,000 people. The war in Yugoslavia resulted in a drastic increase in their numbers, although the majority of movements took place between one Yugoslav republic and another, partly because of simple reasons of geographical proximity but also due to the policies of 'ethnic cleansing' pursued by various warlords in an attempt to reverse centuries of history overnight for the purpose of creating ethnically homogeneous states in the area. Quite simply the war in former Yugoslavia resulted in the creation of the biggest displaced persons crisis in Europe since the end of the Second World War so that, recalling the situation in Germany in 1945, Yugoslavia in the early 1990s resembled a vast refugee camp. By August 1992 one in ten Yugoslavs was a refugee, either within his or her own Yugoslav state, in a neighbouring one or in another European country. [117] By 1995 UNHCR was assisting 3,700,000 people affected by the war, [118] bringing the figure close to 20 per cent of the population of Yugoslavia, which stood at 22,427,600 in 1981. [119]

As the most ethnically mixed republic and the one which faced the most prolonged and violent experience of war, the greatest number of refugees originated from Bosnia-Herzegovina. One estimate placed their numbers within the former Yugoslav states at 1,496,648 at the end of 1992. [120] The greatest displacement here took place after the Serb invasion of the area in the summer of 1992, a situation in which people left their homes with whatever possessions they could grab. [121] The following describes the experiences of one teenager, who lived in Sarajevo:

> On 30 April I took the last train out of Sarajevo. I went to Jajce, where I joined my parents. We all thought the war would soon stop and that we would get back to our normal lives. But the war spread like wildfire, and at the end of May we found ourselves surrounded by the Serb Army. The only way out of the besieged town was past the gunfire between the two front lines. We managed to escape by running. The elderly and children were killed because they could not run fast enough. My father was badly wounded when he tried to protect me. [122]

But Bosnians formed just one element of the total number of people displaced by the war in Yugoslavia. In all over a million Croats, Macedonians, Montenegrins and Serbians and Slovenes were also affected, not just during the conflict but also at its end, as the solution sponsored by the USA legalised the exchange of populations.

Victims of the Yugoslav conflict who fled abroad, totalling 531,412 in August 1992, generally made their way either to neighbouring countries or to states which had liberal asylum policies as well as an established Yugoslav community. In the former category were Austria, which accepted 57,500 refugees, and Hungary, taking 50,000. States which fit the second description include Sweden (47,600) and Germany (220,000). [123] The meanest countries, in terms of the size of their own populations and their consequent ability to absorb refugees, were Britain and France, which had accepted just 2000 and 1106 respectively in August 1992, [124] although this tied in with the draconian asylum procedures which both of these countries pursue.

Hungary also experienced further influxes of ethnic Hungarians moving towards its borders in the early 1990s, especially after violence against this group in early 1990 in Transylvania, which caused 7848 to flee between March and May of that year. [125] Austria, because of its geographical location, experienced a dramatic increase in the number of foreigners within its borders as a result of the post Cold War refugee crisis, so that the figure increased from 299,000 in 1988 to 518,000 in 1991. [126]

This increase remains small compared with the millions of people, from a variety of origins, who moved into Germany in the late 1980s and early 1990s. Geographical location, bordering eastern Europe, provides one major explanation. Another is Article 16 of the Constitution of the Federal Republic which offers a right of asylum to refugees, although we should not overestimate its importance: all western European states, having signed the Geneva Convention, should accept refugees. Article 116 of the Federal Constitution, accepting ethnic Germans from eastern Europe, offers a third explanation for the level of immigration into Germany during the early 1990s. The actual intake between 1990 and 1992 totalled 887,366 asylum seekers and 849,606 ethnic Germans, averaging out at over half a million newcomers per year for these three years alone, [127] although the figures were comparatively high in the late 1980s and declined only gradually after 1992. These numbers are even more striking when we consider that in 1992 Germany received 92 per cent of all applications for asylum to EU countries. [128] Yet if we put the above figures into the perspective of the history of migration into the Federal Republic, annual increases of the scale indicated above have not been uncommon.

The high rate of immigration into Germany in the early 1990s did not look good to European policy-makers who, by this time, had moved towards the development of a unified strategy for European migration, with the creation of a fortress where those within could move as they wished, with internal border controls virtually disappearing; while those outside, especially to the south and east, had great difficulty entering. These developments, especially free movement within the European Union, had a history stretching over several decades.

Articles 48 and 49 of the Treaty of Rome, which established the original European Economic Community in 1957, aimed at achieving free movement of labour by the end of 1968 as a necessary part of the economic and political integration envisaged. This provision suited both Italy, wishing to export people, and the labour hungry economies north of the Alps. The accomplishment of free movement began to become a reality from the early 1960s with Regulations 15/61 and 38/64 of the Council of Ministers of 1961 and 1964 respectively. Consequently, by 1968 workers could move from one country to another in search of work. Further regulations in the late 1960s and early 1970s allowed workers to bring their families to their new places of residence and also to claim social security benefits. [129]

Free movement of labour has not led to substantial increases in the level of migration between member states, although the richer states, such as Germany, have the power to attract people from southern Europe and even Ireland. Restaurants in Stuttgart, for instance, made use of Irish waitresses during the early 1990s. The relative lack of migration between EU states can be explained by the fact that differences between the richest and poorest states within the Union are small compared with differences between the EU and African, Asian or many East European states, which have a far greater labour surplus. Migration which does takes place includes commuters (moving, for instance, from Holland to Germany, Belgium to France and France to Germany), academics, students and professionals, as well as young people broadening their experience of life.

The Council of Ministers did not begin to regard the immigration of people into Europe as an issue until 1974, but in 1976 it put forward a resolution stating that members of the Community should eventually aim at reaching an agreement on immigration policy. The first concrete development did not occur, however, until 14 June 1985 when the governments of France, West Germany and the Benelux countries signed the Schengen Agreement, which aimed at abolishing internal border controls and implementing stronger ones outside. Five years later the Schengen Implementation Agreement placed more stress upon the latter than the former proposal, aiming also at the processing of asylum applications which would affect all member countries in one state, although only nine governments had signed this by the end of 1993. By the late 1990s we have reached a situation in which Fortress Europe seems to have become a reality.

The contrast with Europe in 1945 cannot be starker, a situation in which a refugee was almost the normal human condition in central Europe. After passing through a period of large-scale labour immigration, we have now reached a stage in which the European Union attempts to prevent as much migration as it can. This is in accordance with the wishes of its members, most of whom strive towards excluding as many people as possible, making every effort to deter genuine asylum seekers.

Ultimately, the European Union cannot succeed in keeping people out for several reasons. First, the survival of black economies which exist in every European state but are larger in southern Europe. Secondly, the impossibility of closely controlling the entire length of the external border. Inevitably 'illegal' immigrants will enter via the Oder-Neisse rivers or using the Mediterranean. These have become the equivalent of the Rio Grande and the Atlantic as points of entry in the case of the USA.

The third reason why western Europe cannot succeed may be the most important: demography and economics, which have been fundamental push factors in all migrations, are against it. Whereas European states have reached a situation of stable or even negative natural population growth, the developing world is expanding at a rate which Europe experienced during the nineteenth century. As Paul Kennedy has pointed out: 'The southern European states of Spain, Portugal, France, Italy and Greece, whose combined populations are estimated to increase by a mere five million between 1990 and 2025, lie close to North African countries (Morocco, Algeria, Tunisia, Libya, Egypt) whose populations are forecast to grow by 108 million in those years.'[130] Economic pressures also make some sort of migration likely. In 1990 the developed world had a per capita GNP twenty-four times greater than that of poor countries.[131]

One possible solution to this conflict would be the collapse of Europe, in the same way as the Roman Empire, with the flooding towards it of disenfranchised people from beyond its borders. Or to give another analogy: can it be that European citizens, even though they do not realise this, are rather like the French aristocracy in the late eighteenth century? They have, along with other advanced states, cornered the world's resources, fixed the market and control political power, just as the aristocracy did in France before 1789. Of course not all Europeans are equally wealthy, but neither were French nobles. Could it be that Europeans will suffer the same fate as the French aristocracy?

Ultimately, this is unlikely to happen, but in a time of increasing globalisation and ease of transportation it seems doubtful that Europe will be able to keep out foreigners in the ruthless manner it wishes to in the late 1990s. The increasingly ageing, infertile and educated European population will need people to do its menial work for it. European governments are trying to stop an inevitability in human history. Just as the 'indigenous' populations of Europe were succeeded by those who moved towards it in the age of migration during the Dark Ages, so it is quite likely that, sooner or later, if European birth rates keep falling (which seems an irreversible process), the European continent will be predominantly, and ultimately overwhelmingly, populated by fertile black and brown people. European governments in the late twentieth century are, in the long run, fighting a losing battle. The only alternative scenario is for the Third World to reach the level of development of the west, which would reduce the number of people wishing to migrate.

Whatever may or may not happen in the future, five decades of migration have transformed the demography of Europe, especially its western sections. Ethnic communities have emerged in the cities throughout the continent to which the post-war migrants moved, either as a result of economic or political factors, or a combination of both. While those with ethnic characteristics similar to the dominant population may have disappeared quite quickly, newcomers who have moved to Europe from outside the continent have formed distinct ethnic communities. Not only do they look different, and face hostility from both the state which imported them and the dominant population within it, they also find themselves employed in occupations which autochthonous people shun.

The future evolution of the post-war immigrants and refugees remains open to speculation. Will they survive as distinct groups for centuries in the same way that dispersed peoples and localised populations have done? Or will they assimilate into the surrounding populations? The latter process will be easier for some than others: groups such as the Irish in Britain or Italians, Spaniards and Portuguese in France. West Indians in Britain or Africans in France may never disappear, always to remain a distinct population within these two nation states.

Notes

Chapter 1: Minorities, States and Nationalism

1. Adrian Hastings, *The Construction of Nationhood: Ethnicity, Religion and Nationalism* (Cambridge, 1997).
2. Peter Alter, *Nationalism* (2nd edn, London, 1994), p. 39.
3. John Breuilly, *Nationalism and the State* (Manchester, 1982), p. 45.
4. Gérard Chaliand, 'Minority Peoples in the Age of Nation States', in Chaliand (ed.), *Minority Peoples in the Age of Nation States* (London, 1989), p. 1.
5. Ernest Gellner, *Nations and Nationalism* (Oxford, 1983) p. 1.
6. Alexander J. Motyl, *Will the Non-Russians Rebel? State, Ethnicity and the Stability in the USSR* (London, 1987), pp. 38–39; René Tangac, 'The Soviet Response to the Minority Problem', in Chaliand, *Minority Peoples*, p. 105; Walker Connor, *The National Question in Marxist-Leninist Theory and Strategy* (Princeton, 1984), pp. 392–407.
7. See Eric Hobsbawm, 'Mass-Producing Traditions: Europe, 1870–1914', in Eric Hobsbawn and Terence Ranger (eds), *The Invention of Tradition* (Cambridge, 1983) pp. 283–91.

Chapter 2: Dispersed Minorities

1. James Parkes, *A History of the Jewish People* (Harmondsworth, 1964), p. 32.
2. Cecil Roth, *A Short History of the Jewish People* (2nd edn, London, 1969), p. 137.
3. Roth, *Short History of the Jewish People*, pp. 138, 141; Parkes, *History of the Jewish People*, pp. 34–39; Abram Leon Sachar, *A History of the Jews* (5th edn, New York, 1967), p. 121.
4. Werner Keller, *Diaspora: The Post-Biblical History of the Jews* (London, 1971), p. 112.
5. Roth, *Short History of the Jewish People*, p. 139.
6. Angus Fraser, *The Gypsies* (Oxford, 1992), pp. 10–44; Jean-Paul Clebert, *The Gypsies* (London, 1964), pp. 15–29; Felipe Fernández-Armesto (ed.), *The Times Guide to the Peoples of Europe* (London, 1994), pp. 394–35; David M. Crowe, *A History of Gypsies of Eastern Europe* (London, 1995), p. 1; Hugh Poulton, *The Balkans: Minorities and States in Conflict* (2nd edn, London, 1993), p. 87.
7. Noel Malcolm, *Bosnia: A Short History* (London, 1994), p. 114.
8. Sam Beck, 'Ethnicity, Class and Public Policy: Tsigani-Gypsies in Socialist Romania', *Gießener Heft für Tsiganologie* (1986), p. 111. For the history of Gypsy

slavery see Ian Hancock, *The Pariah Syndrome: An Account of Gypsy Slavery and Persecution* (London, 1987), especially pp. 16–29.

9. Gérard Chaliand and Jean-Pierre Rageau, *The Penguin Atlas of Diasporas* (London, 1995), p. 97.

10. *National Minorities in Hungary* (London, 1979), p. 11.

11. Teresa San Román, 'Kinship, Marriage, Law and Leadership in Two Urban Gypsy Settlements in Spain', in Farnham Rehfisch (ed.), *Gypsies, Tinkers and Other Travellers* (London, 1975), p. 169.

12. Rainer Heheman, '"Jederzeit gottlose böse Leute": Sinti und Roma zwischen Duldung und Vernichtung', in Klaus J. Bade (ed.), *Deutsche im Ausland – Fremde in Deutschland: Migration in Geschichte und Gegenwart* (Munich, 1992), p. 272.

13. Clebert, *Gypsies*, p. 29.

14. Brian Vesey-Fitzgerald, *Gypsies of Britain: An Introduction to their History* (2nd edn, Newton Abbot, 1973), pp. 20–32.

15. Ibid., pp. 32–42; Bettina Barnes, 'Irish Travelling People', in Rehfisch, *Gypsies, Tinkers and Other Travellers*, pp. 231–32; Andrew McCormick, *The Tinkler Gypsies* (London, 1907), pp. 386–456.

16. Adam Heymowski, *Swedish 'Travellers' and Their Ancestry: A Social Isolate or an Ethnic Minority* (Uppsala, 1969), pp. 80, 96; C. H. Tillhagen, 'The Gypsy Problem in Finland', *Journal of the Gypsy Lore Society*, 37 (1958), p. 41.

17. The above account of the Ottoman Empire is based upon Stanford Shaw, *History of the Ottoman Empire and Modern Turkey*, i, *Empire of the Gazis: The Rise and Decline of the Ottoman Empire, 1208–1808* (Cambridge, 1976); Lord Kinross, *The Ottoman Centuries: The Rise and Fall of the Turkish Empire* (London, 1977); Barbara Jelavich, *History of the Balkans*, i, *Eighteenth and Nineteenth Centuries* (Cambridge, 1983).

18. Huey Louis Kostanick, *Turkish Resettlement of Bulgarian Turks, 1950–1953* (Berkeley and Los Angeles, 1957), pp. 76–78; Erhard Franz, 'The Exodus of Turks from Bulgaria, 1989', *Asian and African Studies*, 25 (1991), pp. 83–84.

19. One useful but biased account of the Turkish population of Cyprus is Kiamran Halil, 'The Structure of the Turkish-Cypriot Race', *Mankind Quarterly*, 15 (1974), pp. 124–34.

20. See, for instance, David Morgan, *The Mongols* (Oxford, 1986); and J. J. Saunders, *The History of the Mongol Conquest* (London, 1971).

21. Walter Schmidt, 'The Nation in German History', in Mikuláš Teich and Roy Porter (eds), *The National Question in Europe in Historical Context* (Cambridge, 1993), p. 151.

22. Roger P. Bartlett, *Human Capital: The Settlement of Foreigners in Russia, 1762–1804* (Cambridge, 1979), p. 15.

23. Hans Fenske, 'International Migration: Germany in the Eighteenth Century', *Central European History*, 13 (1980), p. 346.

24. Fernández-Armesto, *The Peoples of Europe*, pp. 389–90; Roth, *Short History of the Jewish People*, pp. 188–89; Paul Hymans, 'The Jewish Community in Medieval England, 1066–1290', *Journal of Jewish Studies*, 25 (1974), pp. 270–93. The quote

is from Joseph Jacobs, *The Jews of Angevin England: Documents and Records* (London, 1893), p. 112.

25. Malcolm, *Bosnia*, pp. 107–8.

26. The beginning of Jewish settlement in Poland is open to speculation. See Bernard D. Weinryb, *The Jews of Poland: A Social and Economic History of the Jews of Poland from 1100 to 1800* (Philadelphia, 1976).

27. See Stanford J. Shaw, *The Jews of the Ottoman Empire and the Turkish Republic* (London, 1991).

28. Fernández-Armesto, *The Peoples of Europe*, pp. 390–91; Clifford R. Barnett, *Poland: Its People, its Society, its Culture* (New York, 1958), pp. 49–50.

29. See David S. Katz, *The Jews in the History of England* (Oxford, 1994).

30. See, for instance, John Doyle Klier, *Russia Gathers Her Jews: The Origins of the 'Jewish Question' in Russia, 1772–1825* (DeKalb, Illinois, 1986); and Henry-Dietrich Löwe, *The Tsars and the Jews: Reform, Reaction and Antisemitism in Imperial Russia, 1772–1917* (Chur, 1992).

31. See, for instance, Jacob Katz, *Out of the Ghetto: The Social Background to Jewish Emancipation* (Cambridge, Massachusetts, 1973).

32. See Hehemann, 'Jederzeit gottlose böse Leute', pp. 272–73; Vesey-Fitzgerald, *Gypsies of Britain*, pp. 301; Clebert, *Gypsies*, pp. 58–62.

33. British Refugee Council, London, Q21.1, N. Gheorghe and T. A. Acton, 'Minority, Ethnic and Human Rights: Varieties of Strategy and Interest in Romany (Gypsy) Politics in Different Countries as a Case Study in the Sociology of Conflict', unpublished paper, n.d.

34. Willy Guy, 'Ways of Looking at Roms: The Case of Czechoslovakia', in Rehfisch, *Gypsies, Tinkers and Other Travellers*, pp. 206–7.

35. Hancock, *Pariah Syndrome*, pp. 16–36.

36. P. W. R. Rishi, *Roma* (Patiala, 1976), p. 39.

37. George Borrow, *The Zincali: or An Account of the Gypsies of Spain* (London, 1841), p. 261; Hancock, *Pariah Syndrome*, pp. 53–55.

38. Hancock, ibid., pp. 155–57.

39. David Mayall, *English Gypsies and State Politics* (Hertford, 1995), pp. 18–27.

40. Malcolm, *Bosnia*, p. 7.

41. See ibid., pp. 51–69.

42. Ibid., p. 58.

43. Dominik J. Mandić, 'The Ethnic and Religious History of Bosnia and Hercegovina', in Francis H. Eterovich and Christopher Spalatin (eds), *Croatia: Land, People, Culture*, ii (Toronto, 1970), pp. 373–74.

44. Justin McCarthy, 'Ottoman Bosnia, 1800 to 1878', in Mark Pinson (ed.), *The Muslims of Bosnia-Herzegovina: Their Historic Development from the Middle Ages to the Dissolution of Yugoslavia* (Cambridge, Massachusetts, 1993), p. 58.

45. Galaba Palikrusheva, 'Ethnographic Conditions in Macedonia', in M. Apostolski and Haralampie Polenakovich (eds), *The Socialist Republic of Macedonia* (Skopje, 1974); Hugh Poulton, *Minorities in the Balkans* (London, 1989), pp. 23–29.

46. Ramadan Marmullaku, *Albania and the Albanians* (London, 1975), p. 16.

47. Viktor Kozlov, *The Peoples of the Soviet Union* (London, 1988), pp. 22–23.

48. Anne Sheehy, *The Crimean Tatars and Volga Germans: Soviet Treatment of Two National Minorities* (London, 1971), p. 8.

49. Gustav Burbiel, 'The Tatars and the Tatar ASSR', in Zev Katz, Rosemarie Rogers and Frederic Harned (eds), *Handbook of Major Soviet Nationalities* (New York, 1975), p. 392.

50. See Frank Huddle Jr, 'Azerbaidjhan and the Azerbaidjhanis', in Katz, Rogers and Harned, *Handbook of Major Soviet Nationalities*, pp. 191–92.

51. Robert A Kann, *The History of the Habsburg Empire, 1526–1918* (Berkeley, 1974).

52. One of the best histories of German settlement in eastern Europe is G. C. Paikert, *The Danube Swabians: German Populations in Hungary, Rumania and Yugoslavia and Hitler's Impact on their Patterns* (The Hague, 1967).

53. Radoye L. Knejevitch, 'The Ethnical Structure of Yugoslavia', *Yugoslav Observer*, 2 (1956), p. 15.

54. This figure is from Gerard Israel, *The Jews in Russia* (London, 1975), p. 22.

55. Much has been written about Jewish life and the antisemitic pogroms in late Tsarist Russia. The best accounts include John D. Klier, *Imperial Russia's Jewish Question* (Cambridge, 1995), and John D. Klier and S. Lambroza (eds), *Pogroms: Anti-Jewish Violence in Modern Russian History* (Cambridge, 1992).

56. This comes from an English newspaper entitled *In Darkest Russia*, 15 July 1891.

57. Nancy L. Green, *The Pletzl of Paris: Jewish Immigrant Workers in the Belle Epoque* (London, 1986).

58. See Panikos Panayi, *Immigration, Ethnicity and Racism in Britain, 1815–1945* (Manchester, 1994), pp. 31–32, for tables giving the number of Poles and Russians (in both cases overwhelmingly Jews) in Britain in 1901 and 1931.

59. See Jack Wertheimer, *Unwelcome Strangers: East European Jews in Imperial Germany* (Oxford, 1987).

60. Such claims led to much resentment amongst German Jews, who had fought alongside Gentiles. An organisation called the Reichsbund Jüdischer Frontsoldaten came into existence and published a book entitled *Gefallene deutsche Juden: Frontbriefe, 1914–1918* (Berlin, 1935). See also Jacob Segall, *Die deutschen Juden als Soldaten im Kriege, 1914–1918* (Berlin, 1921), which gives precise statistical details of Jewish participation in the front line, as well as Jewish deaths there. For antisemitism in Britain during the First World War see Colin Holmes, *Antisemitism in British Society, 1876–1939* (London, 1979), pp. 121–40.

61. Kenneth C. Farmer, et al., 'National Minorities in Poland', in Stephan M. Horak (ed.), *Eastern European National Minorities, 1919–1980: A Handbook* (Littleton, Colorado, 1985), pp. 39, 51.

62. Alec Nove and J. A. Newth, 'The Jewish Population: Demographic Trends and Occupational Patterns', in Lionel J. Kochan (ed.), *The Jews in Soviet Russia since 1917* (Oxford, 1978), pp. 137–45.

63. Pèteris Zvidriņš, 'Changes in the Ethnic Composition of Latvia', *Journal of Baltic Studies*, 23 (1992), pp. 359–60.

64. Robert Lee Wolff, *The Balkans in Our Time* (Cambridge, Massachusetts, 1974), p. 48.

65. Martin L. Kovacs, 'National Minorities in Hungary', in Horak, *Eastern European National Minorities*, p. 167.

66. H. Renner, 'The National Minorities in Czechoslovakia after the End of the Second World War', *Plural Societies*, 7 (1976), p. 23.

67. Laslo Sekelj, 'Antisemitism and Nationalist Conflicts in Former Yugoslavia', *Patterns of Prejudice*, 27 (1993), p. 64.

68. Peter John Georgeoff, 'National Minorities in Bulgaria, 1919–1980', in Horak, *Eastern European National Minorities*, p. 282.

69. Shaw, *Jews of the Ottoman Empire*, p. 246.

70. Lucy S. Dawidowicz, *The War against the Jews, 1933–45* (Harmondsworth, 1987), pp. 447–51.

71. Michael R. Marrus, *The Unwanted: European Refugees in the Twentieth Century* (Oxford, 1985), p. 130.

72. Bernard Wasserstein, *Britain and the Jews of Europe* (Oxford, 1979), p. 7.

73. An anonymous personal reminiscence from Karen Gershon (ed.), *We Came as Children: A Collective Autobiography* (London, 1966), p. 26.

74. Dawidowicz, *War against the Jews*, p. 448.

75. Constantin Goschler, 'The Attitude towards Jews in Bavaria after the Second World War', *Leo Baeck Institute Yearbook*, 36 (1991), p. 445.

76. Celia S. Heller, *On the Edge of Destruction: Jews of Poland between the Two World Wars* (Detroit, 1994).

77. Abraham Lewin, *A Cup of Tears: A Diary of the Warsaw Ghetto* (Oxford, 1988), p. 233.

78. L. Dobroszycki, 'Restoring Jewish Life in Post-War Poland', *Soviet Jewish Affairs*, 3 (1973), p. 59; Farmer et al., 'National Minorities in Poland', p. 51.

79. Zev Katz, 'The Jews of the Soviet Union', in Katz, Rogers and Harned, *Handbook of Major Soviet Nationalities*, p. 363; Nove and Newth, 'The Jewish Population', p. 149.

80. Randolph L. Braham, *The Politics of Genocide: The Holocaust in Hungary*, i (New York, 1981).

81. Kovacs, 'National Minorities in Hungary', pp. 167–68.

82. Renner, 'National Minorities in Czechoslovakia', p. 30.

83. Dawidowicz, *War against the Jews*, pp. 458–61.

84. Sekelj, 'Antisemitism and Nationalist Conflicts in Former Yugoslavia', pp. 65–69.

85. Harriet Pass Freidenreich, *The Jews of Yugoslavia: A Quest for Community* (Philadelphia, 1979), pp. 192–93.

86. Mark Mazower, *Inside Hitler's Greece: The Experience of Occupation, 1941–44* (London, 1993), p. 256.

87. Wolff, *The Balkans in Our Times*, p. 49.

88. Wasserstein, *Britain and the Jews of Europe*, p. 82.

89. Avni Haim, *Spain, the Jews and Franco* (Philadelphia, 1982), p. 186.

90. Shaw, *Jews of the Ottoman Empire*, pp. 255–58, makes much of Turkish rescue efforts on behalf of Jews during the Second World War, but provides no figures.

91. Harald Runbloom, 'Immigration to Scandinavia after World War II', in Sven

Tägil (ed.), *Ethnicity and Nation Building in the Nordic World* (London, 1995), pp. 293–96.

92. Richard A. Stein, 'Antisemitism in the Netherlands: Past and Present', *Patterns of Prejudice*, 19 (1985), p. 19.

93. Simon P. Sibelman, '*Le Renouvellement Juif:* French Jewry on the Eve of the Centenary of the *Affaire Dreyfus*', *French Cultural Studies*, 3 (1992), p. 265; Robert S. Wistrich, *Anti-Semitism: The Longest Hatred* (London, 1992), pp. 132–34.

94. Davidowicz, *War against the Jews*, pp. 441–43.

95. See Jonathan Steinberg, *All or Nothing: The Axis and the Holocaust, 1941–43* (London, 1990).

96. Dawidowicz, *War against the Jews*, p. 480.

97. Panayi, *Immigration, Ethnicity and Racism in Britain*, p. 51.

98. Quoted in Bernard Wasserstein, *Vanishing Diaspora: The Jews in Europe since 1945*, p. 2 (London, 1996).

99. Georgeoff, 'National Minorities in Bulgaria', p. 284.

100. See Bozena Szaynok, 'The Pogrom of the Jews in Kielce, July 4, 1946', *Yad Vashem Studies*, 22 (1992), pp. 199–235.

101. See, for instance, Josef Banas, *The Scapegoats: The Exodus of the Remnants of Polish Jewry* (London, 1979).

102. See V. Zaslavsky and R. J. Brym, *Soviet Jewish Emigration and Soviet Nationality Policy* (London, 1983); and Mikhael A. Chlevnov, 'Jewish Communities and Jewish Identities in the Former Soviet Union', in Jonathan Webber (ed.), *Jewish Identities in the New Europe* (London, 1994), p. 130.

103. See Wasserstein, *Vanishing Diaspora*, pp. 85–102.

104. Geoffrey Alderman, *Modern British Jewry* (Oxford, 1992), pp. 322–26.

105. Yoram Govlizki, 'The Jews', in Graham Smith (ed.), *The Nationalities Question in the Post-Soviet States* (London, 1996), pp. 436–61.

106. W. D. Rubinstein, *A History of the Jews in the English Speaking World: Great Britain*, pp. 364–427 (London, 1996).

107. Zoltan D. Barany, 'Hungary's Gypsies', *Report on Eastern Europe*, 29, 20 July 1990, p. 27.

108. Crowe, *History of the Gypsies of Eastern Europe*, p. 11.

109. Andreas Mari Shuka, *With Gypsies in Bulgaria* (Liverpool, 1916), pp. 102–3.

110. David M. Crowe, 'Romania', in David M. Crowe and J. Kolsti (eds), *The Gypsies of Eastern Europe* (Armonk, New York, 1991), p. 61; Brigitte Mihok, *Ethnostratifikation im Sozialismus, aufgezeigt an den Beispielländern Ungarn und Rumänien* (Frankfurt, 1990), p. 62.

111. Otto Ulč, 'Communist National Minority Policy: The Case of the Gypsies in Czechoslovakia', *Soviet Studies*, 20 (1969), p. 421; Jiří Lípa, 'The Fate of Gypsies in Czechoslovakia under Nazi Domination', in Michael Berenbaum (ed.), *A Mosaic of Victims: Non-Jews Persecuted and Murdered by the Nazis* (London, 1990), p. 208.

112. Jerzy Ficowski, *The Gypsies in Poland: History and Customs* (Warsaw, 1989).

113. Malcolm, *Bosnia*, pp. 116–17.

114. See David Mayall, *Gypsy-Travellers in Nineteenth-Century British Society* (Cambridge, 1988); Mayall, *English Gypsies and State Politics*, pp. 47–54. The quote comes from John Hoyland, *A Historical Survey of the Customs, Habits and Present Status of the Gypsies* (New York, 1846), p. 178.

115. Clebert, *The Gypsies*, pp. 87–91.

116. Fraser, *The Gypsies*, p. 253.

117. Borrow, *Zincali*, passim.

118. Guy, 'Ways of Looking at Roms', p. 211.

119. John Kolsti, 'Albania', in Crowe and Kolsti, *Gypsies of Eastern Europe*, p. 52.

120. Crowe, *History of the Gypsies*, pp. 176–80.

121. Hehemann, 'Jederzeit gottlose böse Leute', p. 275; Isabel Fonseca, *Bury Me Standing: The Gypsies and their Journey* (London, 1995), pp. 255–57; Michael Burleigh and Wolfgang Wippermann, *The Racial State: Germany, 1933–1945* (Cambridge, 1991), pp. 114–20. The quote is my translation of a passage from Alfred Lessing, *Mein Leben in Versteck: Wie ein deutscher Sinti den Holocaust überlebte* (Düsseldorf, 1993), p. 30.

122. Donald Kenrick and Grattan Puxon, *The Destiny of Europe's Gypsies* (London, 1972), pp. 183–84.

123. Grattan Puxon, 'Forgotten Victims: Plight of the Gypsies', *Patterns of Prejudice*, 11 (1977), p. 26.

124. Fonseca, *Bury Me Standing*, pp. 265–71; Burleigh and Wippermann, *Racial State*, pp. 125–26.

125. Hehemann, 'Jederzeit gottlose böse Leute', p. 277.

126. Ficowski, *Gypsies in Poland*, p. 49.

127. Guy, 'Ways of Looking at Roms', p. 215; Lípa, 'Fate of Gypsies in Czechoslovakia'; David J. Kostelancik, 'The Gypsies of Czechoslovakia: Political and Ideological Considerations in the Development of Policy', *Studies in Comparative Communism*, 22 (1989), p. 309.

128. Crowe, *History of the Gypsies*, p. 186.

129. See the relevant contributions on Albania, Hungary and Rumania in Crowe and Kolsti, *Gypsies of Eastern Europe*.

130. Crowe, *History of the Gypsies*, pp. 220–21.

131. See Chaliand and Rageau, *Penguin Atlas of Diasporas*; Kveta Kalibova, Tomas Haisman and Jitka Gjuricova, 'Gypsies in Czechoslovakia: Demographic Development and Policy Perspectives', in John O'Loughlin and Herman van der Wusten (eds), *The New Political Geography of Eastern Europe* (London, 1993), pp. 133–44; Zoltan D Barnay, 'Hungary's Gypsies', *Report on Eastern Europe*, 20 July 1990, p. 26.

132. The best book on English gypsies is Judith Okely, *The Traveller Gypsies* (London, 1983).

133. See Crowe, *History of the Gypsies*.

134. Kostanick, *Turkish Resettlement*; Poulton, *The Balkans*, pp. 111–27; Wolff, *The Balkans*, pp. 476–77; Kemal. H. Karpat, 'Introduction: Bulgarian Way of Nation Building and the Turkish Minority', in idem (ed.), *The Turks of Bulgaria: The*

History, Culture and Political Fate of a Minority (Istanbul, 1990), pp. 1–22; Ilker Alp, *Bulgarian Atrocities: Documents and Photographs* (London, 1988), pp. 1–10; Wolfgang Höpken, 'From Religious Identity to Ethnic Mobilisation: The Turks of Bulgaria before, under and since Communism', in Hugh Poulton and Suha Taji Farowki (eds), *Muslim Identity and the Balkan State* (London, 1997), pp. 54–81; Ali Eminov, *Turkish and Other Muslim Minorities of Bulgaria* (London, 1997).

135. Barbara Jelavich, *History of the Balkans,* ii, *Twentieth Century* (Cambridge, 1983), p. 151.

136. Robert Donia and John V. A. Fine, Jr, *Bosnia and Herzegovina: A Tradition Betrayed* (London, 1994), pp. 86–87.

137. Poulton, *The Balkans,* p. 39.

138. For the events of the 1990s see, for instance: Laura Silber and Alan Little, *The Death of Yugoslavia* (London, 1985); and Human Rights Watch, *A Failure in the Making: Human Rights and the Dayton Agreement* (New York, 1996).

139. A good account of this period is Miranda Vickers, *The Albanians: A Modern History* (London, 1995), pp. 32–76.

140. A. Angelopoulos, 'Population Distribution of Greece Today According to Language, National Consciousness and Religion', *Balkan Studies,* 20 (1979), p. 125.

141. Figures vary. These are taken from Helsinki Watch, *Destroying Ethnic Identity: The Turks of Greece* (New York, 1990), p. 1; and Tozun Bahcheli, *Greek-Turkish Relations since 1955* (Boulder, Colarado, 1990), p. 170.

142. For disputes about figures see, for example, Poulton, *Minorities in the Balkans,* p. 32; and, a Greek view, K. G. Andreades, *The Moslem Minority in Western Thrace* (Thessaloniki, 1956), pp. 9–10.

143. Robin Oakley, 'The Turkish Peoples of Cyprus' in M. Bainbridge (ed.), *The Turkic Peoples of the World* (London, 1993), pp. 88–91.

144. Floya Anthias and Ron Ayres, 'Ethnicity and Class in Cyprus', *Race and Class* 25 (1983), p. 61.

145. Joseph S. Joseph, *Cyprus: Ethnic Conflict and International Concern* (New York, 1985), p. 29.

146. The best account of the movement for Enosis is Nancy Crawshaw, *The Cyprus Revolt: An Account of the Struggle for Union with Greece* (London, 1978).

147. A good account of these years can be found in Stavros Panteli, *A New History of Cyprus: From the Earliest Times to the Present* (London, 1984), pp. 345–410.

148. See Alexandre Bennigsen and S. Enders Wimbush, *Muslims of the Soviet Empire: A Guide* (London, 1985); and Richard Pipes, 'Muslims of Soviet Central Asia: Trends and Prospects: Part 1', *Middle East Journal,* 9 (1955), pp. 147–62.

149. Alan W. Fisher, *The Crimean Tatars* (Stanford, 1978), p. 138.

150. Anne Sheehy, *The Crimean Tatars and the Volga Germans: Soviet Treatment of Two National Minorities* (London, 1971), pp. 9–12.

151. See, for instance, Edward J. Lazzerini, 'The Crimean Tatars', in Smith, *Nationalities Question,* pp. 420–33.

152. Burbiel, 'Tatars', pp. 393–94; Marie Bennigsen Boxrup, 'Tatarstan and the Tatars', in Smith, *Nationalities Question,* pp. 75–93.

153. See: Christopher J. Walker (ed.), *Armenia and Karabagh: The Struggle for Unity* (London, 1991); and Jonathan Davis, 'Spontaneous Pogroms or State-Sponsored Racial Violence? Assessing the Nature of Ethnic Violence in Nagorno-Karabkh' (unpublished Master of Social Science Dissertation, University of Birmingham, 1997).

154. Alfred Bohman, 'Deutsche in Polen', in Manfred Straka (ed.), *Handbuch der europäischen Volksgruppen* (Vienna and Stuttgart, 1970), p. 445.

155. Farmer, 'National Minorities in Poland', pp. 46–47.

156. Alfred-Maurice de Zayas, *The German Expellees: Victims in War and Peace* (London, 1993), p. 21.

157. Farmer, 'National Minorities in Poland', p. 50.

158. Quoted in de Zayas, *German Expellees*, p. 22.

159. Farmer, 'National Minorities in Poland', p. 55.

160. Marrus, *The Unwanted*, pp. 325–26.

161. Theodor Schieder (ed.), *The Expulsion of the German Population from the Territories East of the Oder-Neisse-Line* (Bonn, 1960), pp. 47, 62.

162. Barnett, *Poland*, p. 47.

163. See Meic Stephens, *Linguistic Minorities in Western Europe* (Llandysul, 1976), p. 235; and Jørgen Elklit, Johan Peter Noack and Ole Tonsgaard, 'A National Group or a Social System: The Case of the German Minority in North Schleswig', *Journal of Intercultural Studies*, 1 (1980), pp. 5–18.

164. 'Die deutsche Volksgruppe in Ostbelgien', in Straka, *Handbuch der europäischen Volksgruppen*, p. 329.

165. Stephens, *Linguistic Minorities*, p. 520.

166. See two articles by Laurence Cole: 'Aufklärung – Nationalgefühl – Frühromantik: das Beispiel der patriotischen Mobilisierung Tirols, 1790–1810', *Historicum* (Frühling, 1997), pp. 16–21; and 'Province and Patriotism: German National Identity in Tirol, 1850–1914', *Österreichische Zeitschrift für Geschichtswissenschaften*, 6 (1995), pp. 61–83.

167. Viktoria Stadlymayer, 'Die Südtiroler Volksgruppe', in Straka, *Handbuch der europäischen Volksgruppen*, p. 356.

168. Flavia Pristinger, 'Ethnic Conflict and Modernization in the South Tyrol', in C. R. Foster (ed.), *Nations without a State: Ethnic Minorities in Western Europe* (New York, 1980), p. 167.

169. Anthony Alcock, 'Trentino and Tyrol: From Austria Crownland to European Region', in Seamus Dunn and T. G. Fraser (eds), *Europe and Ethnicity: World War I and Contemporary Ethnic Conflict* (London, 1996), pp. 73–85.

170. The figure is from Kalvoda, 'National Minorities in Czechoslovakia', p. 123.

171. Kovacs, 'National Minorities in Hungary', p. 164.

172. Minority Rights Group and TWEEC, *Minorities in Central and Eastern Europe* (London, 1993), p. 40.

173. Theodor Schieder (ed.), *The Fate of the Germans in Rumania* (Bonn, 1961), p. 16.

174. Ibid., p. 54.

175. Leo Paul, 'The Stolen Revolution: Minorities in Romania after Ceaçescu', in

O'Loughlin and van der Wusten, *New Political Geography of Eastern Europe*, p. 146.

176. Toussaint Hoćevar, 'National Minorities in Yugoslavia, 1919–1980: Linguistic Minorities from an Economic Perspective', in Horak, *Eastern European National Minorities*, p. 224.

177. Joseph B. Schectman, 'The Elimination of the German Minorities in Southeastern Europe', *Journal of Central European Affairs*, 6 (1946), pp. 161–62.

178. Hoćevar, 'National Minorities in Yugoslavia', p. 229.

179. Detlef Brandes, 'Die Deutschen in Russland und der Sowjetunion', in Bade, *Deutsche im Ausland*, p. 85.

180. Benjamin Pinkus, 'The Germans in the Soviet Union since 1945', in I. Fleischauer, B. Pinkus and E. Frankel (eds), *The Soviet Germans Past and Present* (London, 1986), pp. 103–53; Schieder, *The Expulsion of the German Population from the Territories East of the Oder-Neisse-Line*, p. 120; Brandes, 'Die Deutschen in Russland und der Sowjetunion', pp. 130–34

Chapter 3: Localised Minorities

1. These figures are from Lars-Anders Baer, 'The Sami: An Indigenous People in Their Own Land', in Birgitta Jahresog (ed.), *The Sami National Minority in Sweden* (Stockholm, 1982), p. 12. See also Mervyn Jones, *The Sami of Lapland* (London, 1982).

2. Victor Kiernan 'The British Isles: Celt and Saxon', in Mikuláš Teich and Roy Porter (eds), *The National Question in Europe in Historical Context* (Cambridge, 1993), p. 7.

3. Meic Stephens, *Linguistic Minorities in Western Europe* (Llandysul, 1976), p. 51.

4. 'Welsh', in Minority Rights Group, *World Directory of Minorities* (London, 1989), p. 102.

5. Outline histories of England and its relationship with Scotland, Wales and Ireland include Kiernan, 'British Isles'; Michael Hechter, *Internal Colonialism: The Celtic Fringe in British Development, 1546–1966* (London, 1975); Hugh Kearney, *The British Isles: A History of Four Nations* (Cambridge, 1989); and Keith Robbins, *Great Britain: Identities, Institutions and the Idea of Britishness* (London, 1998).

6. A good introduction to Russian history is Lionel Kochan and Richard Abraham, *The Making of Modern Russia* (2nd edn, Harmondsworth, 1983).

7. The total figures can be found in Richard Pipes, *The Formation of the Soviet Union: Communism and Nationalism, 1917–1923* (Cambridge, Massachsetts, 1970), pp. 300–1.

8. See Viktor Kozlov, *The Peoples of the Soviet Union* (London, 1988), p. 23.

9. Oscar I. Janowsky, *Nationalities and National Minorities* (New York, 1945), p. 74.

10. See Hugh Seton-Watson, *The Russian Empire, 1801–1917* (Oxford, 1967), pp. 267–74, 485–505, 663–76.

11. The above account of Stalinist persecution is based upon Robert Conquest,

Soviet Nationalities Policy in Practice (London, 1967); Robert Conquest, *The Nation Killers: The Soviet Deportation of Nationalities* (New York, 1970); Nikolai K. Deker and Andrei Lebed (eds), *Genocide in the USSR: Studies in Group Destruction* (New York, 1958); and Dina Rome Spechler, 'Russia and the Russians', in Zev Katz, Rosemarie Rogers and Frederic Harned (eds), *Handbook of Major Soviet Nationalities* (New York, 1975), pp. 9–20.

12. For figures see, Oleh R. Martovych, *National Problems in the USSR* (Edinburgh, 1953).

13. Bernard Comrie, *The Languages of the Soviet Union* (Cambridge, 1981), p. 1.

14. Barbara Anderson and Brian D. Silver, 'Some Factors in the Linguistic and Ethnic Russification of Soviet Nationalities: Is Everyone Becoming Russian?', in Lubomyr Hajda and Mark Beissinger (eds), *The Nationalities Question in Soviet Politics and Society* (Boulder, Colorado, 1990), p. 96.

15. See, for instance, Donna Bahry and Carol Nechemias, 'Half Full or Half Empty? The Debate over Soviet Regional Equality', in Rachel Denber (ed.), *The Soviet Nationality Reader: The Disintegration in Context* (Boulder, Colorado, 1992), pp. 287–304.

16. See contributions to Katz, Rogers and Harned, *Handbook of Major Soviet Nationalities*.

17. See, for instance, contributions to Graham Smith (ed.), *The Nationalities Question in the Post-Soviet States* (London, 1996).

18. G. Paul Holman, Jr, 'Russo-Ukrainian Relations: The Containment Legacy', in W. Raymond Duncan and G. Paul Holman (eds), *Ethnic Nationalism and Regional Conflict* (Boulder, Colorado, 1994), p. 77.

19. John S. Reshetar, 'Ukrainian Nationalism and the Orthodox Church', *American Slavic and East European Review*, 10 (1951), p. 39.

20. Walter Dushnyck, 'Discrimination and Abuse of Power in the USSR', in Willem A. Veenhoven et al. (eds), *Case Studies in Human Rights and Fundamental Freedoms: A World Survey* (The Hague, 1975), p. 468.

21. Two excellent sources, of completely different scales, on the Ukraine, are Roman Szporluk, 'The Ukraine and the Ukrainians', in Katz, Rogers and Harned, *Handbook of Major Soviet Nationalities*, pp. 21–48; and Paul Robert Magocsci, *A History of Ukraine* (Toronto, 1997).

22. An outline of Lithuanian history can be found in Frederic T. Harned, 'Lithuania and the Lithuanians', in Katz, Rogers and Harned, *Handbook of Major Soviet Nationalities*, pp. 120–23.

23. Ibid., pp. 119–20.

24. Vladis Gaidys, 'Russians in Lithuania', in Vladimir Shlapentokh, Munir Sendich and Emil Payin (eds), *The New Russian Diaspora: Russian Minorities in the Former Soviet Republics* (Armonk, New York, 1994); Saulius Girnius, 'Migration to and from Lithuania', *Report on the USSR*, 14 September 1990, p. 25.

25. Paul Kolstoe, *Russians in the Former Soviet Republics* (London, 1995), pp. 139–41.

26. The figure is from J. Dreifelds, 'Immigration and Ethnicity in Latvia', *Journal of Soviet Nationalities*, 1, p. 44. For an introduction to the history of Latvians

and Estonians see the essays by Frederic T. Harned and Rein Taagepera in Katz, Rogers and Harned, *Handbook of Major Soviet Nationalities.*

27. See Romuald Misiunas and Rein Taagepera, *The Baltic States: Years of Dependence* (London, 1993); and Anatol Lieven, *The Baltic Revolution: Estonia, Latvia, Lithuania and the Path to Independence* (London, 1994).

28. For an outline of Belorussian history see Jan Zaprudnik, *Belarus: At a Crossroad of History* (Boulder, Colarado, 1993); Steven L. Guthier, 'The Belorussians: National Identity and Assimilation, 1897–1970', *Soviet Studies*, 29 (1977), pp. 37–61, 270–83. See also Jakub Zejinis, 'Belarus in the 1920s: Ambiguities of National Formation', *Nationalities Papers*, 25 (1977), pp. 243–54; and David R. Marples, *Belarus: From Soviet Rule to Nuclear Catastrophe* (London, 1996).

29. Peter Hodges, 'The Georgians', in G. Ashworth (ed.), *World Minorities*, i (Sunbury, 1977), p. 68; Ronald Grigor Suny, 'The Emergence of Political Society in Georgia', in Suny (ed.), *Transcaucasia, Nationalism and Social Change* (Ann Arbor, Michigan, 1996), pp. 109–40; Suzanne Goldenberg, *Pride of Small Nations: The Caucasus and the Post-Soviet Disorder* (London, 1994), pp. 81–114.

30. See Stephen Fischer-Galati, 'Moldavia and the Moldavians', in Katz, Harned and Rogers, *Handbook of Major Soviet Nationalities*, pp. 415–33.

31. John Lowell Armstrong, 'Policy toward the Polish Minority in the Soviet Union', *Polish Review*, 35 (1990), pp. 51–65.

32. The West Frisians are covered by Stephens, *Linguistic Minorities.*

33. Douglas Johnson, 'The Making of the French Nation', in Teich and Porter, *The National Question in Europe*, pp. 40, 41.

34. Felipe Fernández-Armesto (ed.), *The Times Guide to the Peoples of Europe* (London, 1994), p. 41.

35. See, for example, M. McDonald, *'We Are Not Fench!' Language, Culture and Identity in Brittany* (London, 1989).

36. All French groups are covered in Stephens, *Linguistic Minorities in Western Europe*, pp. 295–402.

37. One of the best accounts of this period remains J. H. Elliot, *Imperial Spain, 1469–1716* (Harmondsorth, 1970).

38. Michael Keating, 'Spain: Peripheral Nationalism and State Response', in John McGarry and Brendan O'Leary (eds), *The Politics of Ethnic Conflict Regulation* (London, 1993), p. 210.

39. See the first chapter of Roger Collins, *The Basques* (Oxford, 1987).

40. The figure is from Marianne Heiberg, *The Making of the Basque Nation* (Cambridge, 1989), p. 74.

41. Ibid., pp. 76, 77.

42. John Sullivan, *ETA and Basque Nationalism: The Fight for Euskadi, 1890–1986* (London, 1988), p. 20.

43. See, for instance, Cyrus Ernesto Zirakzadeh, *A Rebellious People: Basques, Protests and Politics* (Reno and Las Vegas, Nevada, 1991).

44. See, for instance, Keating, 'Spain', pp. 212, 219.

45. For details on the above and other minority languages in Italy see three sources in

particular: Commission of the European Community, *Linguistic Minorities in Countries Belonging to the European Community* (Luxemburg, 1986), pp. 35–118; Stephens, *Linguistic Minorities in Western Europe*, pp. 479–552; Anna Laura Lepschy, Giulio Lepschy and Miriam Voghera, 'Linguistic Variety in Italy', in Carl Levy (ed.), *Italian Regionalism: History, Identity and Politics* (Oxford, 1996), pp. 69–80.

46. Fernández-Armesto, *The Peoples of Europe*, p. 31.

47. See Roger Portal, *The Slavs* (London, 1969), pp. 1–25; and Marija Gimbutas, *The Slavs* (London, 1971).

48. Gerald Stone, *The Smallest Slavonic Nation: The Sorbs of Lusatia* (London, 1972), p. 9, although on p. 5 he seems to contradict this view, stating that 'The Sorbs have occupied their present homeland since the beginning of recorded history', by which, however, he may mean the sixth and seventh centuries in the case of Lusatia.

49. See Stone, *Smallest Slavonic Nation*, passim. For the Nazi period see Todd Huebner, 'Ethnicity Denied: Nazi Policy towards the Lusatian Sorbs, 1933–1945', *German History*, 6 (1988), pp. 250–77. For the post-Unification period see Leoš Šatava, 'The Lusatian Sorbs in Eastern Germany', in Minority Rights Group and TWEEC, *Minorities in Central and Eastern Europe* (London, 1993), p. 33.

50. This phrase is used by František Kavka, *An Outline of Czechoslovak History* (Prague, 1960), p. 71.

51. Josef Kalvoda, 'National Minorities in Czechoslovakia, 1919–1980', in Stephan M. Horak (ed.), *Eastern European National Minorities, 1919–1980: A Handbook* (Littleton, Colorado, 1985), p. 117.

52. For the above see, for example: Kavka, *Outline of Czechoslovak History*; Vlastislav Häufler, *The Ethnographic Map of the Czech Lands* (Prague, 1973); and contributions to Jiří Musil (ed.), *The End of Czechoslovakia* (Budapest, 1995).

53. The history of the Yugoslav peoples can be traced in Barbara Jelavich, *History of the Balkans*, i, *Eighteenth and Nineteenth Centuries* (Cambridge, 1983).

54. George Schöpflin, 'The Rise and Fall of Yugoslavia', in McGarry and O'Leary, *Politics of Ethnic Conflict Regulation*, p. 175.

55. Raymond Pearson, *National Minorities in Eastern Europe* (London, 1983), p. 152.

56. Radoye L. Knejevitch, 'The Ethnical Structure of Voyvodina', *Yugoslav Oberver*, 2 (1956), p. 16.

57. Pearson, *National Minorities in Eastern Europe*, p. 157.

58. Fred Singleton, *Twentieth-Century Yugoslavia* (London, 1976), pp. 86, 88.

59. Countless books have appeared on the death of Yugoslavia. One of the very best is Christopher Bennet, *Yugoslavia's Bloody Collapse* (London, 1995). An excellent modern history pre-dating the war of the 1990s is Singleton, *Twentieth-Century Yugoslavia*.

60. See Max Engman, 'Finns and Swedes in Finland', in Sven Tägil (ed.), *Ethnicity and Nation Building in the Nordic World* (London, 1995), pp. 179–216.

61. Einar Niemi, 'The Finns in Northern Scandinavia and Minority Policy', in Tägil, *Ethnicity and Nation Building*, pp. 145–78.

62. Stephens, *Linguistic Minorities in Western Europe*, p. 692.

63. Bogdan C. Novak, *Trieste, 1941–1954: The Ethnic, Political and Ideological Struggle* (Chicago, 1970); Meic Stephens, 'The Slovenes of Trieste', in Georgina Ashworth (ed.), *World Minorities*, ii (Sunbury, 1978), p. 118.

64. Thomas M. Barker, 'The Croatian Minority of Burgenland', *Journal of Central European Affairs*, 19 (1959), pp. 32–56; Österreichische Rektorenkonferenz, *Bericht der Arbeitsgruppe Lage und Perspektiven der Volksgruppen in Österreich* (Vienna, 1969), pp. 68–71; Stephens, *Linguistic Minorities*, pp. 14–17.

65. Bojo Grafenauer, *Ethnic Conditions in Carinthia* (Ljubljana, 1946), p. 10.

66. Thomas M. Barker, *The Slovene Minority of Carinthia* (New York, 1984), p. 265.

67. *Hungarian Minority in Czechoslovakia/Slovakia* (Bratislava, 1993), p. 3.

68. Kalman Janics, *Czechoslovak Policy and the Hungarian Minority, 1945–1948* (New York, 1982), p. 66.

69. H. Renner, 'The National Minorities in Czechoslovakia after the Second World War', *Plural Societies*, 7 (1976), pp. 26–27.

70. Josef Kalvoda, 'National Minorities under Communism: The Case of Czechoslovakia', *Nationalities Papers*, 16 (1988), p. 4.

71. Renner, 'National Minorities in Czechoslovakia', p. 28.

72. Kalvoda, 'National Minorities in Czechoslovakia', p. 126.

73. Stephan M. Horak, 'Eastern European National Minorities', in Horak, *Eastern European National Minorities*, p. 3.

74. Pearson, *National Minorities in Eastern Europe*, p. 163.

75. Kenneth C. Farmer et al., 'National Minorities in Poland, 1919–1980', in Horak, *Eastern European National Minorities*, p. 48.

76. Ibid., p. 53.

77. Horak, 'Eastern European National Minorities', p. 3.

78. Farmer et al., 'National Minorities in Poland', p. 53.

79. See the essays by Alfred Bohman on 'Die Tschechen in Polen' and 'Die Slowaken in Polen', in Manfred Straka (ed.), *Handbuch der europäischen Volksgruppen* (Vienna, 1970), pp. 500–6.

80. Keith Hitchens, *Rumania, 1866–1947* (Oxford, 1994); Jelavich, *History of the Balkans*, i, pp. 98–112, 204–14, 264–98.

81. R. J. Crampton, *Eastern Europe in the Twentieth Century* (London, 1994), p. 107.

82. Pearson, *National Minorities in Eastern Europe*, p. 163.

83. Brigitte Mihok, *Ethnostrazifikation im Sozialismus aufgezeigt an den Beispielländern Ungarn und Rumänien* (Frankfurt, 1990), p. 62.

84. Elemér Illyés, *National Minorities in Romania: Change in Transylvania* (New York, 1982), p. 22.

85. Ibid., p. 23.

86. Leo Paul, 'The Stolen Revolution: Minorities in Romania after Ceaçescu', in John O'Loughlin and Hermann van der Wusten (eds), *The New Political Geography of Eastern Europe* (London, 1993), p. 146.

87. Stephen Fischer-Galati, 'National Minorities in Romania, 1919–1980', in Horak, *Eastern European National Minorities*, p. 198.

88. Mihok, *Ethnostrazifikation im Sozialismus*, p. 101.

89. The Greek word for the period of Ottoman rule which literally translates as Turkocracy.

90. The best introduction of the expansion of the Greek state is Richard Clogg, *A Concise History of Modern Greece* (Cambridge, 1992).

91. A. Angelopoulos, 'Population Distribution of Greece Today According to Language, National Consciousness and Religion', *Balkan Studies*, 20 (1979), p. 131.

92. Hugh Poulton, *The Balkans: Minorities and States in Conflict* (2nd edn, London, 1993), p. 36. The best account of Greeks in Albania is Christodoulos Stavrou, *Die griechische Minderheit in Albanien* (Frankfurt, 1993).

93. Evangelos Kofos, 'The Macedonian Question: The Politics of Mutation', *Balkan Studies*, 27 (1986), p. 159.

94. See Hugh Poulton, *Who Are the Macedonians?* (London, 1995).

95. For details of the Greek and other small minorities in Bulgaria not mentioned above see two articles by John Georgeoff: 'National Minorities in Bulgaria, 1919–1980', in Horak, *Eastern European National Minorities*, pp. 274–85; and 'Ethnic Minorities in the People's Republic of Bulgaria', in D. Klein and Milan J. Reban (eds), *The Politics of Ethnicity in Eastern Europe* (Boulder, Colorado, 1991), pp. 49–84. For the evolution of Bulgaria see R. J. Crampton, *A Short History of Modern Bulgaria* (Cambridge, 1987).

96. The history of ethnic politics in Belgium can be traced in the following: R. E. Irving, *The Flemings and Walloons of Belgium* (London, 1980); Maureen Covell, 'Belgium: The Variability of Ethnic Relations', in McGarry and O'Leary, *Politics of Ethnic Conflict Regulation*, pp. 275–95; Liesbert Hooghe, *A Leap in the Dark: Nationalist Conflict and Federal Reform in Belgium* (Ithaca, New York, 1991); and John Fitzmaurice, *The Politics of Belgium: A Unique Federalism* (London, 1996).

97. The above account of Switzerland is based upon the following: Jonathan Steinberg, *Why Switzerland?* (2nd edn, Cambridge, 1996); K. B. Mayer, *The Population of Switzerland* (New York, 1952); and Christopher Hughes, *Switzerland* (London, 1975).

98. T. J. Winnifrith, *The Vlachs: The History of a Balkan People* (London, 1987), p. 1.

99. Angelopoulos, 'Population Distribution of Greece Today', p. 131.

100. J. Trifunowski, 'Die Aroumanen in Mazedonien', *Balcanica*, 2 (1971), p. 341.

101. Poulton, *The Balkans*, p. 96.

102. Türkkaya Ataöv, 'The Vlach Minority in Greece and Bulgaria', unpublished paper held by Amnesty International, International Secretariat, London, n.d.

103. Constantin Papanace and Aldo Dami, 'Die aroumanische Volksgruppe in den Balkanländern', in Straka, *Handbuch der europäischen Volksgruppen*, p. 247.

104. Miranda Vickers and James Pettifer, *Albania: From Anarchy to a Balkan Identity* (London, 1997), pp. 200–2.

105. See John A. Petropoulos, 'The Compulsory Exchange of Populations: Greek-Turkish Peacemaking, 1922–1930', *Byzantine and Modern Greek Studies*, 2 (1976), pp. 135–60; Clogg, *Concise History of Modern Greece*, pp. 93–108.

106. The recent history of the two islands is comprehensively dealt with by Alexis

Alexandris, 'Imbros and Tenedos: A Study of Turkish Attitudes toward Two Ethnic Greek Island Communities since 1923', *Journal of the Hellenic Diaspora*, 7 (1980), pp. 5–31.

107. Alexis Alexandris, *The Greek Minority of Istanbul and Greek-Turkish Relations* (Athens, 1983); Tozun Bahcheli, *Greek-Turkish Relations since 1955* (Boulder, Colorado, 1990), pp. 169–76.

108. For an outstanding outline of Armenian history see Christopher J. Walker, *Armenia: The Survival of a Nation* (2nd edn, London, 1990). The genocide is one of the central themes of Armenia historiography, especially in view of the Turkish state's denial that it ever happened. Two of the most important books on the subject are Vahakn Dadrian, *The History of the Armenian Genocide* (Oxford, 1995); and Richard G. Hovanissian (ed.), *The Armenian Genocide* (London, 1992).

109. This figure is from: Yvo J. D. Peters, 'The Rights of Minorities in Present-Day Turkey', *Europa Ethnica*, 44 (1987), p. 131.

110. David McDowall, *The Kurds* (London, 1989), p. 7.

111. See, for example Kendal, 'Kurdistan in Turkey', in G. Chaliand (ed.), *A People Without a Country: The Kurds and Kurdistan* (London, 1980); David McDowall, *A Modern History of the Kurds* (London, 1996); Jonathan Rugman and Roger Hutchings, *Atatürk's Children: Turkey and the Kurds* (London, 1996); Kemal Kirişci and Gareth M. Winrow, *The Kurdish Question in Turkey: An Example of Trans-State Ethnic Conflict* (London, 1997).

Chapter 4: Post-War Arrivals

1. Michael Marrus, *The Unwanted: European Refugees in the Twentieth Century* (Oxford, 1985), p. 297.

2. Eugene M. Kulischer, *Europe on the Move: War and Population Changes, 1917–1947* (New York, 1948), p. 305.

3. For the work of these bodies see two works by Louise W. Holborn: *Refugees: A Problem of Our Times*, i (Metuchen, New Jersey, 1975); and *The International Refugee Organization: A Specialized Agency of the United Nations* (London, 1956).

4. Ulrich Herbert, *A History of Foreign Labour in Germany, 1880–1980: Seasonal Workers/Forced Labourers/Guest Workers* (Ann Arbor, Michigan, 1990), pp. 127–92; Edward L. Homze, *Foreign Labour in Nazi Germany* (Princeton, 1967); Hans Pfahlmann, *Fremdarbeiter und Kriegsgefangene in der deutschen Kriegswirtschaft, 1939–1945* (Darmstadt, 1968); Eva Seeber, *Zwangsarbeiter in der faschistischen Kriegswirtschaft* (Berlin, 1964).

5. Wolfgang Jacobmeyer, 'Jüdische Überlebende als "Displaced Persons": Untersuchungen zur Besatzungspolitik in den deutschen Westzonen und zur Zuwanderung osteuropäischer Juden, 1945–1947', *Geschichte und Gesellschaft*, 9 (1983), p. 421.

6. Koppel S. Pinson, 'Jewish Life in Liberated Germany', *Jewish Social Studies*, 9 (1947), p. 103.

7. For brief details of the scale and effects of the bombing see, Martin Kitchen, *Nazi Germany at War* (London, 1995), pp. 87–98. The aim of these raids was to kill as many German civilians as possible, indicating that the Second World War was fought in the name of nationalism on *all* sides. If this was not the case the Allies could have used a few of the 1800 bombs which fell on Dresden on Ash Wednesday of 1945 to destroy the death camps in Poland.

8. Quoted in Alfred-Maurice de Zayas, *The German Expellees: Victims in War and Peace* (London, 1993), p. 83.

9. Siegfried Bethlehem, *Heimatvertreibung, DDR-Flucht, Gastarbeiterwanderung: Wanderungsströme und Wanderungspolitik in der Bundesrepublik Deutschland* (Stuttgart, 1982), p. 22.

10. Hartmut Berghoff, 'Population Change and its Repercussions on the Social History of the Federal Republic', in Klaus Larres and Panikos Panayi (eds), *The Federal Republic of Germany since 1949: Politics, Society and Economics before and after Unification* (London, 1996), p. 40.

11. Klaus J. Bade, 'Einführung: Wege in die Bundesrepublik', in Bade (ed.), *Neue Heimat im Westen: Vertriebene, Flüchtlinge, Aussiedler* (Münster, 1990), p. 5.

12. Berghoff, 'Population Change', p. 40.

13. Hansåke Persson, 'German Refugees after 1945: A British Dilemma', in Anna C. Bramwell (ed.), *Refugees in the Age of Total War* (London, 1988), p. 182.

14. G. Biffl, 'Structural Shifts in the Employment of Foreign Workers in Austria', *International Migration*, 23 (1985), p. 45; Tony Radspieler, *The Ethnic German Refugee in Austria, 1945 to 1954* (The Hague, 1955).

15. Klaus J. Bade, *Vom Auswanderungsland zum Einwanderungsland? Deutschland, 1880–1980* (Berlin, 1983), p. 66.

16. Johannes Dieter Steinert, 'Drehscheibe Westdeutschland: Wanderungspolitik im Nachkriegsjahrzehnt', in Klaus J. Bade (ed.), *Deutsche im Ausland: Fremde in Deutschland* (Munich, 1992), p. 386.

17. James R. McDonald, 'Labour Immigration into France, 1946–1965', *Annals of the Association of American Geographers*, 59 (1969), p. 119.

18. Johannes Dieter Steinert, *Migration und Politik: Westdeutschland – Europa – Übersee* (Osnabrück, 1995), p. 45.

19. 'German Free Workers in France', *International Labour Review*, 58 (1948), p. 230.

20. The best essay on immediate post-war German immigration to Britain is Johannes Dieter Steinert, 'British Recruitment of German Labour', in Panikos Panayi (ed.), *Germans in Britain since 1500* (London, 1996), pp. 171–86.

21. M. R. Elliot, *Pawns of Yalta: Soviet Refugees and America's Role in Their Repatriation* (Chicago, 1982), p. 134.

22. These phrases were used in polls conducted amongst Baltic DPs and are quoted in Kim Saloman, *Refugees in the Cold War: Toward a New International Refugee Regime in the Early Post-War Era* (Lund, 1991), p. 146.

23. Nicholas Bethell, *The Last Secret: Forcible Repatriation to Russia* (London, 1974), p. 92.

24. The two books on this subject are J. A. Tannahill, *European Volunteer Workers*

in Britain (Manchester, 1958); and Diana Kay and Robert Miles, *Refugees or Migrant Workers? European Volunteer Workers in Britain, 1946–1951* (London, 1992).

25. Creslaw's testimony comes from Ethnic Communities Oral History Project, *Passport to Exile: The Polish Way to London* (London, 1988), p. 21.

26. J. B. Schechtman, *The Refugee in the World: Displacement and Integration* (London, 1963), p. 68.

27. See British Refugee Council, London, QIT 59. 2, United Nations pamphlet entitled 'The Refugee Problem in Italy'.

28. See Holborn, *International Refugee Organization*, pp. 180–81.

29. British Refugee Council, London, QH 46, Stergios Babanasis, 'Returning Political Refugees and their Employment Needs and Possibilities', unpublished paper, May 1984; Jacques Vernant, *The Refugee in the Post-War World* (London, 1953), p. 225.

30. Joseph B. Schechtman, 'Compulsory Transfer of the Turkish Minority from Bulgaria', *Journal of Central European Affairs*, 12 (1952), pp. 157–58.

31. Ibid., p. 158.

32. Huey Louis Kostanick, *The Turkish Resettlement of Bulgarian Turks, 1950–1953* (Berkeley and Los Angeles, 1957), pp. 106–8.

33. Holborn, *Refugees*, i, pp. 391–418; UNHCR, *A Mandate to Protect and Assist Refugees: Twenty Years of Service in the Cause of Refugees* (Geneva, 1971), pp. 67–72; R. J. Crampton, *Eastern Europe in the Twentieth Century* (London, 1994), pp. 288–393; Marrus, *Unwanted*, pp. 359–61.

34. See, for instance, Bade, *Neue Heimat im Westen*; and Radspieler, *Ethnic German Refugee in Austria*.

35. See Sheila Patterson, 'The Poles: An Exile Community in Britain', in James L Watson (ed.), *Between Two Cultures: Migrants and Minorities in Britain* (Oxford, 1977), pp. 214–41; Lothar Kettenacker, 'The Germans after 1945', in Panayi, *Germans in Britain since 1500*, pp. 187–208.

36. Stephen Castles, *Here for Good: Western Europe's New Ethnic Minorities* (London, 1987), pp. 20–21.

37. Derek H. Aldcroft, *The European Economy, 1914–1980* (London, 1980), p. 161.

38. Eric Hobsbawm, *Industry and Empire* (Harmondsworth, 1969), pp. 208, 262–63.

39. Panikos Panayi, 'Race in the Federal Republic of Germany: Immigration, Ethnicity and Racism since the Second World War', in Larres and Panayi, *Federal Republic of Germany*, pp. 197–98.

40. John Salt, 'International Labour Migration: The Geographical Pattern of Demand', in John Salt and Hugh Clough (eds), *Migration in Post-War Europe* (London, 1976), p. 82.

41. See, for instance, Patrick Ireland, *The Policy Challenge of Ethnic Diversity: Immigrant Policies in France and Switzerland* (London, 1994), pp. 34–36.

42. See Philip L. Martin, *The Unfinished Story: Turkish Labour Migration to Western Europe* (Geneva, 1991); Ahmet Akgündüz, 'Labour Migration from Turkey to Western Europe, 1960–1974: An Analytical Review', *Capital and Class*, 51 (1993),

pp. 153–93; Nermin Abadan-Unat (ed.), *Turkish Workers in Europe, 1960–1975: A Socio-Economic Reappraisal* (Leiden, 1976).

43. Ivo Baučić, *The Effects of Emigration from Yugoslavia and the Problems of Returning Emigrant Workers* (The Hague, 1972), pp. 1–16.

44. Nicholas Hopkinson, *Migration into Western Europe* (London, 1992), p. 13.

45. Stephen Castles and Godula Kosack, *Immigrant Workers and Class Structure in Western Europe* (London, 1973), pp. 27–28.

46. R. King, 'Italian Migration to Great Britain', *Geography*, 62 (1977), p. 178; Terri Colpi, *The Italian Factor: The Italian Community in Great Britain* (Edinburgh, 1991), pp. 134–35.

47. Judy Chance, 'The Irish in London: An Exploration of Ethnic Boundary Maintenance', in Peter Jackson (ed.), *Essays in Social Geography* (London, 1987), pp. 145–46; John Solomos, *Race and Racism in Britain* (2nd edn, London, 1993), p. 54; Colin Holmes, *John Bull's Island: Immigration and British Society, 1871–1971* (London, 1988), pp. 216–17.

48. McDonald, 'Labour Immigration in France, p. 119.

49. Alec G. Hargreaves, *Immigration, 'Race' and Ethnicity in Contemporary France* (London, 1995), p. 16.

50. Lutz Hoffmann, *Die unvollendete Republik: Zwischen Einwanderungsland und deutschem Nationalstaat* (2nd edn, Cologne, 1992), pp. 28–91.

51. W. R. Böhning, *The Migration of Workers in the United Kingdom and the European Community* (London, 1972), pp. 41–42.

52. Castles, *Here for Good*, pp. 66–69; K. B. Mayer, 'Post-War Migration to Switzerland', *International Migration*, 3 (1968), pp. 122–33; Anne Sue Matasar, 'Labour Transfers in Western Europe: The Problem of Italian Migrant Workers in Switzerland' (unpublished Ph.D thesis, Columbia University, New York, 1968), pp. 3, 14, 54–55, 61.

53. Jonas Widgren, 'Sweden', in R. E. Krane (ed.), *International Labour Migration in Europe* (New York, 1979), pp. 19–25; British Refugee Council, London, QSW 44. 2, Ministry of Labour, 'Swedish Immigration Policy'(1984) p. 7; Harald Runblom, 'Immigration to Scandinavia after World War II', in Sven Tägil (ed.), *Ethnicity and Nation Building in the Nordic World* (London, 1995), pp. 283–303.

54. For British immigration in the immediate post-war period see Kathleen Paul, *Whitewashing Britain: Race and Citizenship in the Postwar Era* (Ithaca, New York, 1997); and Ian R. G. Spencer, *British Immigration Policy: The Making of Multi-Racial Britain* (London, 1997).

55. Pamela Constantinides, 'The Greek Cypriots: Factors in the Maintenance of Ethnic Identity', in Watson, *Between Two Cultures*, p. 271.

56. I am essentially describing the feelings of my mother here.

57. Holmes, *John Bull's Island*, p. 226.

58. *Black Birmingham* (Birmingham, 1987), p. 14.

59. Edward Pilkington, *Beyond the Mother Country: West Indians and the Notting Hill White Riots* (London, 1988), looks at both the immigration process and the disappointment faced by the new arrivals.

60. Holmes, *John Bull's Island*, p. 226.
61. Ibid., pp. 223–25; Muhamad Anwar, *The Myth of Return: Pakistanis in Britain* (London, 1979); Badr Dahya, 'Pakistanis in Britain: Transients or Settlers', *Race*, 14 (1972), pp. 241–77.
62. David Killingray (ed.), *Africans in Britain* (London, 1993).
63. David Parker, 'Chinese People in Britain', in Gregor Benton and Frank N Pieke (eds), *The Chinese in Europe* (London, 1998), pp. 74–78.
64. See Neil MacMaster, *Colonial Migrants and Racism: Algerians in France, 1900–62* (London, 1997).
65. Hargeaves, *Immigration, 'Race' and Ethnicity in Contemporary France*, p. 14.
66. McDonald, 'Labour Immigration into France', p. 126.
67. Stephanie A. Condon and Philip E. Ogden, 'Emigration from the French Caribbean: The Origins of an Organized Migration', *International Journal of Urban and Regional Research*, 15 (1991), pp. 505–23; Ceri Peach, *The Caribbean in Europe: Contrasting Patterns of Migration and Settlement in Britain, France and the Netherlands* (Coventry, 1991), pp. 14–15.
68. Heinrich M. Dreyer, 'Immigration of Foreign Workers into the Federal Republic of Germany', *International Labour Review*, 84 (1961), p. 1.
69. Böhning, *Migration of Workers*, p. 33.
70. Berghoff, 'Population Change', p. 52; Castles, *Here for Good*, p. 72; Heather Booth, *The Migration Process in Britain and West Germany* (Aldershot, 1992), p. 110; Herbert, *History of Foreign Labour in Germany*, p. 224.
71. G. E. Völker, 'Labour Migration: Aid to the West German Economy?', in Ronald E Krane (ed.), *Mobility Across Cultural Boundaries* (Leiden, 1975), pp. 12–13, 19; Bethlehem, *Heimatvertreibung*, p. 125.
72. Hans-Joachim Hoffmann-Nowotny, 'European Migration after World War II', in W. H. McNeill and R. S. Adams (eds), *Human Migration: Patterns and Policies* (Bloomington, Indiana, 1978), pp. 90–91.
73. Castles, *Here for Good*, p. 60.
74. For West Indian migration to the Netherlands see Peach, *The Caribbean in Europe*, pp. 15, 20; Hans van Amersfoort, 'West Indian Migration to the Netherlands', in H. van Honte and W. Melgert (eds), *Foreigners in Our Community* (Amsterdam, 1972), pp. 50–65; Colin Brock, 'The West Indian Dimension in Western Europe', in Brock (ed.), *The Caribbean in Europe: Aspects of West Indian Experiences in Britain, France and the Netherlands* (London, 1986), pp. 8–11; and the contributions by Malcolm Cross and Hans Entzinger, Gert J. Oostindie and Theo Reubsaet to Cross and Entzinger (eds), *Lost Illusions: Caribbean Minorities in Britain and the Netherlands* (London, 1988).
75. See Biffl, 'Structural Shifts in the Employment of Foreign Workers in Austria', pp. 45–71; and Rainer Bauboeck and H. Wimmer, 'Social Partnership and Foreigner Policy: On Special Features of Austria's Guest-Worker System', *European Journal of Political Research*, 116 (1988), pp. 659–80.
76. Castles, *Here for Good*, pp. 62–65; Karlin Goppers, *Migration and Economy: Yugoslav-Swedish Relations* (Stockholm, 1983), pp. 32–33; Sahlin Alpay and

Halil Saviaslan, *Effects of Immigration: The Effects of Immigration on the Town of Kulu in Central Turkey of Emigration to Sweden* (Stockholm, 1984), pp. 1, 11, 37–42.

77. Laila Kvisler, 'Immigrants in Norway', in G. Ashworth (ed.), *World Minorities*, ii (Sunbury, 1978), pp. 54–55; Khalid Salimi, 'Norway's National Racism', *Race and Class*, 32 (1991), pp. 111–12; Ragnar Naess, 'Refugees and National Policies: The Norwegian Case', in Daniéle Joly and Robin Cohen (eds), *Reluctant Hosts: Europe and its Refugees* (Aldershot, 1989), p. 68.

78. Quoted in Solomos, *Race and Racism in Contemporary Britain* p. 67.

79. Panikos Panayi, 'Refugees in Twentieth-Century Britain: A Brief History', in Vaughan Robinson (ed.), *The International Refugee Crisis: British and Canadian Responses* (London, 1993), p. 108.

80. Berghoff, 'Population Change', pp. 59–67.

81. Quoted in Rudolf Spiegel, 'Mitburger: Vorurteile und kulturelle Unterschiede als Hemmnise der Integration', in Winifried Schlaffke and Rudiger von Voss (eds), *Vom Gastarbeiter zum Mitarbeiter: Ursachen, Folgen und Konsequensen der Ausländerbeschäftigung in Deutschland* (Cologne, 1982), p. 226.

82. Hoffmann-Nowotny, 'Switzerland', pp. 53–61; Lucio Boscardin, *Die italienische Einwanderung in die Schweiz mit besonderer Berücksichtigung der Jahre 1946–1959* (Basel, 1962), pp. 30–41, 56–57; Ireland, *Policy Challenge of Ethnic Diversity*, pp. 153, 157, 166.

83. Castles, *Here for Good*, pp. 47–48.

84. Bouscaren, *International Migrations*, pp. 87–88; Biffl, 'Structural Shifts in the Employment of Foreign Workers in Austria', pp. 45–55; Bauboeck and Wimmer, 'Social Partnership and "Foreigners Policy"', pp. 659–63.

85. See Dirk Jasper, 'Ausländerbeschäftigung in der DDR', in Marianne Krüger-Portratz (ed.) *Anderssein gab es nicht: Ausländer und Minderheiten in der DDR* (Münster, 1991), pp. 151–64; A. W. Stack and S. Hussain, *Ausländer in der DDR: Ein Ruckblick* (Berlin, 1991), pp. 4–15.

86. Ellie Vasta, 'Rights and Racism in a New Country of Immigration: The Italian Case', in John Wrench and John Solomos (eds), *Racism and Migration in Western Europe* (Oxford, 1993), p. 83; Böhning, *Migration of Workers*, p. 39; *Social Europe*, Supplement 1/91, *Immigration of Citizens from Third Countries to Southern Member States of the European Community* (Luxembourg, 1991), p. 54.

87. Giovanna Campani, 'Immigration and Racism in Southern Europe: The Italian Case', *Ethnic and Racial Studies*, 16 (1993), pp. 512–14; British Refugee Council, London, QIT 44. 2, Simpson Snowden, 'Asylum Seekers and Illegal Labour in Southern Italy and Sicily', 1992.

88. Hopkinson, *Migration into Western Europe*, p. 33.

89. *The Times*, 20 March 1997.

90. *Trends in International Migration* (Paris, 1992), pp. 76–77; Maria José Santa Cruz Robles, 'Refugees from South-East Asia in Spain: The Challenge of Hope', in Joly and Cohen, *Reluctant Hosts*, pp. 54–66; *Social Europe*, Supplement 1/91, *Immigration of Citizens from Third Countries*, pp. 67, 57–59.

91. Maria Beatriz Rocha Trindade, 'Portugal', in Krane, *International Labour Migration*, pp. 164–71.

92. Martin Eaton, 'Foreign Residents and Illegal Immigrants: *Os Negros em Portugal*', *Ethnic and Racial Studies*, 16 (1993), pp. 536–48.

93. Ira Emke-Poulopoulos, 'The Causes of Entry of Immigrants and Refugees into Greece', *Migration*, 16 (1992), pp. 55–84; *Trends in International Migration*, pp. 64–66; *Social Europe*, Supplement 1/91, *Immigration of Citizens from Third Countries*, p. 61; Sotiris Soulis, 'Illegal Immigration to Greece', in OECD (ed.), *The Future of Migration* (Paris, 1987), pp. 315–19; British Refugee Council, London, QH 46, Stergios Babanasis, 'Returning Political Refugees and Emigrants and their Employment Needs and Possibilities', May 1984; Krystyna Romanszyn, 'The Invisible Community: Undocumented Polish Workers in Athens', *New Community*, 22 (1996), pp. 321–33.

94. For more details on the 1981 Act, see Satvinder S. Suss, *Immigration, Nationality and Citizenship* (London, 1993), pp. 53–55.

95. Panayi, 'Refugees in Twentieth-Century Britain', p. 107.

96. *Prisoners Without a Voice: Asylum-Seekers Detained in the United Kingdom* (London, 1994), p. 42.

97. These figures are from two sources, which contradict each other: Hopkinson, *Migration into Western Europe*, p. 32; and Hargreaves, *Immigration, 'Race' and Ethnicity in Contemporary France*, p. 22.

98. Jonas Widegren, *Report to OECD (SOPEMI) on Immigration to Sweden in 1978 and the First Half of 1979* (Stockholm, 1979), p. 2.

99. *Trends in International Migration*, pp. 77–78.

100. Aleksandra Ålund, 'The Thorny Road to Europe: Swedish Immigrant Policy in Transition', in Wrench and Solomos, *Racism and Migration in Western Europe*, pp. 101–2.

101. Naess, 'Refugees and National Policies', p. 68.

102. See Zara Kamalkamia, *Iranian Immigrants and Refugees in Norway* (Bergen, 1988); *Trends in International Migration*, pp. 72–73; British Refugee Council, London, QNO44. 253, 'Country Report Norway to the ECRE Meeting in Geneva on 2–3 October 1994'.

103. Eszter Körmendi, *Refugees in Denmark* (Copenhagen, 1987), p. 6; British Refugee Council, London, QD 44. 2523, 'Denmark: ECRE Biannual Country Report First Half 1994'.

104. Runblom, 'Immigration to Scandinavia', p. 285.

105. British Refugee Council, London, QF 44. 2523, 'Finland: ECRE Report for the Biannual Meeting Geneva, 1–2 October 1994'.

106. British Refugee Council, 'Closing Doors: The European Response to Refugees from the Third World, Open Space, BBC2, October 1986'.

107. This paragraph is based upon Stephen Castles and Mark J. Miller, *The Age of Migration: International Population Movements in the Modern World* (London, 1993), p. 84; Danièle Joly, *Refugees: Asylum in Europe?* (London, 1992), pp. 24, 28; Barbara Marshall, 'Migration into Germany: Asylum Seekers and Ethnic

Germans', *German Politics*, 1 (1992), p. 125; Vaughan Robinson, 'The Nature of the Crisis and the Academic Response', in Robinson, *International Refugee Crisis*, pp. 3–6.

108. George Schöpflin and Hugh Poulton, *Rumania's Ethnic Hungarians* (London, 1990), pp. 17–19; Rudolf Joó, *The Hungarian Minority Situation in Ceaçescu's Rumania* (New York, 1994), pp. 101–8.

109. Darina Vasileva, 'Bulgarian Turkish Migration and Return', *International Migration Review*, 26 (1992), pp. 342–52; Erhard Franz, 'The Exodus of Turks from Bulgaria', *Asian and African Studies*, 25 (1991), pp. 91–94.

110. Hopkinson, *Migration into Western Europe*, p. 16.

111. Solon Ardittis, 'East-West Migration: An Overview of Trends and Issues', in Ardittis (ed.), *The Politics of East-West Migration* (London, 1994), pp. 12–13.

112. *Welt am Sonntag*, 16 August 1992.

113. *Stern*, 7 October 1993.

114. British Refugee Council, London, R20. 5, Gil Loescher, 'Forced Migration within and from the Former USSR: The Policy Challenges Ahead', unpublished typescript, pp. 1–2; United Nations High Commission for Refugees, *The State of the World's Refugees* (Oxford, 1995), p. 25; Paul Kolstoe, *Russians in the Former Soviet Republics* (London, 1995), pp. 290–99.

115. United Nations High Commission for Refugees, *The State of the World's Refugees*, p. 24.

116. United Nations High Commission for Refugees, *The State of the World's Refugees, 1997–98* (Oxford, 1997), p. 200.

117. *Observer*, 15 August 1992.

118. United Nations High Commission for Refugees, *The State of the World's Refugees*, p. 12.

119. Vladimir Grecic, 'Former Yugoslavia', in Ardittis, *Politics of East-West Migration*, p. 131.

120. Roy Gutman, *A Witness to Genocide: The First Inside Account of the Horrors of 'Ethnic Cleansing' in Bosnia* (Shaftesbury, 1993), p. 107.

121. *Financial Times*, 21–22 November 1992.

122. Zdenko Lešić (ed.), *Children of Atlantis: Voices from the Former Yugoslavia* (Budapest, 1995), p. 67.

123. These figures are from Grecic, 'Former Yugoslavia', p. 127.

124. *Observer*, 16 August 1992.

125. *World Refugee Survey 1991* (Washington, DC, 1991), p. 73.

126. R. Bauboeck, 'Austria', in Ardittis, *Politics of East-West Migration*, p. 158.

127. Cornelia Schmalz-Jacobsen, Holger Hinte and Georgios Tsapanos, *Einwanderung und Dann: Perspektiven einer Neuen Ausländerpolitik* (Munich, 1993), p. 314.

128. *Guardian*, 1 June 1993.

129. See Arnold M. Rose, *Migrants in Europe: Problems of Acceptance and Adjustment* (Minneapolis, 1969), pp. 45–46; Böhning, *Migration of Workers*, pp. 10–20.

130. Paul Kennedy, *Preparing for the Twenty-First Century* (London, 1994), p. 44.

131. Eric Hobsbawm, *Age of Extremes: The Short Twentieth Century, 1914–1991*

(London, 1994), p. 361. Another reason why migration will continue, according to Saskia Sassen, lies in the increasing globalisation taking place in the world economy and the development of transnational organisations. See her essay entitled 'The *De Facto* Transnationalizing of Immigration Policy', in Christian Joppke (ed.), *Challenge to the Nation-State: Immigration in Western Europe and the United States* (Oxford, 1998), pp. 49–85.

Bibliography

The following list of books represents the most important used in this study and does not aim to be a complete source of information on the history of European minorities, which would take up a whole volume on its own. Many of the books were used in more than one section.

Chapter 1: Minorities, States and Nationalism

Alter, Peter, *Nationalism* (2nd edn, London, 1994).

Anderson, Benedict, *Imagined Communities: Reflections on the Origin and Spread of Nationalism* (London, 1991).

Breuilly, John, *Nationalism and the State* (Manchester, 1982).

Chaliand, Gérard (ed.), *Minority Peoples in the Age of Nation States* (London, 1989).

Chaliand, Gérard, and Rageau, Jean-Pierre, *The Penguin Atlas of Diasporas* (London, 1995).

Claude, I. L., *National Minorities: An International Problem* (2nd edn, Cambridge, Massachusetts, 1969).

Connor, Walker, 'A Nation is a Nation, is a State, is an Ethnic Group is a ...', *Ethnic and Racial Studies*, 1 (1978).

Connor, Walker, *The National Question in Marxist-Leninist Theory and Strategy* (Princeton, 1984).

Gellner, Ernest, *Nations and Nationalism* (Oxford, 1983).

Hastings, Adrian, *The Construction of Nationhood: Ethnicity, Religion and Nationalism* (Cambridge, 1997).

Hobsbawm, Eric, 'Mass Producing Traditions: Europe, 1870–1914', in Eric Hobsbawm and Terence Ranger (eds), *The Invention of Tradition* (Cambridge, 1983).

Hobsbawm, Eric, *Nations and Nationalism since 1780: Programme, Myth, Reality* (2nd edn, Cambridge, 1992).

Kellas, James G., *The Politics of Nationalism and Ethnicity* (Basingstoke, 1991).

Smith, Anthony D., *The Ethnic Origins of Nations* (Oxford, 1983).

Stalin, Joseph, *Marxism and the National and Colonial Question* (London, 1936).

Chapter 2: Dispersed Minorities

a) Jews

Alderman, Geoffrey, *Modern British Jewry* (Oxford, 1992).

Banas, Josef, *The Scapegoats: The Exodus of the Remnants of Polish Jewry* (London, 1979).

Braham, Randolph L., *The Politics of Genocide: The Holocaust in Hungary*, i (New York, 1981).

Dawidowicz, Lucy S., *The War against the Jews, 1933–45* (Harmondsworth, 1987).

Dobroszycki, L., 'Restoring Jewish Life in Post-War Poland', *Soviet Jewish Affairs*, 3 (1973).

Freidenreich, Harriet Pass, *The Jews of Yugoslavia: A Quest for Community* (Philadelphia, 1979).

Green, Nancy L., *The Pletzl of Paris: Jewish Immigrant Workers in the Belle Epoque* (London, 1986).

Haim, Avni, *Spain, the Jews and Franco* (Philadelphia, 1982).

Heller, Celia S., *On the Edge of Destruction: Jews of Poland between the Two World Wars* (Detroit, 1994).

Holmes, Colin, *Antisemitism in British Society, 1876–1939* (London, 1979).

Hymans, Paul, 'The Jewish Community in Medieval England, 1066–1290', *Journal of Jewish Studies*, 25 (1974).

Israel, Gerard, *The Jews in Russia* (London, 1975).

Katz, David S., *The Jews in the History of England* (Oxford, 1994).

Keller, Werner, *Diaspora: The Post-Biblical History of the Jews* (London, 1971).

Klier, John Doyle, *Imperial Russia's Jewish Question* (Cambridge, 1995).

Kochan, Lionel J. (ed.), *The Jews in Soviet Russia since 1917* (Oxford, 1978).

Löwe, Henry-Dietrich, *The Tsars and the Jews: Reform, Reaction and Antisemitism in Imperial Russia, 1772–1917* (Chur, 1992).

Mazower, Mark, *Inside Hitler's Greece: The Experience of Occupation, 1941–44* (London, 1993).

Parkes, James, *A History of the Jewish People* (Harmondsworth, 1964).

Roth, Cecil, *A Short History of the Jewish People* (2nd edn, London, 1969).

Rubinstein, W. D., *A History of the Jews in the English-Speaking World: Great Britain* (London, 1996).

Sachar, Abram Leon, *A History of the Jews* (5th edn, New York, 1967).

Shaw, Stanford J., *The Jews of the Ottoman Empire and the Turkish Republic* (London, 1991).

Sibelman, Simon P., 'Le Renouvellement Juif: French Jewry on the Eve of the Centenary of the *Affaire Dreyfus*', *French Cultural Studies*, 3 (1992).

Stein, Richard A., 'Antisemitism in the Netherlands – Past and Present', *Patterns of Prejudice*, 19 (1985).

Steinberg, Jonathan, *All or Nothing: The Axis and the Holocaust, 1941–43* (London, 1990).

Szaynok, Bozena, 'The Pogrom of the Jews in Kielce, July 4, 1946', *Yad Vashem Studies*, 22 (1992).

Wasserstein, Bernard, *Vanishing Diaspora: The Jews in Europe since 1945* (London, 1996).

Webber, Jonathan (ed.), *Jewish Identities in the New Europe* (London, 1994).

Weinryb, Bernard D., *The Jews of Poland: A Social and Economic History of the Jews of Poland from 1100 to 1800* (Philadelphia, 1976).

Wertheimer, Jack, *Unwelcome Strangers: East European Jews in Imperial Germany* (Oxford, 1987).

Wistrich, Robert S., *Anti-Semitism: The Longest Hatred* (London, 1992).

Zaslavsky, V., and Brym, R. J., *Soviet Jewish Emigration and Soviet Nationality Policy* (London, 1983).

b) Gypsies

Barany, Zoltan D., 'Hungary's Gypsies', *Report on Eastern Europe*, 29 (20 July 1990).

Beck, Sam, 'Ethnicity, Class and Public Policy: Tsigani-Gypsies in Socialist Romania', *Gießener Heft für Tsiganologie* (1986).

Borrow, George, *The Zincali: or An Account of the Gypsies of Spain* (London, 1841).

Clebert, Jean-Paul, *The Gypsies* (London, 1964).

Crowe, David M., *A History of Gypsies of Eastern Europe* (London, 1995).

Crowe, David M., and Kolsti, J. (eds), *The Gypsies of Eastern Europe* (Armonk, New York, 1991).

Ficowski, Jerzy, *The Gypsies in Poland: History and Customs* (Warsaw, 1989).

Fonseca, Isabel, *Bury Me Standing: The Gypsies and Their Journey* (London, 1995).

Fraser, Angus, *The Gypsies* (Oxford, 1992).

Hancock, Ian, *The Pariah Syndrome: An Account of Gypsy Slavery and Persecution* (London, 1987).

Heheman, Rainer, '"Jederzeit gottlose böse Leute" – Sinti und Roma zwischen Duldung und Vernichtung', in Klaus J. Bade (ed.), *Deutsche im Ausland – Fremde in Deutschland: Migration in Geschichte und Gegenwart* (Munich, 1992).

Heymowski, Adam, *Swedish 'Travellers' and Their Ancestry: A Social Isolate or an Ethnic Minority* (Uppsala, 1969).

Hoyland, John, *A Historical Survey of the Customs, Habits and Present Status of the Gypsies* (New York, 1846).

Kalibova, Kveta, Haisman, Tomas and Gjuricova, Jitka, 'Gypsies in Czechoslovakia: Demographic Development and Policy Perspectives', in John O'Loughlin and Herman van der Wusten (eds), *The New Political Geography of Eastern Europe* (London, 1993).

Kenrick, Donald and Puxon, Grattan, *The Destiny of Europe's Gypsies* (London, 1972).

Kostelancik, David J., 'The Gypsies of Czechoslovakia: Political and Ideological Considerations in the Development of Policy', *Studies in Comparative Communism*, 22, (1989).

Lípa, Jiří, 'The Fate of Gypsies in Czechoslovakia under Nazi Domination', in Michael Berenbaum (ed.), *A Mosaic of Victims: Non-Jews Persecuted and Murdered by the Nazis* (London, 1990).

Mayall, David, *English Gypsies and State Politics* (Hertford, 1995).

Mayall, David, *Gypsy-Travellers in Nineteenth-Century British Society* (Cambridge, 1988).

McCormick, Andrew, *The Tinkler Gypsies* (London, 1907).

Okely, Judith, *The Traveller-Gypsies* (London, 1983).

Rehfisch, Farnham (ed.), *Gypsies, Tinkers and Other Travellers* (London, 1975).

Shuka, Andreas Mari, *With Gypsies in Bulgaria* (Liverpool, 1916).

Tillhagen, C. H., 'The Gypsy Problem in Finland', *Journal of the Gypsy Lore Society*, 37 (1958).

Ulč, Otto, 'Communist National Minority Policy: The Case of the Gypsies in Czechoslovakia', *Soviet Studies*, 20 (1969).

Vesey-Fitzgerald, Brian, *Gypsies of Britain: An Introduction to their History* (2nd edn, Newton Abbot, 1973).

c) Muslims

Andreades, K. G., *The Moslem Minority in Western Thrace* (Thessaloniki, 1956).

Anthias, Floya and Ayres, Ron, 'Ethnicity and Class in Cyprus', *Race and Class*, 25 (1983).

Bahcheli, Tozun, *Greek-Turkish Relations since 1955* (Boulder, Colorado, 1990).

Bainbridge, M. (ed.), *The Turkic Peoples of the World* (London, 1993).

Bennigsen, Alexandre and Wimbush, S. Embers, *Muslims of the Soviet Empire: A Guide* (London, 1985).

Donia, Robert and Fine, John V. A., Jr, *Bosnia and Herzegovina: A Tradition Betrayed* (London, 1994).

Eminov, Ali, *Turkish and Other Muslim Minorities of Bulgaria* (London, 1997).

Franz, Erhard, 'The Exodus of Turks from Bulgaria, 1989', *Asian and African Studies*, 25 (1991).

Halil, Kiamran, 'The Structure of the Turkish-Cypriot Race', *Mankind Quarterly*, 15 (1974).

Helsinki Watch, *Destroying Ethnic Identity: The Turks of Greece* (New York, 1990).

Joseph, Joseph S., *Cyprus: Ethnic Conflict and International Concern* (New York, 1985).

Karpat, Kemal H. (ed.), *The Turks of Bulgaria: The History, Culture and Political Fate of a Minority* (Istanbul, 1990).

Kostanick, Huey Louis, *Turkish Resettlement of Bulgarian Turks, 1950–1953* (Berkerley and Los Angeles, 1957).

Malcolm, Noel, *Bosnia: A Short History* (London, 1994).

Mandić, Dominik J., 'The Ethnic and Religious History of Bosnia and Hercegovina', in Francs H. Eterovich and Christopher Salatin (eds), *Croatia: Land, People, Culture*, ii (Toronto, 1970).

Marmullaku, Ramadan, *Albania and the Albanians* (London, 1975).

Palikrusheva, Galaba, 'Ethnographic Conditions in Macedonia', in M. Apostolaki and Haralampie Polekanovich (eds), *The Socialist Republic of Macedonia* (Skopje, 1974).

Panteli, Stavros, *A New History of Cyprus: From the Earliest Times to the Present* (London, 1984).

Pinson, Mark (ed.), *The Muslims of Bosnia-Herzegovina: Their Historic Development from the Middle Ages to the Dissolution of Yugoslavia* (Cambridge, Massachusetts, 1993).

Pipes, Richard, 'Muslims of Soviet Central Asia: Trends and Prospects: Part 1', *Middle East Journal*, 9 (1955).

Poulton Hugh, and Farowki, Suha Taji (eds), *Muslim Identity and the Balkan State* (London, 1997).

Shaw, Stanford, *History of the Ottoman Empire and Modern Turkey*, i, *Empire of the Gazis: The Rise and Decline of the Ottoman Empire, 1208–1808* (Cambridge, 1976).

Vickers, Miranda, *The Albanians: A Modern History* (London, 1995).

d) Germans

Alcock, Anthony, 'Trentino and Tyrol: From Austrian Crownland to European Region', in Seamus Dunn and T. G. Fraser (eds), *Europe and Ethnicity: World War I and Contemporary Ethnic Conflict* (London, 1996).

Bade, Klaus J. (ed.), *Deutsche im Ausland – Fremde in Deutschland: Migration in Geschicte und Gegenwart* (Munich, 1992).

Bartlett, Roger P., *Human Capital: The Settlement of Foreigners in Russia, 1762–1804* (Cambridge, 1979).

Cole, Laurence, 'Aufklärung – Nationalgefühl – Frühromantik: Das Beispiel der patriotischen Mobilisierung Tirols, 1790–1810', *Historicum* (Spring, 1997).

Cole, Laurence, 'Province and Patriotism: German National Identity in Tirol, 1850–1914', *Österreichische Zeitschrift für Geschichtswissenschaften*, 6 (1995).

De Zayas, Alfre-Maurice, *The German Expellees: Victims in War and Peace* (London, 1993).

Elklit, Jørgen, Noack, Johan Peter and Tonsgaard, Ole, 'A National Group or a Social System: The Case of the German Minority in North Schleswig', *Journal of Intercultural Studies*, 1 (1980).

Fenske, Hans, 'International Migration: Germany in the Eighteenth Century', *Central European History*, 13 (1980).

Fleischauer, I., Pinkus, B. and Frankel, E. (eds), *The Soviet Germans Past and Present* (London, 1986).

Kann, Robert A., *The History of the Habsburg Empire, 1526–1918* (Berkeley, 1974).

Paikert, G. C., *The Danube Swabians: German Populations in Hungary, Rumania and Yugoslavia and Hitler's Impact on their Patterns* (The Hague, 1967).

Pristinger, Flavia, 'Ethnic Conflict and Modernization in the South Tyrol', in C. R. Foster (ed.), *Nations without a State: Ethnic Minorities in Western Europe* (New York, 1980).

Schechtman, Joseph B., 'The Elimination of the German Minorities in South-Eastern Europe', *Journal of Central European Affairs*, 6 (1946).

Schieder, Theodor (ed.), *The Expulsion of the German Population from the Territories East of the Oder-Neisse-Line* (Bonn, 1960).

Schieder, Theodor (ed.), *The Fate of the Germans in Rumania* (Bonn, 1961).

Chapter 3: Localised Minorities

a) Core Texts

Ashworth, Georgina, *World Minorities*, 3 volumes (Sunbury, 1977–79).

Commission of the European Community, *Linguistic Minorities in Countries Belonging to the European Community* (Luxemburg, 1986).

Crampton, R. J., *Eastern Europe in the Twentieth Century* (London, 1994).

Fernández-Armesto, Felipe (ed.), *The Times Guide to the Peoples of Europe* (London, 1994).

Horak, Stephan M. (ed.), *Eastern European National Minorities, 1919–1980: A Handbook* (Littleton, Colorado, 1985).

Jelavich, Barbara, *History of the Balkans*, 2 volumes (Cambridge, 1983).

Katz, Zev, Rogers, Rosemarie and Harned, Frederic (eds), *Handbook of Major Soviet Nationalities* (New York, 1975).

McGarry, John, and O'Leary, Brendan (eds), *The Politics of Ethnic Conflict Regulation* (London, 1993).

Minority Rights Group (ed.), *World Directory of Minorities* (London, 1989).

Minority Rights Group and TWEEC, *Minorities in Central and Eastern Europe* (London, 1993).

Pearson, Raymond, *National Minorities in Eastern Europe* (London, 1983).

Poulton, Hugh, *The Balkans: Minorities and States in Conflict* (2nd edn, London, 1993).

Smith, Graham (ed.), *The Nationalities Question in the Post-Soviet States* (London, 1996).

Stephens, Meic, *Linguistic Minorities in Western Europe* (Llandysul, 1976).

Straka, Manfred (ed.), *Handbuch der europäischen Volksgruppen* (Vienna and Stuttgart, 1970).

Tägil, Sven (ed.), *Ethnicity and Nation Building in the Nordic World* (London, 1995).

Teich, Mikuláš and Porter, Roy (eds), *The National Question in Europe in Historical Context* (Cambridge, 1993).

Veenhoven, Wilhelm A. et al. (eds), *Case Studies in Human Rights and Fundamental Freedoms: A World Survey*, i (The Hague, 1975).

b) Specfic Texts

Alexandris, Alexis, *The Greek Minority of Istanbul and Greek-Turkish Relations* (Athens, 1983).

Alexandris, Alexis, 'Imbros and Tenedos: A Study of Turkish Attitudes toward Two Ethnic Greek Island Communities since 1923', *Journal of the Hellenic Diaspora*, 7 (1980).

Angelopoulos, A., 'Population Distribution of Greece Today According to Language, National Consciousness and Religion', *Balkan Studies*, 20 (1979).

Armstrong, John Lowell, 'Policy Toward the Polish Minority in the Soviet Union', *Polish Review*, 35 (1990).

Baer, Lars-Anders, 'The Sami: An Indigenous People in Their Own Land', in Birgitta Jahreshog (ed.), *The Sami National Minority in Sweden* (Stockholm, 1982).

Barker, Thomas M., *The Slovene Minority of Carinthia* (New York, 1984).

Bennett, Christopher, *Yugoslavia's Bloody Collapse: Causes, Course and Consequences* (London, 1995).

Clogg, Richard, *A Concise History of Modern Greece* (Cambridge, 1992).

Collins, Roger, *The Basques* (Oxford, 1989).

Comrie, Bernard, *The Languages of the Soviet Union* (Cambridge, 1981).

Conquest, Robert, *Soviet Nationalities Policy in Practice* (London, 1967).

Conquest, Robert, *The Nation Killers: The Soviet Deportation of Nationalities* (New York, 1970).

Crampton, R. J., *A Short History of Modern Bulgaria* (Cambridge, 1987).

Dadrian, Vahakn, *The History of the Armenian Genocide* (Oxford, 1995).

Deker, Nikolai K. and Lebed, Andrei (eds), *Genocide in the USSR: Studies in Group Destruction* (New York, 1958).

D'Encausse, Hélène Carrère, *The Great Challenge: Nationalities and the Bolshevik State, 1917–1930* (New York, 1992).

Denber, Rachel (ed.), *The Soviet Nationality Reader: The Disintegration in Context* (Boulder, Colorado, 1992).

Druškovič, Drago, *Carinthian Slovenes: Some Aspects of Their Situation* (Ljubljana, 1973).

Fisher, Alan W., *The Crimean Tatars* (Stanford, 1978).

Fitzmaurice, John, *The Politics of Belgium: A Unique Federalism* (London, 1996).

Georgeoff, John, 'Ethnic Minorities in the People's Republic of Bulgaria', in D. Klein and Milan J. Reban (eds), *The Politics of Ethnicity in Eastern Europe* (Boulder, Colorado, 1991).

Goldenberg, Suzanne, *Pride of Small Nations: The Caucasus and the Post-Soviet Disorder* (London, 1994).

Grafenauer, Bojo, *Ethnic Conditions in Carinthia* (Ljubljana, 1946).

Guthier, Steven L., 'The Belorussians: National Identification and Assimilation, 1897–1970', *Soviet Studies*, 29 (1977).

Hajda, Lubomyr, and Beissinger, Mark (eds), *The Nationalities Question in Soviet Politics and Society* (Boulder, Colorado, 1990).

Hechter, Michael, *Internal Colonialism: The Celtic Fringe in British Development, 1546–1966* (London, 1975).

Heiberg, Marianne, *The Making of the Basque Nation* (Cambridge, 1989).

Hitchens, Keith, *Rumania, 1866–1947* (Oxford, 1994).

Holman, G. Paul, Jr, 'Russo-Ukrainian Relations: The Containment Legacy', in W. Raymond Duncan and G. Paul Holman (eds), *Ethnic Nationalism and Regional Conflict* (Boulder, Colorado, 1994).

Hooghe, Liesbert, *A Leap in the Dark: Nationalist Conflict and Federal Reform in Belgium* (Ithaca, New York, 1991).

Hovanissian, Richard G. (ed.), *The Armenian Genocide* (London, 1992).

Huebner, Todd, 'Ethnicity Denied: Nazi Policy towards the Lusatian Sorbs, 1933–1945', *German History*, 6 (1988).

Hughes, Christopher, *Switzerland* (London, 1975).

Illyés, Elemér, *National Minorities in Romania: Change in Transylvania* (New York, 1982).

Irving, R. E. M., *The Flemings and Walloons of Belgium* (London, 1980).

Janics, Kalman, *Czechoslovak Policy and the Hungarian Minority, 1945–1948* (New York, 1982).

Jones, Mervyn, *The Sami of Lapland* (London, 1982).

Kalvoda, Josef, 'National Minorities under Communism: The Case of Czechoslovakia', *Nationalities Papers*, 16 (1988).

Kavka, František, *An Outline of Czechoslovak History* (Prague, 1960).

Kearney, Hugh, *The British Isles: A History of Four Nations* (Cambridge, 1989).

Kendal, 'Kurdistan in Turkey', in G. Chaliand (ed.), *A People Without a Country: Kurds and Kurdistan* (London, 1980).

Kirişci, Kemal and Winrow, Gareth M., *The Kurdish Question in Turkey: An Example of Trans-State Ethnic Conflict* (London, 1997).

Knejevitch, Radoye L., 'The Ethnical Structure of Voyvodina', *Yugoslav Oberver*, 2 (1956).

Kochan, Lionel and Abraham, Richard, *The Making of Modern Russia* (2dn edn, Harmondsworth, 1983).

Kofos, Evangelos, 'The Macedonian Question: The Politics of Mutation', *Balkan Studies*, 27 (1986).

Kolstoe, Paul, *Russians in the Former Soviet Republics* (London, 1995).

Kozlov, Viktor, *The Peoples of the Soviet Union* (London, 1988).

Levy, Carl (ed.), *Italian Regionalism: History, Identity and Politics* (Oxford, 1996).

Lieven, Anatol, *The Baltic Revolution: Estonia, Latvia, Lithuania and the Path to Independence* (2nd edn, London, 1994).

McDonald, M., *'We Are Not French!' Language, Culture and Identity in Brittany* (London, 1989).

McDowall, David, *The Kurds* (London, 1989).

McDowall, David, *A Modern History of the Kurds* (London, 1996).

Magocsci, Paul Robert, *A History of Ukraine* (Toronto, 1997).

Marples, David R., *Belarus: From Soviet Rule to Nuclear Catastrophe* (London, 1996).

Mayer, K. B., *The Population of Switzerland* (New York, 1952).

Medrano, Juan Díez, *Divided Nations: Class, Politics and Nationalism in the Basque Country and Catalonia* (Ithaca, New York, 1995).

Mihok, Brigitte, *Ethnostrazifikation im Sozialismus, aufgezeigt an den Beispielländern Ungarn und Rumänien* (Frankfurt, 1990).

Misiunas, Romuald and Taagepera, Rein, *The Baltic States: Years of Depedence* (London, 1993).

Musil, Jiří (ed.), *The End of Czechoslovakia* (Budapest, 1995).

Novak, Bogdan C., *Trieste, 1941–1954: The Ethnic, Political and Ideological Struggle* (Chicago, 1970).

Österreichische Rektorenkonferenz, *Bericht der Arbeitsgruppe Lage und Perspektiven der Volksgruppen in Österreich* (Vienna, 1969).

Paul, Leo, 'The Stolen Revolution: Minorities in Romania after Ceaçescu', in John O'Loughlin and Hermann van der Wusten (eds), *The New Political Geography of Eastern Europe* (London, 1993).

Peters, Yvo J. D., 'The Rights of Minorities in Present-Day Turkey', *Europa Ethnica*, 44 (1987).

Petropoulos, John A., 'The Compulsory Exchange of Populations: Greek-Turkish Peacemaking, 1922–1930', *Byzantine and Modern Greek Studies*, 2 (1976).

Pipes, Richard, *The Formation of the Soviet Union: Communism and Nationalism, 1917–1923* (Cambridge, Massachusetts, 1970).

Poulton, Hugh, *Who Are the Macedonians?* (London, 1995).

Renner, H., 'The National Minorities in Czechoslovakia after the End of the Second World War', *Plural Societies*, 7 (1976).

Robbins, Keith, *Great Britain: Identities, Institutions and the Idea of Britishness* (London, 1998).

Rugman, Jonathan and Hutchings, Roger, *Atatürk's Children: Turkey and the Kurds* (London, 1996).

Schöpflin, George and Poulton, Hugh, *Rumania's Ethnic Hungarians* (London, 1990).

Seton-Watson, Hugh, *The Russian Empire, 1801–1917* (Oxford, 1967).

Shlapentokh, Vladimir, Sendich, Munir and Payin, Emil (eds), *The New Russian Diaspora: Russian Minorities in the Former Soviet Republics* (Armonk, New York, 1994).

Siguan, Manuel, *Linguistic Minorities in the European Economic Community: Spain, Portugal, Greece* (Luxembourg, 1990).

Singleton, Fred, *Twentieth-Century Yugoslavia* (London, 1976).

Stavrou, Christodoulos, *Die griechische Minderheit in Albanien* (Frankfurt, 1993).

Steinberg, Jonathan, *Why Switzerland?* (2nd edn, Cambridge, 1996).

Stone, Gerald, *The Smallest Slavonic Nation: The Sorbs of Lusatia* (London, 1972).

Sullivan, John, *ETA and Basque Nationalism: The Fight for Euskadi, 1890–1986* (London, 1988).

Suny, Ronald Grigor (ed.), *Transcaucasia: Nationalism and Social Change* (Ann Arbor, Michigan, 1996).

Trifunowski, J., 'Die Aroumanen in Mazedonien', *Balcanica*, 2 (1971).

Walker, Christopher J., *Armenia: The Survival of a Nation* (2nd edn, London, 1990).

Winnifrith, T. J., *The Vlachs: The History of a Balkan People* (London, 1987).

Zaprudnik, Jan, *Belarus: At a Crossroads of History* (Boulder, Colorado, 1993).

Zirakzadeh, Cyrus Ernesto, *A Rebellious People: Basques, Protests and Politics* (Reno and Las Vegas, Nevada 1991).

Chapter 4: Immigrants

a) Core Texts

Ardittis, Solon (ed.), *The Politics of East-West Migration* (London, 1994).

Böhning, W. R., *The Migration of Workers in the United Kingdom and the European Community* (London, 1972).

Bramwell, Anna C. (ed.), *Refugees in the Age of Total War* (London, 1988).

Brock, Colin (ed.), *The Caribbean in Europe: Aspects of West Indian Experiences in Britain, France and the Netherlands* (London, 1986).

Castles, Stephen, *Here for Good: Western Europe's New Ethnic Minorities* (London, 1987).

Castles, Stephen, and Kosack, Godula, *Immigrant Workers and Class Structure in Western Europe* (London, 1973).

Castles, Stephen, and Miller, Mark J., *The Age of Migration: International Population Movements in the Modern World* (London, 1993).

Holborn, Louise W., *Refugees: A Problem of Our Times*, i (Metuchen, New Jersey, 1975).

Hollifield, James F., *Immigrants, Markets, and States: The Political Economy of Postwar Europe* (Cambridge, Massachusetts, 1992).

Hopkinson, Nicholas, *Migration into Western Europe* (London, 1992).

Ireland, Patrick, *The Policy Challenge of Ethnic Diversity: Immigrant Politics in France and Switzerland* (London, 1994).

Joly, Daniéle, *Refugees: Asylum in Europe?* (London, 1992).

Joppke, Christian (ed.), *Challenge to the Nation-State: Immigration in Western Europe and the United States* (Oxford, 1998).

Kulischer, Eugene M., *Europe on the Move: War and Population Changes, 1917–1947* (New York, 1948).

Marrus, Michael R., *The Unwanted: European Refugees in the Twentieth Century* (Oxford, 1985).

Martin, Philip L., *The Unfinished Story: Turkish Labour Migration to Western Europe* (Geneva, 1991).

Salt, John and Clough, Hugh (eds), *Migration in Post-War Europe* (London, 1976).

Schechtman, Joseph B., *The Refugee in the World: Displacement and Integration* (London, 1963)

b) Specific Texts

Abadan-Unat, Nermin (ed.), *Turkish Workers in Europe, 1960–1975: A Socio-Economic Reappraisal* (Leiden, 1976).

Akgündüz, Ahmet, 'Labour Migration from Turkey to Western Europe, 1960–1974: An Analytical Review', *Capital and Class*, 51 (1993).

Alpay, Sahlin and Halil, Saviaslan, *Effects of Immigration: The Effects of Immigration on the Town of Kulu in Central Turkey of Emigration to Sweden* (Stockholm, 1984).

Anthias, Floya, *Ethnicity, Class, Gender and Migration: Greek Cypriots in Britain* (Aldershot, 1992).

Anwar, Muhamad, *The Myth of Return: Pakistanis in Britain* (London, 1979).

Bade, Klaus J., 'Einführung: Wege in die Bundesrepublik', in Bade (ed.), *Neue Heimat im Westen: Vertriebene, Flüchtlinge, Aussiedler* (Münster, 1990).

Bade, Klaus J., *Vom Auswanderungsland zum Einwanderungsland? Deutschland, 1880–1980* (Berlin, 1983).

Bauboeck, Rainer and Wimmer, H., 'Social Partnership and Foreigner Policy: On

Special Features of Austria's Guest-Worker System', *European Journal of Political Research*, 116 (1988).

Baučić, Ivo, *The Effects of Emigration from Yugoslavia and the Problems of Returning Emigrant Workers* (The Hague, 1972).

Berghoff, Hartmut, 'Population Change and its Repercussions on the Social History of the Federal Republic', in Klaus Larres and Panikos Panayi (eds), *The Federal Republic of Germany since 1949: Politics, Society and Economy before and after Unification* (London, 1996).

Bethell, Nicholas, *The Last Secret: Forcible Repatriation to Russia* (London, 1974).

Bethlehem, Siegfried, *Heimatvertreibung, DDR-Flucht, Gastarbeiterwanderung: Wanderungsströme und Wanderungspolitik in der Bundesrepublik Deutschland* (Stuttgart, 1982).

Biffl, G., 'Structural Shifts in the Employment of Foreign Workers in Austria', *International Migration*, 23 (1985).

Booth, Heather, *The Migration Process in Britain and West Germany* (Aldershot, 1992).

Boscardin, Lucio, *Die italienische Einwanderung in die Schweiz mit besonderer Berücksichtigung der Jahre 1946–1959* (Basel, 1962).

Campani, Giovanna, 'Immigration and Racism in Southern Europe: The Italian Case', *Ethnic and Racial Studies*, 16 (1993).

Chance, Judy, 'The Irish in London: An Exploration of Ethnic Boundary Maintenance', in Peter Jackson (ed.), *Race and Racism: Essays in Social Geography* (London, 1987).

Colpi, Terri, *The Italian Factor: The Italian Community in Great Britain* (Edinburgh, 1991).

Condon, Stephanie A., and Ogden, Philip E., 'Emigration from the French Caribbean: The Origins of an Organized Migration', *International Journal of Urban and Regional Research*, 15 (1991).

Cross, Malcolm, and Entzinger, Hans (eds), *Lost Illusions: Caribbean Minorities in Britain and the Netherlands* (London, 1988).

Dahya, Badr, 'Pakistanis in Britain: Transients or Settlers', *Race*, 14 (1972).

Dreyer, Heinrich M., 'Immigration of Foreign Workers into the Federal Republic of Germany', *International Labour Review*, 84 (1961).

Eaton, Martin, 'Foreign Residents and Illegal Immigrants: Os Negros em Portugal', *Ethnic and Racial Studies*, 16 (1993).

Elliot, M. R., *Pawns of Yalta: Soviet Refugees and America's Role in Their Repatriation* (Chicago, 1982).

Emke-Poulopoulos, Ira, 'The Causes of Entry of Immigrants and Refugees into Greece', *Migration*, 16 (1992).

Goppers, Karlin, *Migration and Economy: Yugoslav-Swedish Relations* (Stockholm, 1983).

Hargreaves, Alec G., *Immigration, 'Race' and Ethnicity in Contemporary France* (London, 1995).

Herbert, Ulrich, *A History of Foreign Labour in Germany, 1880–1980: Seasonal Workers/Forced Laborers/Guest Workers* (Ann Arbor, Michigan, 1990).

Hjarnø, Jan, 'Migrants and Refugees on the Danish Labour Market', *New Community*, 18 (1991).

Hoffmann, Lutz, *Die unvollendete Republik: Zwischen Einwanderungsland und Deutschem Nationalstaat* (2nd edn, Cologne, 1992).

Hoffmann-Nowotny, Hans-Joachim, 'European Migration after World War II', in W. H. McNeill and R. S. Adams (eds), *Human Migration: Patterns and Policies* (Bloomington, Indiana, 1978).

Holmes, Colin, *John Bull's Island: Immigration and British Society, 1871–1971* (London, 1988).

Homze, Edward L., *Foreign Labour in Nazi Germany* (Princeton, 1967).

Jacobmeyer, Wolfgang, 'Jüdische Überlebende als "Displaced Persons": Untersuchungen zur Besantzungspolitik in den deutschen Westzonen und zur Zuwanderung osteuropäischer Juden, 1945–1947', *Geschichte und Gesellschaft*, 9 (1983).

Joly, Daniéle and Cohen, Robin (eds), *Reluctant Hosts: Europe and its Refugees* (Aldershot, 1989).

Kamalkamia, Zara, *Iranian Immigrants and Refugees in Norway* (Bergen, 1988).

Kay, Diana and Miles, Robert, *Refugees or Migrant Workers? European Volunteer Workers in Britain, 1946–1951* (London, 1992).

Killingray, David (ed.), *Africans in Britain* (London, 1993).

King, R., 'Italian Migration to Great Britain', *Geography*, 62 (1977).

Körmendi, Eszter, *Refugees in Denmark* (Copenhagen, 1987).

Krane, R. E. (ed.), *International Labour Migration in Europe* (New York, 1979).

Krüger-Portratz, Marianne (ed.) *Anderssein gab es nicht: Ausländer und Minderheiten in der DDR* (Münster, 1991).

Layton-Henry, Zig, *The Politics of Immigration: Immigration, 'Race' and 'Race' Relations in Post-War Britain* (Oxford, 1992).

McDonald, James R., 'Labor Immigration into France, 1946–1965', *Annals of the Association of American Geographers*, 59 (1969).

MacMaster, Neil, *Colonial Migrants and Racism: Algerians in France, 1900–62* (London, 1997).

Marshall, Barbara, '"Migration into Germany": Asylum Seekers and Ethnic Germans', *German Politics*, 1 (1992).

Matasar, Anne Sue, 'Labor Transfers in Western Europe: The Problem of Italian Migrants in Switzerland' (unpublished Ph.D. thesis, New York, Columbia University Press, 1968).

Mayer, Kurt B., 'Post-War Migration to Switzerland', *International Migration*, 3 (1968).

Ogden, Philip E. and White, Paul E. (eds), *Migrants in Modern France* (London, 1989).

Panayi, Panikos, (ed.), *Germans in Britain since 1500* (London, 1996).

Panayi, Panikos, 'Race in the Federal Republic of Germany: Immigration, Ethnicity and Racism since the Second World War', in Klaus Larres and Panikos Panayi (eds), *The Federal Republic of Germany since 1949: Politics, Society and Economy before and after Unification* (London, 1996).

Panayi, Panikos, 'Refugees in Twentieth-Century Britain: A Brief History', in Vaughan Robinson (ed.), *The International Refugee Crisis: British and Canadian Responses* (London, 1993).

Parker, David, 'Chinese People in Britain', in Gregor Benton and Frank N. Pieke (eds), *The Chinese in Europe* (London, 1998).

Paul, Kathleen, *Whitewashing Britain: Race and Citizenship in the Postwar Era* (Ithaca, New York, 1997).

Peach, Ceri, *The Caribbean in Europe: Contrasting Patterns of Migration and Settlement in Britain, France and the Netherlands* (Coventry, 1991).

Pfahlmann, Hans, *Fremdarbeiter und Kriegsgefangene in der deutschen Kriegswirtschaft, 1939–1945* (Darmstadt, 1968).

Pilkington, Edward, *Beyond the Mother Country: West Indians and the Notting Hill White Riots* (London, 1988).

Pinson, Koppel S., 'Jewish Life in Liberated Germany', *Jewish Social Studies*, 9 (1947).

Radspieler, Tony, *The Ethnic German Refugee in Austria, 1945 to 1954* (The Hague, 1955).

Romanszyn, Krystyna, 'The Invisible Community: Undocumented Polish Workers in Athens', *New Community*, 22 (1996).

Salimi, Khalid, 'Norway's National Racism', *Race and Class*, 32 (1991).

Saloman, Kim, *Refugees in the Cold War: Toward a New International Refugee Regime in the Early Post-War Era* (Lund, 1991).

Seeber, Eva, *Zwangsarbeiter in der faschistischen Kriegswirtschaft* (Berlin, 1964).

Solomos, John, *Race and Racism in Britain* (2nd edn, London, 1993).

Spencer, Ian R. G., *British Immigration Policy: The Making of Multi-Racial Britain* (London, 1997).

Stack, A. W. and Hussain, S., *Ausländer in der DDR: Ein Ruckblick* (Berlin, 1991).

Steinert, Johannes Dieter, *Migration und Politik: Westdeutschland -Europa – Übersee* (Osnabrück, 1995).

Tannahill, J. A., *European Volunteer Workers in Britain* (Manchester, 1958).

van Amersfoort, Hans ,'West Indian Migration to the Netherlands', in H. van Honte and W. Melgert (eds), *Foreigners in Our Community* (Amsterdam, 1972).

Watson, James L. (ed.), *Between Two Cultures: Migrants and Minorities in Britain* (Oxford, 1977).

Widegren, Jonas, *Report to OECD (SOPEMI) on Immigration to Sweden in 1978 and the First Half of 1979* (Stockholm, 1979).

Wrench, John, and Solomos, John (eds), *Racism and Migration in Western Europe* (Oxford, 1993).

Index